Praise for *Tangled Vines*

"Dinkelspiel is at her best . . . page-turning."

—*San Francisco Chronicle*

"Once you pick up Dinkelspiel's stunning new look at the dark side of California wine, you won't want to get up until you've devoured the entire book . . . [An] uncommon page-turner. Dinkelspiel has woven skillfully three distinct yet inextricable narratives into a book that will inform and fascinate readers for years to come. While the stories she tells are engrossing on their own, it is her steady journalistic tone, backed by prodigious and painstaking research, that gives this book its power and allure."

—*Berkeleyside Nosh*

"An engaging read."

—*The Mercury News* (San Jose)

"More than just a crime story, this is a book about the wealth, passion, and murky reality shaped by life inside the twisted vines of California's most revered crop. . . . An enjoyable read for wine connoisseurs and neophytes alike."

—*Kirkus Reviews*

"The author's gripping descriptions of the fire and its aftermath, her unflinching narrative, and her vast knowledge of the subject matter make this a page-turner for both wine aficionados and casual tasters."

—*Publishers Weekly*

"*Tangled Vines* is a captivating account of how a wine connoisseur became one of the most notorious wine criminals in history. Dinkelspiel deftly weaves his true tale into the rich, colorful, and at times shady history of California wine. A delicious read."

—Allison Hoover Bartlett, author of *The Man Who Loved Books Too Much: The True Story of a Thief, a Detective, and a World of Literary Obsession*

"The author is deeply rooted in the Golden State's financial history, as anyone knows who read her excellent *Towers of Gold*. Now we find that *terroir's* part of that story, too. A family member's bottled heirlooms passed down through generations fall victim to a bizarre crime, and the author's drawn in by a sense of loss, anger, and curiosity. How could even an unhinged perpetrator of the worst case of wine arson in California history destroy vintages bearing some of the biggest names in West Coast viticulture, and apparently get away with it? Dinkelspiel weaves together strands of past and present in an enthralling narrative that binds the reader to the investigation and to her personal triumph."

—James Conaway, *New York Times* bestselling author of *Napa: The Story of an American Eden*

"History, wine, and crime intertwine in this fascinating page-turner. Dinkelspiel travels in time to create a dark and deep portrait of three centuries of California wine culture." —Davia Nelson, NPR's The Kitchen Sisters

"I gulped down this page-turning chronicle of big egos, bold Cabernets, and brazen wine wars. Frances Dinkelspiel vividly captures the wild early years of California's wine industry as well as the modern crime revealing the dark obsession some people have for wine. I'll never look at a bottle of Napa Valley Cabernet in quite the same way again."

—Julia Flynn Siler, *New York Times* bestselling author of *The House of Mondavi: The Rise and Fall of an American Wine Dynasty*

TANGLED
VINES

TANGLED VINES

GREED, MURDER, OBSESSION,
AND AN ARSONIST IN THE
VINEYARDS OF CALIFORNIA

FRANCES DINKELSPIEL

 ST. MARTIN'S GRIFFIN NEW YORK

www.stmartins.com

Map by Jeffrey Ward

Designed by Steven Seighman

The Library of Congress has cataloged the hardcover edition as follows:

Dinkelspiel, Frances, author.
   Tangled vines : greed, murder, obsession, and an arsonist in the vineyards of California / Frances Dinkelspiel. — First edition.
     p. cm.
   Includes bibliographical references and index.
   ISBN 978-1-250-03322-2 (hardcover)
   ISBN 978-1-250-03321-5 (e-book)
   1. Wine industry—California—History.   2. Wine and wine making—Corrupt practices—California—History.
3. Crime—California—History.   I. Title.
   HD9377.C2D56 2015
   338.4'76632009794—dc23

                            2015018648

ISBN 978-1-250-11389-4 (trade paperback)

First St. Martin's Griffin Edition: October 2016

10 9 8 7 6 5 4 3 2 1

For my daughters, Charlotte and Juliet

CONTENTS

PART FOUR: EXPANSION

PART FIVE: DECEPTION

PART SIX: REDEMPTION

MAJOR CHARACTERS

TWENTY-FIRST CENTURY

Mark Anderson—A Sausalito photographer and owner of Sausalito Cellars, a boutique wine storage company. Anderson was a civic leader and bon vivant, known for his knowledge of wine and patronage of the town's best Japanese restaurant.

Delia Viader—An Argentina-born winemaker whose 1997 Viader Napa Valley was named the number two wine in the world by the *Wine Spectator* magazine. Viader was one of the first in the Napa Valley to plant vertical rows on steep hillsides.

Dick Ward—A cofounder of Saintsbury, one of the first wineries to make wine from Pinot Noir grapes grown in the Carneros district in southern Napa County.

Ted Hall—A former management consultant who started Long Meadow Ranch in the Mayacamas Mountains with his wife, Laddie, and son, Chris.

Miranda Heller—A fifth-generation Californian who inherited numerous bottles of wine made in 1875 by her great-great-grandfather, Isaias Hellman.

R. Steven Lapham—An assistant United States attorney for the Eastern District of California. Lapham specializes in arson, terrorism, and wine fraud.

Debbie Polverino—A longtime Napa Valley resident and the manager of Wines Central in 2005 at the time of the fire.

Brian O. Parker—Special agent for the Bureau of Alcohol, Tobacco, Firearms, and Explosives. Parker was the lead agent on the Mark Anderson investigation, a case that would consume seven years of his life.

Yoshi Tome—The owner of Sushi Ran in Sausalito, regarded as one of the top restaurants in the Bay Area.

Ron Lussier—A web designer whose first taste of Sine Qua Non, a California cult wine, changed his attitude about wine forever. Lussier stored his wine at Sausalito Cellars.

Michael Bales—A Latin teacher from Toronto who had built up a small but superb collection of California cult wine, including multiple bottles of the hard-to-buy Screaming Eagle. Bales rented a storage space at Sausalito Cellars so he could get direct delivery.

Samuel Maslak—Maslak's south San Francisco restaurant, Bacchanal, was known for its wine list. After the restaurant went bankrupt in 2001, Maslak entrusted 756 cases into Mark Anderson's care.

Michael Liccardi—A prominent wine broker from Stockton who masterminded a scheme to pass off cheap wine grapes as more expensive Zinfandel grapes.

Fred Franzia—The owner of Bronco Wines, one of the largest wine companies in the world and the producer of "Two-Buck Chuck," sold at Trader Joe's. Franzia pleaded guilty to fraud in 1999 for substituting cheap grapes for Zinfandel grapes. He paid a $500,000 fine and was barred from the wine business for five years.

Rudy Kurniawan—An Indonesian who came to the United States to go to college, but overstayed his visa. After tasting a bottle of Opus One, Kurniawan became interested in wine and used his family's considerable wealth to acquire—and then sell—a cellar full of rare French wines. Much of it was fake. Kurniawan was convicted of fraud in 2014 and sentenced to ten years in prison.

William I. Koch—Koch, an energy magnate worth $4 billion and the brother of David and Charles Koch, who contribute widely to conservative causes, has one of the world's great wine collections. He bought numerous bottles of rare wine from Kurniawan, only to discover they were fake. His lawsuits have played a large role in revealing the scope of wine fraud around the world.

Mark Reichel—Mark Anderson's Sacramento-based defense attorney.

Fred Dame—A wine expert whose palate is so advanced that he passed the test for Master Sommelier on the first try—an accomplishment only fourteen other people in the world have achieved.

NINETEENTH AND TWENTIETH CENTURIES

Tiburcio Tapia—The original grantee of the 13,000-acre Rancho Cucamonga in southern California. A descendant of some of the area's earliest Spanish settlers, Tapia was given the rancho by the Mexican government in 1839. He was the first to plant grapes there.

Jean-Louis Vignes—A French immigrant who arrived in Los Angeles around 1831, when California was part of Mexico. Vignes was widely considered the most important winemaker of his time and a spur to French emigration to southern California. His 104-acre vineyard along the banks of the Los Angeles river was a showplace and a center of Los Angeles society.

Jean Louis Sainsevain—Along with his younger brother, Pierre, Sainsevain bought his uncle Vignes's vineyard in 1855. Sainsevain became one of the most important wine merchants of the 1860s, opening stores in San Francisco and New York. After going bankrupt, he took over management of Cucamonga Vineyard. He was the winemaker for the 1875 Port and Angelica that was destroyed in the 2005 wine warehouse fire.

John Rains—A southern sympathizer who gained control of thousands of acres of land when he married Maria Merced de Williams. Rains purchased the 13,000-acre Rancho Cucamonga in 1858 using his wife's money, but did not put her name on the deed. His murder set off a chain of violence throughout the region.

Maria Merced Williams de Rains—The daughter of one of southern California's richest cattle barons, Merced grew up in luxury on Rancho Chino during the height of the rancho era. Raised to be wife and mother, Merced married John Rains when she was sixteen and was ill equipped to deal with the world after his death.

Robert Carlisle—When his brother-in-law John Rains was murdered, Carlisle led the hunt for his killers, often going outside the law. He took over Maria Merced Williams de Rains's business affairs after her husband's death and used the position to his advantage.

Benjamin Hayes—As the judge for the First Judicial District of Southern California, which included Los Angeles, San Bernardino, and San

Diego counties in the 1860s, Hayes was intimately involved in the hunt for Rains's killer. He became obsessed with the case—and with Rains's widow—and documented it thoroughly in his diaries and scrapbooks, which are a major source of information about southern California in the mid-nineteenth century.

Andrew J. King—King came from a notoriously violent family in El Monte, a secessionist stronghold east of Los Angeles. As undersheriff for Los Angeles, King hunted for Rains's killer. He eventually took over management of Rancho Cucamonga, with deadly results.

Ramón Carrillo—A descendant of an old *Californio* family who fought for Mexico in the war against the United States, Carrillo became John Rains's majordomo in 1861. As tensions between Americans and *Californios* heightened after Rains's death, Carrillo was vilified in the press and named a prime suspect in the murder.

Isaias W. Hellman—A German-Jewish immigrant who acquired Rancho Cucamonga in a sheriff's sale in 1870. Hellman, who became one of California's most prominent financiers, eventually overseeing Wells Fargo Bank, owned the Cucamonga Vineyard for more than forty years. One hundred seventy-five bottles of his Port and Angelica from 1875 were destroyed in the Wines Central warehouse fire. He is the author's great-great-grandfather.

Benjamin Dreyfus—From a single vineyard in Anaheim, Dreyfus built one of the country's largest wholesale wine firms, B. Dreyfus & Co., which had sales around the world. Dreyfus became a partner in the Cucamonga Vineyard and took over management in 1878. He is credited with selling the first kosher wine in California.

Leland Stanford—A railroad baron, California governor, and U.S. senator, Stanford built Vina Ranch in northern California, which became the largest wine operation in the world in the 1880s.

Percy Morgan—An English accountant who brought together seven of San Francisco's biggest wine houses in 1894 to create the California Wine Association. By 1911, the time Morgan stepped down from the presidency of the CWA, the company had crushed its competitors and controlled more than 80 percent of the winemaking in California.

Pietro Rossi—An Italian chemist who came to San Francisco and assumed the helm of the Italian Swiss Colony, a large wine operation based in Asti in northern Sonoma County. Rossi fought hard against the avarice of the California Wine Association, but capitulated to its power in the end.

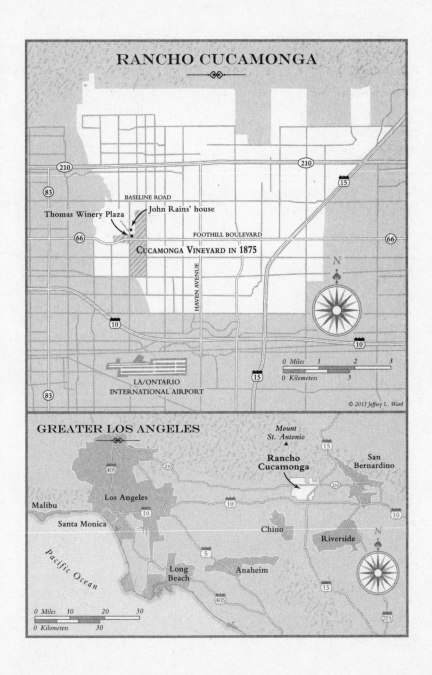

RANCHO CUCAMONGA

Thomas Winery Plaza

John Rains' house

BASELINE ROAD

FOOTHILL BOULEVARD

CUCAMONGA VINEYARD IN 1875

HAVEN AVENUE

N

210

83

66

210

15

66

10

15

10

83

0 Miles 1 2 3

0 Kilometers 3

LA/ONTARIO
INTERNATIONAL AIRPORT

© 2015 Jeffrey L. Ward

GREATER LOS ANGELES

Mount
St. Antonio

**Rancho
Cucamonga**

San
Bernardino

405

210

15

210

Los Angeles

Malibu

10

10

Santa Monica

Chino

Riverside

N

15

Pacific Ocean

5

Long
Beach

Anaheim

405

15

215

0 Miles 10 20 30

0 Kilometers 30

PROLOGUE: A FIRE IS SET

The three-hundred-pound man walked slowly up the steps to the mezzanine area of the cavernous wine warehouse, pausing to rest on a cane when his breath grew short. It was a warm fall afternoon in October 2005, right in the middle of the grape harvest, and the black sweatpants and t-shirt that were the man's signature look clung damply to his heavy frame.

As he hobbled down the hallway leading to his storage locker, the man could look down onto the main floor of Wines Central, which was packed with millions of bottles of California's finest wines. Pallets stacked forty feet high stretched the length of two football fields, with wine as varied as that from Beaulieu Vineyards, one of state's oldest wineries, to cases from boutique wineries like the one owned by the Italian race car driver Mario Andretti.

The man, however, did not pause to consider the vast array of wine below him. He was in a hurry. And he was angry. He regarded this enormous warehouse in Vallejo, fifteen miles south of Napa, to be his domain. But he was soon to be an outcast.

The man stopped in front of Bay 14, a 2,500-square foot area he had been renting for the previous thirteen months. The space had once been filled with wines from the great châteaux of Burgundy and Bordeaux, as well as from the cult wineries of California like Sine Qua Non and Harlan Estate. But now it was almost empty. Wooden pallets perched haphazardly on the floor. Cardboard boxes and Styrofoam inserts leaned against a chain-link fence. Just 4,700 bottles, seven pallets of shrink-wrapped wine, remained, a bitter reminder of how the man's business had fallen apart during the previous year. While he had once been sought out for his knowledge of wine, asked to join boards and commissions, and invited to Bacchanalian feasts around the world featuring gourmet food and rare vintages, the man was now a pariah, ignored by his longtime friends and under investigation by police.

The mezzanine was quiet, the sound dampened by the three-foot-thick concrete walls that had been constructed to hold Navy torpedoes. The man wiped his sweaty brow and took a final look around. The area was empty. He unlocked the gate into his storage area and went inside. There was no one to see him reach into his canvas bag and bring out a plastic bucket filled with gasoline-soaked rags. He removed a propane torch and pulled its trigger, which sent a small flame surging from the brass tip. The man held the torch against a piece of cloth until a flame took hold.

As the man clamored down the stairs toward the warehouse's exit, the flame flickered, and then flickered some more, before it leaped up and caught on a nearby pile of cardboard. The tongues of fire grew as they gobbled up the wooden crates and Styrofoam nearby. Within a few minutes, the fire had spread up to the ceiling.

At 3:34 p.m., about nineteen minutes after the man had rushed out of the warehouse, walking faster than any of those inside had ever seen, fire alarms started to blare. The lights flashed. A piercing alarm went off. The warehouse manager and three workers ran to the front door and struggled to get out. Then an enormous explosion rocketed through the building, shattering thousands of windows. A railway portal toppled. The sudden rush of oxygen created a fireball that consumed everything it touched, scorching shrink-wrapped pallets of wine that fell upon one another like rows of dominos. Glass bottles shattered everywhere.

The firefighters from Vallejo who rushed to the scene would later comment that there was so much black smoke it looked as if a 747 airliner had crashed. For eight hours they fought the blaze, bringing in companies from around the San Francisco Bay Area as the fire grew larger. By the time the flames were out, the warehouse was a smoky, soggy mess. More than four and a half million bottles of premium wine stored inside, worth more than a quarter billion dollars on the retail market, were now worthless. It was the greatest crime involving wine in history.

Mark Anderson—the man in black—was nowhere to be found.

INTRODUCTION

Mark Anderson was wearing prison orange, not black, when I looked at him through the glass of the jail's visiting room window. Under the glare of a harsh fluorescent light, his skin was sallow and his once luxurious blond ponytail had turned an undistinguished gray. Anderson was sitting down so I couldn't see his enormous girth, but the jowls around his face hinted at his size. Anderson's manner was mild, and his face almost cherubic, but, as I would soon learn, that openness was deceptive: he didn't care anything for others. He was the kind of man who thought and talked only about himself.

Anderson had asked me to the Sacramento County Jail to prove his innocence. He had been accused of a heinous crime, one that cost the California economy hundreds of millions of dollars. There was plenty of evidence to suggest he was guilty, but Anderson had been spinning tales about his life for so long he never knew when to stop. Maybe this reporter would believe his version of events, would take the clues he hinted at and go out and uncover the government conspiracy he was sure was after him.

We only had twenty minutes to talk. I didn't have either pen or paper, as I had been ordered to leave my purse in a locker after I had shown my driver's license to a sheriff's deputy ensconced behind bulletproof glass.

I then joined a long line of women and their children, mostly Mexican or Black, who were waiting to see loved ones too poor to make bail.

How do you cram months' worth of questions into a few minutes? How do you steer a man you have never met into a conversation about what might have motivated his crime when he has no intention of admitting anything? Even though I had spent years writing about gruesome murders, cheating husbands, and shady politicians, when I sat across from Mark Anderson I found I couldn't pounce with the hard questions when I needed to. I didn't have any true killer instinct, it turned out.

Instead, Mark and I had a conversation that wouldn't have been out of place around a nice dinner and a glass of wine. Of course, it being Mark, who fancied himself a wine connoisseur, the wine would have to be an old Bordeaux or a hard-to-find Burgundy. I inquired about his living conditions. He described them in detail. I asked about his health. He went on to explain his various physical ailments. He had a back so contorted he spent many hours of each day lying on the ground. He was recovering from prostate cancer. He had sleep apnea. According to him, the jail was a pit, "akin to a prison ship in the 1600s" (a reference, it seemed, designed to impress me with his erudition). From there our conversation meandered to his travels in France, the incompetence of his lawyer, and how I really should track down this particular lead. His role in the crime barely came up.

Mark Anderson wasn't the only person lying. I had gone to him under the pretense of objectivity, a reporter interested in better understanding why he had set such a destructive fire. That was cover enough for me to write an article.

But I obscured my personal motivations, the real reason I wanted him to confess. Yes, I was after a story, like most reporters. But I was also there for myself, to understand a chapter from my family's past, rather than for any scoop I might have scored.

The fire in the Wines Central warehouse in October 2005 had

destroyed 175 bottles of Port and Angelica wine my great-great grand-father had made in 1875. The wine had come from a vineyard forty miles east of Los Angeles, in Rancho Cucamonga, from grapes that had been planted as early as 1839. California was part of Mexico then and the area around Los Angeles, not Napa and Sonoma, produced the bulk of the state's wine. The Cucamonga Vineyard was widely lauded for produc-ing some of the best wine in California.

Numerous wooden boxes of the wine had been handed down through the generations. I hadn't owned the particular bottles that were destroyed in the fire, although I had a few at my home in Berkeley. An-other branch of the family had inherited most of the wine and a cousin had sent the bottles to a winemaker friend in St. Helena for assessment. He had kept the boxes of wine in his caves tunneled into the Mayaca-mas Mountains for months, but got worried that the humidity would ruin the labels. So when he moved his own wine cases to the Wines Central warehouse, he moved her historic wine as well. He had been convinced that there was no safer place for the wine than the old Navy bunker with its thick, earthquake-proof walls.

That must have been one agonizing phone call to make, the one to my cousin, telling her that all her wine had been destroyed.

To me, the loss of the wine felt like the severing of my past, some-thing I had been trying to grab onto for as long as I could remember. I came from a pioneer California family, but had been ripped from its em-brace after my parents' divorce when I was two. In hindsight, I spent much of my life chasing after the security I imagined an intact home would have provided; when the wine burned I felt like one more link to my father, who had died when I was sixteen, and his side of the family had disappeared.

It's not that I didn't seek ways to dig deeper into my roots. I researched the life of the man who made the wine, my great-great-grandfather, Isaias W. Hellman, and published a book in 2008 about his rise to prom-inence. He had been a poor Jewish immigrant when he immigrated to Los Angeles in 1859 and had eventually become a successful banker and financier, even assuming control of Wells Fargo Bank. My research meant that I became the family historian and genealogy expert, the one everyone called to figure out how we were related to this person or that.

The loss of the wine prompted me to think harder about what it had taken to succeed as a winemaker in the nineteenth century when there were no stainless steel tanks or packaged native yeasts or Facebook to connect with customers. Where was Rancho Cucamonga, the place the wine was produced, anyway?

I started to do research and found that the Franciscan fathers, the men who trekked north from Mexico to found missions and colonize the area, were the first to produce wine in California. They essentially enslaved the Native Americans to plant the vines, pick the fruit, and then stomp the grapes suspended in cowhides. The *Californios*, the native-born Mexicans of the state, as well as the earliest American settlers, were no kinder to the Native Americans.

The wine in California was not particularly good in the nineteenth century. It was made with Mission grapes, brought here in 1778. The wine was a deep red, but was low in acidity, making it taste flat and dull. It was livened up with sugar and brandy and, on occasion, more ominous adulterants.

Making wine back in California in the nineteenth century was a fool's errand, an easy way to lose money fast. Yet believers had stuck with it and carved out a respectable industry despite the boom and bust cycles that seemed to hit every decade. But winemaking also brought out men's avarice and search for power. In the late 1880s and 1890s, a group of men, including my ancestor, had created the California Wine Association, a long-forgotten monopoly that bullied small wineries into submission. The company eventually controlled more than 80 percent of the wine production in California and constructed the largest winery in the world on the edge of San Francisco Bay. Prohibition put it out of business. It took decades to rebuild American interest in wine and create one of the largest wine economies in the world, worth an estimated $24.6 billion in 2014.[1]

What, I began to wonder, drove this passion? What kind of determination did it take to make something wonderful from a bunch of grapes? Why were people so passionate about something that was, at the end of the day, one liquid among millions? Why did they go to great lengths to chase down rare bottles or push their way onto the waiting lists of cult wineries? Was it the search for prestige, for status? There was no shortage of Japanese corporate titans and Silicon Valley entrepreneurs who reinvented themselves as country vintners, spending millions on prime Napa Valley real estate and the best vineyard managers and winemakers they could afford. What prompted them?

I found myself on a quest of sorts, one to comprehend why someone would knowingly ruin that much wine, and to better understand the drive it took to make a good bottle of wine. I realized that the journey those particular 1875 bottles had taken was a microcosm of the history of wine in California, and I began to think that if I really understood what went into the making of that wine—the history of the land, the stories of the men and women who owned the vineyard, and those who worked to ensure that California wine culture flourished—I would know more about what I had lost. Was it only a liquid? Was it a heritage? Was it a link to anything that mattered?

PART ONE

DESTRUCTION

CHAPTER ONE

THE MYSTERY OF WINE

The aerial acrobat was dangling from a silky, sea-green rope attached to the ceiling. She wrapped one portion around her foot, used that as an anchor, and slowly turned upside down, arching her back as she slipped down the rope, the better to show off her gold lamé leotard and elbow-length fingerless black satin gloves. Grasping the rope with one hand and a bottle of Raymond Vineyards Chardonnay with the other, she carefully poured wine into the glasses lifted toward her. She didn't spill a drop.

It was the night before the seventeenth Premiere Napa Valley, the annual auction in February that lures big wine retailers, auction houses, and a select number of the very rich to the Napa Valley. The place to be that evening was at the party thrown by Jean-Charles Boisset, a smooth talking, sexy upstart French winemaker who paid no attention to the convention that the California wine lifestyle was laid back and tasteful. Boisset liked big, he liked brash, he liked red. The main room in his Raymond Vineyards winery off the Silverado Trail is called The Red Room, and it is decorated like a fin de siècle French bordello, with stuffed red velvet settees, red velvet walls, leopard-print rugs, crystal chandeliers, and pictures of a scantily clad Marilyn Monroe scattered around. Boisset's Crystal Cellars, where thousands of gallons of wine ferment in enormous stainless steel tanks, is probably the only winery in northern California equipped with a Baccarat crystal chandelier and theatrical lights that can flicker between red, blue, and yellow.

When Boisset first came to the Napa Valley, the scion of a successful French winemaker, and started a buying spree that netted him Raymond Vineyards and the historic Buena Vista Winery, many old-timers rolled their eyes in dismay. But disdain eventually turned to respect. Boisset, who dresses in Tom Ford suits and Louboutin shoes, married Gina Gallo, an heir to E. & J. Gallo, the world's largest wine company. The couple moved with their twin daughters into the hilltop home built by Robert Mondavi for his wife, Magritte, as if to declare that they were the new generation. Boisset then devoted himself to putting the fun back into wine with over-the-top gatherings that included erotic dancers and models bathing in tubs of chocolate. No one could discount Boisset's financial success or ignore the fact that he seemed like a genuinely sweet guy who loved nothing more than throwing a great party.

When I walked into the fête, Boisset was standing by a table covered with colorful feather masks. He greeted me—and everyone else—with kisses on the cheeks as if we were old friends, then encouraged us to disguise ourselves with masks and get our pictures taken. He even jumped into some of the photos. It was classic Boisset—fun and frivolous, with a hint of naughty.

I took a mask and walked slowly through the winery, feasting on a huge spread of shrimp and oysters in one room and cheese, bread, and olives in another room. The Asian buffet was next, and I piled pot stickers, egg rolls, and stir-fried noodles on my plate. My wineglass was never empty, as passing waiters regularly topped it off with a Raymond Vineyards white. I could have had his JCB Champagne made from Burgundian grapes or a nice Cabernet if I had preferred.

All around me the music blared. People were laughing and joking. In the crush of guests and behind the anonymity of the feathered masks, some revelers were tossing aside their inhibitions and openly rubbing against each other. Napa Valley, usually known for its tasteful wineries disguised as rustic barns, its rows of green grapevines under bright blue skies, its olive trees, rosemary bushes, and lavender plants, was the location that night for a party that better resembled a nightclub at a racy Club Med than a dignified occasion for sniffing and swirling.

The lubricant, of course, was wine.

The first recorded mention of wine is in the Bible, which said that one of the first things Noah did after surviving the flood was to plant a vineyard. "And he drank of the wine, and was drunken." The Greeks and the Romans both had wine gods, one called Dionysus, the other Bacchus. Their civilizations celebrated wine at every opportunity, from the planting of the grapes, to the harvest, to drinking until debauched. Wine was so central to the Roman Empire that its leaders believed that everyone, not just the elite, deserved to drink it daily.

The American relationship to wine is more complex. For much of this country's history, people have preferred cider or beer. Early efforts by California winemakers to convince those living on the East Coast that their wine was as good as that of Europe were ignored, at best, or openly scorned. Wine was largely the drink of the wealthy until the 1880s, when a flood of immigrants from France, Spain, and Italy came to the United States. They regarded wine as an everyday beverage, not something limited to special occasions. Consumption picked up, as did wine quality, but those advances were wiped away with Prohibition. It was not until the late 1960s, when men like Robert Mondavi began to promote a lifestyle that included drinking wine and eating good food that wine made deep inroads into the American psyche. First Americans turned to jug wine, those ubiquitous glass gallons labeled "Chianti" or "Burgundy." Then came the switch to 750-milliliter bottles and a rush to drink the slightly sweet Sutter Home white Zinfandel. Then wine moved on to supermarket shelves and Costco. Now the United States is the largest wine consuming country in the world, drinking 13 percent of all the wine produced globally in 2013.

Most people who drink wine reach for bottles that cost less than ten dollars. But there is a smaller, yet influential, group that regards wine as more than just a beverage. Those people think of it as an elixir, something that changes feeling and mood. "Wine can be a portal into the mystic," wrote wine importer Terry Theise. Just as grapes are transformed into wine through fermentation, people are transformed by wine. It warms our bodies as we sip it. It cheers us up. A bottle shared around a dinner can enhance friendships. Taken to the extreme, wine can loosen tongues to let out long-suppressed truths.

For some people, wine is an intellectual journey. The more they drink, the more they want to know—about the grapes used, the place they came from, the vineyard's history, the winemaker's thoughts when blending a wine. They may develop an affinity for a particular varietal or winery. In time, that can evolve into an urgent need, an obsession of sorts. Those who are fanatical hunt down elusive vintages of Domaine de la Romanée Conti or Château Cheval Blanc, two highly regarded French wines. They join waiting lists of the so-called "cult" wineries, like Screaming Eagle, Harlan, or Sine Qua Non in California and patiently wait for years, even decades, until their first allocation. They scour retail stores for rare bottles. They join wine bulletin boards to exchange tasting notes. Then there are the collectors, often extremely rich men who own tens of thousands of bottles, more wine than they can possibly drink in their lifetime.

These oenophiles are fascinated with wine because they see it as a living, breathing thing, a beverage that evolves with age. If you pour wine into a glass it will taste different in an hour and even more different at the end of the evening. If you store it in a cellar, in ten years it will have a completely different character than it does today. Nothing changes like wine.

Matt Kramer, a wine writer, tried to explain in a 2013 article in the *Wine Spectator* magazine why wine enriches life. "Why should you care about fine wine?" Kramer wrote. "The answer is surprisingly simple: Fine wine can—and indeed will—expand your world. It broadens and deepens the reach of your senses. It can help soften the rough edges of daily life and even remind you that beauty exists in moments when it seems least likely to penetrate your daily life."

Maya, a character in the 2004 hit film *Sideways*, rhapsodizes in one scene about wine. Although she is a fictional character, her words could have come out of the mouths of many of the people who flock to Napa Valley on a summer day. "I like to think about the life of wine . . . How it's a living thing. I like to think about what was going on the year the grapes were growing; how the sun was shining; if it rained. I like to think about all the people who tended and picked the grapes. And if it's an old wine, how many of them must be dead by now. I like how wine continues to evolve, like if I opened a bottle of wine today it would taste different than if I'd opened it on any other day, because a bottle of wine is actually alive. And it's constantly evolving and gaining complexity. That is, until it peaks, like your '61. And then it begins its steady, inevitable decline."

For people just as happy with a bottle of Two Buck Chuck from Trader Joe's as a $150 bottle of California Cabernet, all this rhapsodizing may seem ridiculous. And the language around wine, such as tasting notes that talk about essences of chocolate, graphite, and berries, can be over the top. But not for the true believers, men like Mark Anderson. He wrote to me from jail to say that when he drank a particularly good glass of, say, a 1900 Château Lafite Rothschild, which is extremely rare, he liked to close his eyes to intensify the sensations. As the deep red liquid swirled in his mouth, setting off buzzers of taste, he would visualize the sunshine on the Bordeaux vineyard the year the wine was made. He would think about what had happened in 1900. Who had lovingly coaxed the grapes to maturity and transformed them into wine? What had they been dreaming about? And he thought, as he often did when he drank a great vintage, that the wine was "like bottled sunshine, the sweet juice from a small star."[2] Anderson may have been accused of destroying the largest amount of wine in recorded history, but when it came to wine he had a poet's heart and the words to express it.

Anderson was first seduced by wine in the 1960s, when the Napa and Sonoma valleys were coming out of their long Prohibition-induced slumber. The area north of San Francisco was pastoral, with small towns scattered among large fields and grazing land. Vineyards were tucked among prune, pear, and walnut orchards and travelers along Highway 29 were as likely to see farmers cutting wheat as laborers picking grapes. Feed, hay, and fuel stores, not high-end boutiques and tasting rooms, clustered along St. Helena's Main Street.

A few Italian families were making wine then, including the Mondavis and Sebastianis, as were a handful of wineries like Beaulieu and Beringer Brothers. Sweet wines outsold table wines throughout the country, so many growers sent their grapes to the Central Valley to be blended into bulk wine.

The old wineries that had been abandoned during Prohibition still stood unattended, their vineyards overrun with weeds and the yellow mustard that bloomed with the cold winter rains. The aspiring winemakers who would transform Napa Valley into the most sought-after wine destination in the United States during the next two decades had just started to arrive.

Anderson used to drive up to the region from the San Francisco Bay Area with an empty jug in his backseat. Wine tasting was mostly an informal affair. Visitors didn't need appointments. Anderson could wander in to Charles Krug in Napa or old man Pagani's in Sonoma and fill up his bottle for fifty cents. It wasn't hard to spot Robert Mondavi, who had just built his mission-style winery in Oakville, wandering the grounds to greet visitors.

The small-town feeling made it easy to meet winemakers and talk to them about what they were doing. Along with the camaraderie was a sense of discovery that impressed itself upon Anderson. "Those wines weren't rated in points and by today's standards would not even be listed," Anderson recalled much later. "But it was all we had and we enjoyed it. It was inexpensive, vintners were learning, we were all learning. European wines were very difficult to find and not much better." When Anderson sat on the lawn of a winery, eating a picnic lunch under blue skies, and sipping a bright red wine, all while staring out at rows of green vines, he felt like he belonged.

Fifty years later, Napa Valley has perfected that sense of belonging. It is no longer a bucolic secret; it is one of the most visited tourist destinations in California. The valley has seven hundred wineries that pump $13 billion annually into the local economy.[3] The Napa Valley Tourism Bureau spends $4.5 million a year promoting the valley, emphasizing both wine and food with their slogan "Come here to experience the art of living well." Yet people still connect with the valley for the very same reasons Anderson did more than fifty years ago: they feel included.

Winery owners know that nothing sells wine better than a sense of intimacy and connection to the land and to the winemaker. So the valley plays down its corporate-owned wineries, its significant role in the global market of wine. The family story, the tale of determined men and women who have produced stellar wine from unique hillside or valley vineyards, is a dominant theme.

Around three million people visit Napa each year. Most come just for the day, dropping into three or four wineries. They pay anywhere from fifteen to fifty-five dollars to sip, swirl, and spit the valley's many Chardonnays, Cabernet Sauvignons, and Pinot Noirs. In the summertime, when the days are bright and hot, Highway 29 and the Silverado Trail, the north-south roads that traverse the west and east sides of the valley, are bumper to bumper with cars. While the traffic might be frustrating, the scenery is beautiful. The wooded Mayacamas Mountains rise sharply on the west, a natural buffer between the cool fog that rolls off the Pacific Ocean and the inland temperatures that reach into the high nineties. The dryer Howell Mountains form the eastern boundary. Rows of grapevines extend across the valley floor and into the foothills, with their summer clusters of purple grapes peaking from under bright green leaves.

The tourists weave in and out of the traffic to stop at the tasting rooms lining the highways, and then go to eat at Oxbow Market in Napa or Redd in Yountville or Mustards in Oakville. If they are really fortunate, they have snagged a reservation at Thomas Keller's French Laundry.

Day tripping and wine tasting can only go so far, however. As eno-tourism has evolved into a multi-million-dollar industry, true wine lovers seek out experiences, ones that bring them closer to winemakers and the winemaking process. They want to feel a part of the Napa Valley.

Napa has developed ways to meet the expectations of the people Kramer might define as "obsessed." Need help assembling a wine cellar? Soutirage, a personal wine merchant, can help. The private sommeliers will come into your home, assess your cellar, and develop a plan for buying wine for everyday drinking, aging, and investment. With their deep contacts at American and European wineries, they can get their clients rare or hard to find wines, like Colgin, a Napa Valley cult wine made by Ann Colgin, or Château Mouton Rothschild. They can arrange a truffle hunt in Piedmont or a private dinner at a French château. If a client is at a London restaurant trying to choose between two Italian Barolos on the wine list, that person can text the Soutirage staff, many of whom have been sommeliers at restaurants like the French Laundry, for a recommendation. They will take your personal preferences into consideration and tell you which Barolo you will probably like best. If there is a bottle you particularly enjoy while at a restaurant or a friend's house, Soutirage clients can take a photo of it, shoot it to the sommeliers, and Soutirage staff will locate the bottle and put it in your cellar.

Do you have a hankering for your own vineyard? The eighty-acre Napa Valley Reserve is a place where wine lovers who don't have the money (prime vineyard land can cost $300,000 an acre) or the time to grow their own grapes can pretend to be winemakers. Located right next to the Meadowood resort in St. Helena, the Reserve is a perfect expression of Napa Valley's casual luxury, with its artificially weathered wood building, rows of olive trees, an organic garden, and grapevines running up to near the edge of the crushed granite paths.

For a mere $175,000 initiation fee and a promise to buy at least another $7,500 of wine each year, the Reserve's six hundred members get the right to "own" two or three rows of vines made from cloned grapes from Harlan Estate.

In early fall, the Reserve's rows of grapevines are filled with the bankers and doctors and real estate investors—and their children—who are members. They get up early, mimicking the rhythm of the Mexican or

Central American field workers who pick most of the valley's grapes, don thick protective gloves, and use red-handled grape shears to cut off clusters of ripe red grapes. They then sort out the unripe fruit, leaves, and bugs before the grapes are crushed. Once the wine has fermented, each member can work with a master winemaker to blend his or her own vintage, which will then be aged in French oak for two years and bottled with a personalized label.

Membership sales have been brisk. The actors Robert Redford and Nicolas Cage belong. Lance Armstrong, the disgraced seven-time Tour de France winner, and David and Victoria Beckham, the retired British soccer star and his fashionista wife, are members. So is Suze Orman, the financial guru.

All of the members can afford to buy fine wine; it's the lifestyle they want—getting their hands dirty, smelling the ripe grapes, discussing the fine points of a vintage with a world-renowned winemaker. "I love the visceral side—the land, the grapes, the biology," said one New York doctor. "That whole thing is extremely appealing."[4]

"There's a spiritual element to wine," said a Michigan businessman who sold his company for more than $122 million. "You know you're producing something from the earth."[5]

The ultimate expression of the Napa Valley lifestyle is Auction Napa Valley, the annual fund-raiser put on by a trade group, the Napa Valley Vintners, in late May or early June to support local charities. The auction—which has cost $3,000 a couple in recent years—draws some of the world's top collectors, as well as tech and finance moguls enjoying what they have earned.

The auction is held each year under huge white tents set up on the vast lawn of the Meadowood resort in St. Helena. I attended on a scorching bright blue day in June 2013. The theme was orange. The color was everywhere: on signs, on tabletops, on napkins, on the umbrellas providing shade from the relentless sun. Even the expensive race cars parked as eye candy at the auction entrance, like the Audi R8 Spyder convertible, were bright orange. The day started off under one big white tent. Revelers wandered around and nibbled on lamb sliders, grilled cheese sandwiches, ox tongue, and fresh scallops prepared by nine winners of the Bravo! *Top Chef* competition. Winemakers holding magnums of their wine mingled with the guests, and poured glasses for anyone who asked.

I didn't spot any celebrities—in other years Oprah Winfrey, Jay Leno, and Teri Hatcher had attended—but I saw many well-dressed people in bright cotton sundresses and linen shirts and straw panama hats. There were a few tech titans, too, like Steve Case, the founder of AOL, and his wife, Jean. Most of the people I talked to said they returned year after year in part because the auction organizers pampered them and made them feel special. No detail was overlooked, from the glasses of cold sparkling wine that were handed out as guests boarded the shuttle bus to bring them to Meadowood to the gift bags they took home. The guests felt part of a special inner circle, I heard repeatedly.

In the early afternoon, as the heat rose into the mid-nineties, a conga line of vintners danced their way into the auction tent. It was the signal for the beginning of the main event. Big spenders, the people who had purchased lots in previous years, were seated near the front at long rectangular tables covered with orange tablecloths. Bottles of fine wine sat on every table.

The auction got off to a strong start. One bidder paid $350,000 for a trip to Tokyo and Kyoto with Naoko Dalla Valle, the Japanese-born cult winemaker whom the *Wine Spectator* magazine dubbed one of the "Three Graces of Napa," for her beauty and winemaking skills. Another bid $120,000 to travel through Argentina with winemaker Delia Viader (another "Grace") and Aria Mehrabi, the owner of Mithra Winery. But the thousand people gathered under the white tent regarded those lots as mere warm-ups. They had been anticipating Lot #20, a twenty-year vertical of Harlan Estate. Bill Harlan, who owned Meadowood as well as the Napa Reserve, made legendary wines from a thirty-acre vineyard in the Oakville region of Napa. The world's top wine critics were uniformly enthusiastic about Harlan's wines. British wine writer Jancis Robinson called Harlan's lush, intensely concentrated Cabernets "one of the ten best wines of the twentieth century." Robert Parker, who many regard as having the most discriminating palate around, had given

100-point scores to five of Harlan's vintages. The wines are made in such small quantities that they are almost impossible to get. The waiting list is years long. And any wine that made its way to the secondary market commanded thousands of dollars. In short, Lot #20 was *the* lot of the auction.

To start the bidding, auction organizers projected large pictures of Harlan Estate wine on three screens behind the auctioneers. The gavel went down. A handful of people seated at tables near the front thrust their wooden paddles in the air. The opening bid was around $100,000. Within two minutes, the number had shot up, up, up, up into the stratosphere, with a venture capitalist named Gary Rieschel determined to hold his lead. Every time someone bid, Rieschel lifted up paddle #26 with his right hand while nursing a glass of red wine with his left. He seemed calm, but aggressive, meeting and raising each bid. He had clearly done this before. "Do I see $500,000 for this lot," the auctioneer rattled off. Up went a paddle. "Do I see $700,000?" A few bidders waved their paddles around. When the gavel landed, Rieschel had bid $800,000 for an auction lot titled "The Works." The package included a tasting of every Harlan vintage from 1990 to 2009, two nights at Meadowood, and a celebratory dinner for eight prepared by Christopher Kostow, the resort's Michelin three-star chef.

Hours later, as auction attendees left the tent to sit down for a dinner prepared by the executive chef of Blackberry Farm in the Smoky Mountains of Tennessee, Rieschel, then fifty-seven, sat cross-legged on the Meadowood lawn. Dressed in khaki shorts and a beige linen shirt (the only startling splashes of color were his pink-and-yellow argyle socks), the man who had made the day's highest bid waved off auction handlers eager to protect him from nosy journalists. Rieschel was perfectly happy to speak openly about why he dropped so much money on a twenty-year vertical of Harlan Estate wine. Reischel, the founder of Qiming Venture Partners, a $1 billion fund that invests in early-stage companies in China, explained by way of example. A few years earlier he had purchased a vertical tasting at Shafer Vineyards, a 210-acre winery in Napa's Stag's Leap district whose wine Robert M. Parker had anointed as "one of the New World's most profound Cabernet Sauvignons." Rieschel and his friends spent hours with the owner, Doug Shafer, tasting and discussing wines and learning about the ups and downs of each vintage. They walked the hillside vineyards. They wandered among the barrels and fermentation tanks. They shared an excellent meal at the winery. They forged a strong personal connection. Reischel called it "one of the most emotional and special days" he had ever spent in Napa. "It's not about the wine," he said. "It's about the people."

What does it say that a man like Rieschel, a man with millions of dollars at his disposal, chooses to spend his money on wine? He could spend the same amount chartering a private plane to fly to the Seven Wonders of the World, renting a yacht to cruise the Mediterranean, or buying a painting. Yet he chose to spend his money on wine.

It's the pursuit of the experience, the belief that wine opens up worlds and forges friendships that drives people to be so obsessed. Humans have worshipped wine for eons, from Noah to the Greeks to Gary Rieschel. It's what also drove Mark Anderson.

CHAPTER TWO

ALL IS LOST

October 12, 2005

Delia Viader paused at the entrance to Meadowood Resort, taking a moment to get her bearings. It was just after six p.m. on the evening of October 12, 2005, and the Napa Valley air was still warm and pleasant.

Viader looked around. Meadowood was familiar to her, as it had become the center of the Napa Valley social life ever since Bill Harlan and his now-deceased partner Peter Stocker had purchased it in 1979. The two men had poured millions into the 240-acre estate, transforming it from a small country club into a world-class resort where bungalows nestled among ancient oak trees and guests played croquet on a broad and sweeping lawn. Viader had been at Meadowood just a few months earlier when she attended the 2005 Napa Valley auction in June with her boyfriend, Tim Mondavi, son of Robert Mondavi, the man many credited with raising the reputation—and consumption—of Napa wine. That evening had been a bittersweet affair. The Mondavis had just sold their wine empire for $1.03 billion to Constellation Brands, merging the family-owned business with one of the largest beverage companies in the world. All eyes were on the Mondavi family—and Viader—as they entered the white auction tent. What was their reaction to the sale, which signaled the end of an era in Napa Valley history? But the auction had been fun as well. Jay Leno, the host of *The Tonight Show* on NBC, was the host. Everyone had laughed when he deadpanned: "This is a performer's dream. Rich people who have been drinking."

Viader, who was born in Argentina but who had spent a lot of time in France before moving to the United States, was back at Meadowood that evening for another party. This time, Silicon Valley Bank, a lender to Viader and many other Napa Valley winemakers, was celebrating the accomplishments of some of its most successful clients with an elegant evening under the stars.

Viader Vineyards was nineteen years old. In May 1986, when Viader was a single mother of three, including one son with Down syndrome, she had persuaded her father to let her use the land he owned on Howell Mountain on the eastern side of the valley. Viader's father, an Argentinian diplomat who once served as a military attaché to the United Nations, had purchased the hillside property years earlier as an investment.

Viader had always had a head for numbers. It was trait that she might have inherited from her paternal grandfather, a large landowner in Spain who had emigrated to Argentina after the government confiscated his holdings in the name of agrarian reform. He moved there during the first decade of the twentieth century, where he formed a partnership in a tobacco venture with the Greek shipping magnate Aristotle Onassis. Just as her grandfather had learned to re-create himself and prosper, so would Viader.

Viader was well educated but had no experience with wine before she started a winery in 1986. A blond woman with delicate features and green eyes, Viader spoke Spanish, French, German, Italian, Latin, and English and had gotten the equivalent of a PhD in philosophy from the Sorbonne in Paris. She had also studied at the Massachusetts Institute of Technology and at two campuses of the University of California— Berkeley and Davis. But she had never selected a grape variety, plotted out a vineyard, or blended grapes. Because Viader loved to drink wine, particularly French Bordeaux and Burgundy, she had fantasized about bringing that Old World approach to California wine.

The idea seemed a folly. The land on which Viader planned to create a vineyard was so rocky and steep that standing was difficult. Most of the grapes in Napa at that time were planted on the flat valley floor or on hills with a slight incline.

But Viader had seen vertical vineyards on steep slopes in Europe and was convinced it could be done. She hired Dave Abreu—who would later become a famous vineyard manager—to design her vineyard. He planted twelve acres of closely spaced rows of Cabernet Sauvignon and Cabernet Franc grapes running up and down the hill. That, too, was unheard of in the Napa Valley, where most hillside vineyards were terraced. But Viader had heard that a vertical orientation gave the grapes better sun exposure.

Disaster struck early on. Viader used dynamite to crack apart the hill's volcanic rock. During some heavy October rains in 1989, dirt from the exposed hill liquefied. The mud and rocks flowed down the hill and into the Bell Canyon reservoir, the source of St. Helena's water supply, and then buried the shooting range of the St. Helena police. The landslide, many believe, was an impetus for the Napa County Board of Supervisors to adopt a hillside ordinance establishing erosion controls on the hills in 1991.

But matters eventually stabilized. Viader made her first vintage, a combination of Cabernet Sauvignon and Cabernet Franc, a blend that the young winemaker regarded as more restrained than the fruity, high-alcohol Cabernet Sauvignons that were increasingly popular in Napa.

In 2000, *Wine Spectator*, the influential glossy magazine that touted wine and wine country living, named Viader's 1997 red, a blend of Cabernet Sauvignon and Petit Verdot grapes, its number two wine in the world. The renowned wine critic Robert Parker called it "terrific . . . a wine of exceptional finesse and elegance." Her signature "Viader" was selling for $100 a bottle, and her most elite product, V, a Petit Verdot, sold for $150 a bottle.

The evening of October 12 was to be a celebration of all Viader had accomplished the previous nineteen years. Viader, who many regarded as one of the most beautiful women in Napa, with a lilting accented voice that enhanced her mystique, dressed simply, but elegantly, in a black pantsuit. Her home at the top of Howell Mountain near the town of Deer Park was nearby and it had only taken Viader ten minutes to speed down the road to Meadowood. She pulled into the parking lot shortly as the sun was starting to set.

Suddenly her cell phone rang. Viader looked at it, not certain if she should answer. But the call was from her son Alan, the second oldest of her children. He was her vineyard manager and heir apparent, and was poised to take over as head winemaker.

Viader flipped open the cell phone. At first she couldn't quite understand Alan. He was in a panic, his voice strained, his breathing hard. He seemed close to tears. He told her something about a warehouse. He screamed into the phone that everything was on fire.

Viader paused at the entryway to Meadowood. Fire? What fire? What warehouse? What was he talking about? But then she remembered. Alan was talking about the Wines Central warehouse on Mare Island in Vallejo, a place about nineteen miles away from her winery. The warehouse, with its thick concrete walls that served as a natural insulator and bulwark against earthquakes, seemed like a good storage facility. It was right near the highways that led to San Francisco and Sacramento, and close to rail lines that carried cargo to ships. Viader had sent all of her 2003 vintage, about 7,400 cases, there just a few weeks earlier.

As Viader hung up, a feeling of doom flooded over her. She had millions of dollars of wine in that warehouse. She needed to go there to see what was happening. But she still had to face the dinner hosted by Silicon Valley Bank—her creditor, the institution that was rewarding her for her loyalty and accomplishments by hosting a celebratory evening. Viader steeled herself and walked into the banquet room. She saw her personal banker and pulled him aside. "We have to talk," she said.

Ted Hall was bustling around in the office of Long Meadow Ranch headquarters, located on a hill high above the floor of the Napa Valley. It felt good to be back and focusing on his winery and ranch operations after a hiatus. In January 2004, Hall, a heavy man with a round and friendly face, took a yearlong break from overseeing his winery and farm to serve as chairman of the board of the Robert Mondavi winery—the first time in its history an outsider had taken the helm. The company that had elevated the profile of Napa Valley's wines to equal those of France and Italy had been in free fall at the time. Mondavi had stepped down as chairman in 2001 and then, after installing his son Michael as his successor, helped oust him after just a few years. Revenue was falling. Hall, a former McKinsey consultant who had an extensive background in wine and finance, was brought in to stop the decline. Within a year Hall, considered a master strategist and turnaround expert, had negotiated the wine company's sale to Constellation Brands for $1.36 billion, a 61 percent increase in value from the time Hall had stepped in. He pocketed $2.5 million for his efforts.

The work had been intense, but it was over. Hall was at Long Meadow Ranch, which he owned with his wife, Laddie, and son, Christopher. Hall and his family had long lived in San Francisco, where Hall served on the board of the San Francisco Symphony and was a member of the secretive, male-only Bohemian Club. He was also a jazz aficionado who had started his own record company. But Hall had another identity as an amateur vintner. He had grown up in a small farming community in western Pennsylvania and made his first batch of wine in 1971 with two classmates from Stanford Business School. They purchased Carignane and Zinfandel grapes from a longtime grower in Gilroy, south of San Jose, and, in what would become a Silicon Valley tradition, handcrafted the wine in a garage in Santa Clara. Hall made wine as an amateur for seventeen years. Then he and his wife decided to enter the business professionally.

Laddie and Ted scoured the Napa Valley for a suitable place to grow grapes. They fell in love with an old 640-acre parcel that President Ulysses S. Grant had deeded to E. J. Church in 1872 as a land patent grant. The farm was nestled in the foothills of the Mayacamas Mountains with magnificent views looking out over the valley to Howell Mountain. The long meadow that formed the centerpiece of the property gave the farm its name.

Grapes and other crops had first been planted at Long Meadow Ranch in the late nineteenth century and for decades its owners had raised cattle, produced olive oil, and cultivated apples, pears, and other fruit trees. The vineyards were abandoned during Prohibition and by the time the Halls purchased the property in 1989, the farming operations had long lay fallow.

The farm and its history inspired the Halls. They didn't just resurrect the winery, but decided to build an integrated farming operation that harkened back to the ranch's historical roots. They brought in cattle and Appaloosa horses, and bottled olive oil from the property's 125-year-old trees. They also bought land in the small city of St. Helena and converted an old barn into the Farmstead Restaurant, one of St. Helena's first farm-to-table restaurants. It focused on locally sourced and organic food, much of it grown on the property's gardens, and was widely admired.

Hall was pleased with what he and his wife had accomplished. Production had grown steadily and in 2005 Long Meadow Ranch was producing between 12,000 and 15,000 cases of wine a year, including its signature E. J. Church Reserve Cabernet Sauvignon. After fifteen years of work and more than 5,000 visits to stores, restaurants, and wine shops around the country, Long Meadow Ranch wine was carried in some of the best restaurants and stores in New York and San Francisco.

Hall was hoping that the 2005 vintage would be a good one. It had been an exceptionally cool year in California, with early and frequent rains in the spring and summer. Grape growth had been vigorous, which usually leads to less intensely flavored grapes. But the weather had warmed up in September and October, and the sugar level in the grapes still hanging on the vine was steadily increasing. By October 12, some picking had begun, but many winemakers were holding off to let the grape clusters develop as long as possible.

Hall was at his desk tapping away at his computer when Les Dendon, the winery's chief financial officer, popped in his head. Dendon's wife, who was driving up to Napa from the San Francisco peninsula, had just called, said Dendon. She had seen a huge plume of smoke in the air. The radio said there was a massive fire at a wine storage warehouse in Vallejo.

Dendon was concerned. Long Meadow Ranch had most of its inventory in Wines Central, including its 2001 Cabernet, which was getting ready for release, every bottle of the 2002 vintage, and its wine library. In addition, Hall had moved a friend's collection of 1875 wine and port to the warehouse. Dendon suggested that Hall drive down to check up on the fire; he would keep in touch by cell phone.

Hall's heart began to beat more quickly as he raced out of his office and got into his four-wheel-drive pickup truck. He barreled down the steep and twisting driveway until he hit Highway 29, which led south toward Mare Island and Vallejo. After Hall was ten miles down the highway, it was all he could do to keep his eyes on the road. Far ahead he could see a massive column of smoke rising into the sky, a plume so large it could only mean one thing: this was an enormous fire.

Hall pushed down on the accelerator. He crossed the bridge over the Napa River and traveled south on Highway 29 until it intersected with Highway 37. He veered east toward Mare Island. As Hall turned off onto the cratered road that led to the old naval station, he could see fire trucks and fire equipment drive by, their lights and sirens flashing. The Vallejo police had set up a roadblock, but when the officer in charge saw Hall's truck, and Hall dressed in a vest and jeans, for some reason he waved him through.

As Hall pulled closer to the wine warehouse he could see dozens of fire trucks with more arriving by the minute from outlying areas. The fire looked hot, really hot, so hot as to make the building almost unapproachable. Hall spotted one group of firefighters in flame-retardant suits spraying huge metal doors with a cannon of water. When the water hit the superheated doors, it produced a wall of steam so intense that the firefighters were forced to retreat.

Another group of firefighters was on the roof, trying to cut a hole in the concrete to let the heat and smoke dissipate. They didn't have much success. The warehouse, built to store naval parts, was almost indestructible.

By then Hall heard a distinct noise. It was the sound of breaking glass. As the heat and flames melted the shrink-wrap binding together the towering cases of wine stored in the warehouse, the boxes toppled over, hitting other boxes in a domino effect. The crashes were audible over the roar of the fire.

As the bottles broke, the wine mixed with the water the firefighters were using to dwarf the blaze. Soon rivers of red liquid flowed out through the warehouse doors.

Hall couldn't believe the scene. It wasn't chaos, but it was close.

As he sat there in shock and disbelief and watched as firefighters tried to defeat the raging fire, Hall knew his wine was gone.

As Dick Ward was preparing espresso in the kitchen of his St. Helena home, he turned on NPR. Listening to the early morning news was part of his daily ritual, one he and his wife, Linda Reiff, the director of the Napa Valley Vintners Association, enjoyed every morning. They would eat breakfast and discuss the day's plans before Reiff left for her office. She only had to drive a few miles to get to work, where she oversaw the trade association that represented more than 300 wineries and fought to protect and promote the Napa Valley brand around the world. Ward, the cofounder of Saintsbury, a winery in the southern reaches of Napa Valley, had a twenty-five-minute commute.

Around eight a.m. the news came on. The news anchor reported that there had been a massive fire at a wine storage warehouse in Vallejo the day before. The fire had burned for more than eight hours, sending a plume of smoke seven hundred feet high above the area. Firefighters had not had a chance to assess the damage yet, but the warehouse was known to contain millions of bottles of fine wine. Much of it was probably damaged, announced the anchor.

Anxiety flooded Ward's body. Saintsbury wine was in that warehouse, he thought. Ward did a quick mental inventory. He and his partner, David Graves, had sent about 3,000 cases of their library wine, samples of twenty years of vintages, to Wines Central. They had sent the collection of bottles they had made since 1984, as well as two hundred large-format bottles.

Ward ran to the phone. He dialed Graves to find out if he knew any details about the fire. Graves didn't. Neither did any of the staff at the winery. Ward went on to the computer to check the news stories; he found article after article with the same alarming but generic details: the fire was massive and had probably ruined all of the wine that sat inside the building.

Ward, normally a placid man whose modern eyeglasses give him a touch of the avant-garde, couldn't sit still. What was going on with his wine? Was it safe or was it destroyed? Sitting in his house miles away from the winery, plagued by uncertainty, wasn't going to get him answers any faster. It only made him more anxious. Ward jumped into his bronze Honda Element and headed south on Highway 29 to Saintsbury in the Carneros district, the southernmost point of the Napa Valley, right on the edge of San Pablo Bay.

When Ward and Graves had first decided to grow Pinot Noir grapes in the foggy part of the valley, many people thought they were taking a gamble. While some of the best wine in the world is made from Pinot Noir grapes—the wines of Burgundy—very little good Pinot Noir wine was made outside of France at the time. Pinot is a temperamental grape, one susceptible to the elements, and mist, fog, and high winds were endemic in the Carneros district. Most thought it took a master's hand to coax the very best from Pinot grapes.

Ward and Graves weren't masters, just cocky. They had met each other in 1976 at a brewery class in the oenology department at the University of California at Davis, the university that had become the breeding ground for a new generation of modern winemakers and grape growers. Both had degrees in other topics—Ward had studied structural engineering at Tufts University near Boston and Graves had just left a doctoral program in English at the University of Chicago—but they had decided their lives' passion was in pursuit of the grape. There was something mystical about wine, they agreed. Grapes grown next to one another in the same vineyard could produce wines that tasted completely different. That idea of *terroir,* of ground and grape mixing to make something unique, intrigued both men, gripped them, and wouldn't let them free.

Ward and Graves hit it off instantly. They were both literary and enjoyed discussing history and men of letters. How many other people were enamored with *The Lark*, that 1895 literary journal of Gilded Age San Francisco printed on bamboo paper that featured the work of Gelett Burgess, a poet who coined the word "blurb," and others? Or were intrigued by a legendary 1540 Riesling harvest in Germany?

The men also shared a love of Burgundy wine made from Pinot Noir grapes and often lamented that few in California tried to replicate it. The state, particularly Napa Valley, was the land of the big, bold Cabernets, high in alcohol with a rich roll on the tongue.

The conversations inspired Ward and Graves. In 1978, a friend offered them some Cabernet grapes from Nathan Fay's highly regarded vineyard in the Stag's Leap appellation[6] of southeastern Napa. The two men, who had been interning at various Napa Valley wineries, drew on their burgeoning skills to make a barrel of wine. They named it The Lark after that long-ago literary magazine and included a quotation from one of the editions on the label: "Unending flow of dark red Napa claret."

The wine was good, really good. Ward and Graves found that both they and their friends had no difficulty polishing off a bottle and going back for more. So when the experiment was over, the men tried again. This time they bought grapes from the Carneros region on the edge of San Pablo Bay. Sparkling wine producers had long been using Pinot Noir grapes from the Carneros district, but Ward and Graves were among a new generation looking to make red Pinot Noir wine.

Once again the men reached into the literary world for inspiration. They selected the name Saintsbury in homage to the British historian and literary critic George Saintsbury, who at age seventy-five had written his opus, *Notes on a Cellar-Book*, considered one of the best tributes to drinking ever written. The wine was good, prompting the pair to purchase land and plant Pinot Noir grapes in 1981. (They eventually planted Chardonnay as well.) Every year, Ward and Graves set aside a few cases of the vintage for their wine library. They wanted to see how the wine aged. Many wine collectors and critics were skeptical that California wine could get better as it sat in the bottle. Most thought the wine, with its bold flavor and high alcohol content, was best drunk within two or three years. Ward thought otherwise. He thought Saintsbury's reds were as good as French reds, and could deepen and become more complex with time.

Saintsbury Winery would have its twenty-fifth anniversary in 2006. Ward and Graves were planning to host tastings in New York and San Francisco and invite prominent wine critics to a "vertical" tasting, which would offer a sample of every vintage made since the winery's beginnings. The guest list would include luminaries like Jancis Robinson, the British wine writer, whose articles influenced thousands of wine lovers around the globe. Ward had been looking forward to demonstrating how Saintsbury wines stood up over the decades.

But with the news that a fire had broken out in the place where those wines were stored, Ward had the feeling that the twenty-fifth anniversary celebration might never happen.

CHAPTER THREE

THE WRECKED REMAINS

Two days later, as R. Steven Lapham drove his blue Acura into the lot near the Wines Central warehouse, his first thought was that the building didn't look too badly damaged. While Vallejo fire department vehicles were parked nearby, as well as a large white and blue trucks from the Bureau of Alcohol, Tobacco, Firearms, and Explosives, there were no visible smoke stains on the building's outside white walls. The wooden door, with its carvings of grape clusters and a Franciscan friar holding up a glass of wine, was not even singed.

But Lapham's assessment changed as soon as he stepped inside. Wine storage warehouses are usually sterile-looking spaces, with fluorescent lights shining down on rows of shrink-wrapped cardboard wine boxes stacked high on pallets. But parts of the interior of Wines Central looked like they were in a war zone. The electricity had gone out, leaving the cavernous space dim, with light coming only from the gaps three stories up that once held the rows of windows. Case upon case of wine had collapsed in the inferno, sending millions of bottles crashing to the floor where they lay in shattered piles. The flames had burned away the sides of many cardboard boxes, exposing an eerie sight of upside-down wine bottles. The air was pungent, a mix of wine, wood char, smoke, and sodden cardboard.

Lapham stepped gingerly through the water and wine that had pooled on the concrete floor, and within minutes his fine leather loafers were soaking wet. Lapham hadn't expected to be called to investigate the wine fire, so he had dressed that morning in his lawyerly best: a blue suit, white shirt, and shoes more appropriate for the courthouse than a warehouse.

Lapham was an assistant U.S. attorney for the Eastern District of California, a jurisdiction that stretched from the state capital in Sacramento 286 miles south to Bakersfield. On the afternoon of October 14, he had driven from Sacramento to Vallejo to interview a witness for an upcoming racketeering trial against members of the Pitch Dark Family, a notorious Vallejo gang whose members were widely believed to be drug dealers and murderers. But shortly after Lapham completed the hour-long drive down Interstate 80, he got a call from his boss redirecting him to the fire-ravaged Wines Central warehouse. The fire had happened two days earlier and ATF investigators were looking for signs of arson.

It was no surprise that U.S. Attorney McGregor Scott turned to Lapham when a case involved fire. Lapham had spent much of his twenty-one-year career pursuing arsonists. A lithe California native with blue eyes, graying brown hair, and a laid-back demeanor that concealed a sharp prosecutorial instinct, Lapham was expert at understanding the physics behind fire and the mechanics of explosives. Those skills had helped him win numerous convictions, including one against a prominent Sacramento developer who torched his own warehouse to collect $4 million in insurance proceeds. He had also prosecuted three militiamen who planned to blast rocket launchers into two storage tanks that each held twelve million gallons of liquid propane. They were nicknamed the "Twin Sisters." If the right-wingers had succeeded, the explosion might have devastated a five-mile radius, killing 12,000 people.

But Lapham's most absorbing case to date—and the one that brought him a modicum of fame—involved Ted Kaczynski, the brilliant Harvard-trained mathematician turned Montana survivalist also known as the Unabomber. Over a period of seventeen years, Kaczynski had terrorized the United States by sending mail bombs to people and institutions he thought represented modern science and technology run amok. His targets seemed random; he sent bombs to Sacramento, Chicago, and even smuggled one onto an airplane. The bombs had killed three people, including the owner of a computer store in Sacramento, and injured twenty-three others.

Lapham was part of the Sacramento-based federal prosecution team and it was his job to pore through the 40,000 pages that Kaczynski had written in his isolated wooden shack in rural Montana railing against the rise of modern technology. Lapham's task, one that drew on his methodical approach to law, had been to annotate the impenetrable document and see which words or phrases would bolster the federal government's case. It took Lapham eighteen months to pore through the notebooks. He found some appalling evidence, like Kaczynski's reaction to the news that one of his bombs had killed the Sacramento computer storeowner in 1985. "Excellent," wrote Kaczynski. "Humane way to eliminate somebody. He probably never felt a thing. 25,000 reward offered. Rather flattering."[7]

But there was another reason Lapham's boss had called. In addition to being an expert in arson, Lapham was an expert in crimes involving wine. In fact, Lapham was widely looked on as the prosecutor who had made the federal government regard wine fraud as a serious issue. Over a five-year period in the late 1980s and early 1990s, Lapham had overseen a complex fraud prosecution of California grape growers, grape brokers, and winemakers who had passed off cheap grapes and wines as expensive varieties. Lapham won numerous convictions, sent the worst offenders to jail, and forced the others to pay millions in fines.

Lapham liked to visit the scene of a fire. He took his time, wandering around the perimeter of a building, looking at the placement of windows and doors, escape routes and entrapment points, then moving inside to study the path of a blaze. He called the walk his "visual," his time to imprint on his brain the particulars of a fire. Lapham was a physical man by nature, preferring movement to sitting behind a desk (he cycled or skied on weekends) and took the opportunity to go into the field whenever he could. His colleagues would say that his calm demeanor allowed him to absorb more than most; he tamped down his emotions and ramped up his powers of observation. It was the details, after all, that won convictions.

As Lapham shined a flashlight around the dripping interior of Wines Central he could immediately see that if the fire had been deliberately set, this case would be much, much, bigger than the fraud prosecution of the California winemakers and grape growers. His light landed on the wines of dozens of different producers. Sterling Vineyards. Beaulieu Vineyards. Domaine La Due. Justin Winery. Sean Thackrey. Realm Cellars. Sinskey Vineyards. Tres Sabores. Toasted Head. In total, the fire had affected ninety-five wine producers.

Anyone with a small amount of knowledge of the fine wine world of the Napa Valley and other parts of California would have been astonished—and saddened—at the sheer amount of ruined wine in the warehouse, much of it cooked as the concrete building heated up like a kiln. The names on the labels were some of the most respected in the wine world. They ranged from small producers who only made a few hundred cases a year to huge corporations like Diageo, owners of Sterling Vineyards, Beaulieu Vineyards, and Chalone, which made millions of cases annually. As Lapham walked around, he could imagine all the years of work that had gone into that wine—the planting and harvesting of the grapes, the crush, the fermentation and aging in barrels. Now, the flames had erased it.

It was difficult to determine exactly how many bottles the fire ruined or damaged, and it was a figure that investigators would change over time. For many years Lapham thought that 6 million bottles of wine had been affected; he later revised that figure to 4.5 million bottles. In the days after the fire broke out, officials told reporters that the fire had destroyed $100 million worth of wine. As Lapham refined his calculations, later putting the average retail price of each bottle at sixty dollars, his estimate of the dollar value of the wine soared to $277 million or even more. At one point he thought $400 million of wine had been destroyed, making it the most destructive crime involving wine in history.

The fire scene was so big and the fire so extensive that the Vallejo Fire Department quickly realized it did not have sufficient resources to investigate. The fire chief had requested the assistance of agents from the Bureau of Alcohol, Tobacco, Firearms, and Explosives. By the time Lapham arrived, the warehouse was buzzing with activity. Electrical engineers, fire protection engineers, forensic chemists, evidence technicians, and others from the ATF's National Response team were picking through the charred debris and talking to witnesses. A dog sniffed around for the presence of accelerants.

The damage to the building was not uniform. Some edges of the warehouse looked almost untouched, with cartons of shrink-wrapped wine still piled high on pallets. The worst damage appeared to be on the west side of the structure where the Navy had built a three-tiered, heavy timber-and-wood plank mezzanine to store torpedoes and other weapons during World War II. Private collections and library wines were kept on that level. Wineries would set aside a few cases from every vintage to make a historical record of their wines and to watch how they aged over time.

The first firefighters on the scene had noticed an orange glow coming from the mezzanine area and the pattern of damage suggested that the fire had started there. The pallets of wine stored nearby were the most singed. Many of the tall stacks had fallen upon one another, blocking that entire section. Moreover, the flames had eaten away a large portion of the floor, sending huge support beams crashing to the level below.

If the mezzanine was the place the fire had started, Lapham thought as he made his way through the warehouse, who had been up there?

Debbie Polverino, the forty-two-year old dark-haired manager of Wines Central, had been in charge of the warehouse's operation the day of the fire. Less than twenty-four hours after her workplace burned down around her, ATF Special Agent Brian O. Parker brought Polverino back to the building to walk her through the scene. Polverino knew the space intimately. She was a Napa County native, a descendant of a long line of Portuguese grape growers, and had worked in many facets of the industry. Feisty and talkative, Polverino had been hired at Wines Central in 2003 to overhaul the computer system controlling the logistics and tracking mechanisms of the company. With ninety-five wineries, forty private wine collectors, sugar from C & H sugar, loads of raw sugar from Nicaragua, pasta and sauce from Francis Ford Coppola's company, and barrels of olive oil, there were lots of moving parts at the warehouse.

The day of the fire had started like any other, Polverino told Parker, a slender man in his early forties with light brown hair, a boyish face partially covered by a Vandyke beard, and gold-rimmed glasses. He would soon be made the ATF's chief investigator of the fire. It had been a mild summer and harvest had been delayed past its usual early-September start time, which meant that grapes were still sitting on the vines. Twenty to thirty trucks usually delivered wine to the warehouse each day, but the truck traffic was relatively quiet on October 12. So quiet, in fact, that Polverino decided to shut down earlier than the normal four p.m. closing.

In the late afternoon, there was just one truck left at Wines Central. The driver had left the warehouse earlier, but returned when he discovered his load of sugar was too heavy. He parked in a loading dock as a Wines Central workman used a forklift to remove extra bags.

The only other customer in the warehouse was a man Polverino disliked: Mark Anderson. She had long had her suspicions about Anderson—she prided herself on her bullshit detector—and told Parker to take a close look at the man who had vexed her constantly.

Anderson had been difficult from the moment he had become a Wines Central customer in 2004. He had sublet a large space on the mezzanine area for Sausalito Cellars, a boutique wine storage company he had started in 1999 to store collectors' wine. Anderson had brought in around one hundred pallets of wine, about 67,200 bottles, and sequestered them behind a chain-link fence he had erected around his space.

Polverino thought Anderson was a know-it-all, and an annoying one at that. He had a longstanding relationship with Jack Krystal, one of the owners of Wines Central, and that made Anderson feel he had the right to offer his unsolicited opinion about the warehouse's operations. It also made him feel immune to Polverino's request for a detailed inventory of the wine in his storage bay. Every other client was forthright about his or her inventory. Not Anderson.

More annoyingly, Polverino thought Anderson was a braggart, particularly about wine. He would come and sit in her office in his black sweatpants and t-shirt and talk on and on about the oldest vintage he had tasted and how much it cost. He seemed to consider himself a storyteller and, unprompted, would describe marathon tasting sessions he had enjoyed with his wealthy Hong Kong buddies or his many trips to France. Polverino thought he was lying. Anderson didn't seem particularly knowledgeable about wine, nor did he seem like he could afford to pay for the good stuff. He couldn't answer a direct question about wine, either. Instead of a simple yes or no, Anderson would meander and take twenty-five minutes to get to the point. Polverino felt she could never get a clear answer out of him.

Anderson was constantly late on his $1,400 a month rent and recently his Sausalito Cellars clients had started calling Wines Central directly to try to find him. It seemed that Anderson had stopped returning their emails and calls.

Relations between Anderson and Wines Central had gotten so bad that the owners had asked him to move out by September, but Anderson had missed the deadline. Then Polverino noticed that strange things were going on in his storage bay. Anderson started to remove bottles of wine from their wooden boxes. He would place the wine bottles in the middle of the floor and stack the wooden boxes along one edge of the storage bay, creating a visual barrier of sorts. After a few weeks of this, there was a wall of boxes and cardboard twenty feet high running the length of the cage. Polverino told Anderson to remove it. He ignored her admonitions.

Anderson had finally started to move his wine out of Wines Central a few weeks earlier, renting a truck to haul his clients' wine to a warehouse in nearby American Canyon. On the day of the fire, there were only a few pallets left. Anderson came into the building before noon carrying a canvas bag. When Polverino decided to close up early, she sent one of the office workers to the mezzanine to inform Anderson.

A short while later, Anderson rushed through the office, "faster than I have ever seen him," said Polverino. "He was soaking wet and sweating. His eyes were as wide as could be. He didn't want to look at me. I said 'so you are all done?' He didn't say anything to me."

Stranger yet, five to ten minutes later, Anderson telephoned Polverino. He had never called her before. Polverino heard the surprise in Anderson's voice when she picked up the telephone. "You are still there?" he said. Then he launched into a soliloquy about his schedule, telling Polverino he was on his way to Yountville to visit his ailing father and that he wouldn't be back at Wines Central the next day. He would return the following week. Polverino was puzzled and slightly disturbed by the interaction. Why was he telling her this? Anderson had never shared any details about his schedule with her before. She had a feeling Anderson was deliberately trying to keep her on the phone.

Polverino hung up and walked out of her office into the main area of the warehouse to collect the mail. She was standing near the carved wooden door when it suddenly blew open. Polverino went to shut it, but found it hard to close. She yelled to a colleague, who came over. Together they tugged at the door, using all of their strength to shut and lock it.

Polverino returned to her office. Shortly after she sat down at her desk, the fire alarm went off, sending out a high-pitched noise. The lights flickered. Polverino, confused by what was happening, dashed back onto the warehouse floor. She heard a large rushing sound, like all the air was being sucked out of the warehouse. A moaning and then a zapping noise followed. Then one of the Wines Central workmen yelled out, "There's a fire!" Polverino turned around to see a huge ball of orange flame coming toward her from the mezzanine area. She ran to the front door, but it wouldn't open. She pushed it again. It didn't budge. She threw her weight against it, this time looking over her shoulder at the advancing wall of flames. Another Wines Central worker rushed to help. Together they pushed open the door, and the air rushing out of the warehouse lifted Polverino off her feet. She grabbed onto the door handle so she would not be thrown out of the building. Her white tennis shoes flew off. When the air equalized and Polverino crashed to the ground, she ran away from the building. When she turned around, the warehouse was in flames.

The yellow Labrador retriever was racing through the Wines Central warehouse, her snout bounding up and down as she leaped over mounds of glass or swerved to avoid felled timbers. She had started her sniffing at the outer edges of the massive building, where the damage was minimal, but had been slowly led toward the mezzanine where officials thought the fire had started. The dog's nose was incredibly sensitive (dogs have an average of two hundred million cells in their noses compared to a human's five million) and she was working quickly. She was officially known as an accelerant detection canine, or arson dog, but her name was Rosie. She was four years old.

As Rosie made her way with her ATF handler toward the center of the building, she didn't sense gasoline or lighter fluid or lamp oil—any of the accelerants she was trained to detect. But when she was led upstairs to Mark Anderson's storage bay, she sat down and lifted her snout up and down, as if she was nodding a silent yes. That was a sign for the ATF investigators to look more closely through the debris. As they pushed aside burned boxes and shifted beams, they spotted the charred shell of a BernzOmatic brand propane torch, the kind plumbers use to solder copper pipes. That was not something that was usually found in a wine storage facility. The brass nozzle on the torch was slightly melted but still attached, and in a closed position. More digging uncovered some unburned rags and saturated cardboard. Rosie nodded her head vigorously at the items, and was then rewarded with a small treat.

It looked like investigators had found strong evidence that the fire had been deliberately set.

CHAPTER FOUR

A SOGGY, CHARRED MESS

Delia Viader's wine wasn't even supposed to be in the Wines Central storehouse. Normally, she kept her wine at her winery in Deer Park, high up on Howell Mountain, until it was ready to be shipped. Then it went to a wine storage warehouse in American Canyon, just a short jog south of Napa, and then it was sent to stores and restaurants around the world. But in 2005, Viader had shipped out wine that normally would have stayed onsite because she was expanding her wine caves. Viader aged her wine in barrels longer than many winemakers. V, her top wine made from Petit Verdot grapes, stayed in new French oak barrels for thirty months. Her main product, Viader, a blend of Cabernet and Cabernet Franc grapes, spent twenty-four months in barrel. As Viader's operations expanded, she needed more room to age her wine in barrels.

The contractor had promised Viader that he could enlarge the length of the tunnels from 10,000 to 15,000 feet by September, well before the 2005 harvest. But construction fell behind schedule. Viader had to move out her 2003 vintage—all 7,400 cases—or there wouldn't be room for the upcoming harvest. Since her normal wine storage warehouse in American Canyon was full, Viader turned to Wines Central.

As Viader stood outside the scorched and damaged warehouse a few days after the fire, thoughts about her wine ran through her mind. Yellow police tape cordoned off the warehouse. Ever since the fire erupted, anxious winemakers had clustered outside, eager to find out if any of their wine had survived the fire. They waited for days for news because Vallejo police and ATF investigators had shunned their repeated pleas to be let inside. The longer the winemakers waited, the more frustrated—and fearful—they became.

The morning Viader arrived at the warehouse, the only official on site was Polverino, whose job had gone from managing a wine warehouse to managing its cleanup. There were no cops or firefighters around. Polverino was so busy answering phones in the makeshift office in a trailer that she didn't object when Viader said she was going to enter the damaged building.

Viader put a hard hat over her blond hair and picked up a flashlight to navigate her way through the pitch-black warehouse. As she entered, the smell of soot and char and wine overwhelmed her. She could see that towering pallets of wine had toppled over and others were so unstable they were likely to collapse without warning. Her thick, sturdy boots crunched on broken glass. What would she find? she wondered. Broken bottles of Viader? Intact cardboard boxes still surrounded by shrink-wrap?

Viader was certain of one thing. She needed to maintain close control of her bottles to ensure her winery's reputation. She remembered the fire in the Rombauer-Frank Family winery in Calistoga in 2000 in which twenty wineries lost about $40 million of wine. Instead of destroying the ruined wine, an insurance company sold it to a salvage company, which was supposed to remove the labels. But the salvage company sold 9,000 bottles, labels intact, to an import company in San Francisco's North Beach, passing off the wine off as new. Wine lovers bought the damaged wine, expecting it to taste good, only to find that it had a burned flavor. Lawsuits followed and winemakers like Viader made mental notes never to be cavalier about the disposition of fire-damaged wine.[8]

As Viader slogged through the darkness, it was nearly impossible for her to distinguish the names of any of the wine sitting near the center of the warehouse where the damage was greatest. Viader had a sense where some of her wine had been stored and walked up to a pile of bottles in that general vicinity. She started to pull bottle after bottle out of the pile, looking for some telltale mark that it was Viader. But the bottles were covered in a layer of charcoal gray ash. The labels were so burned or blackened that few winery names were visible. Viader scrutinized the lead capsules that covered the corks for clues. Many of those had melted. Other bottles had exploded in the heat and shattered into tiny shards of glass.

While the center of the warehouse was a mess, the outer edges looked almost normal. Viader headed to one side of the building where her portable labeling machine had been working a few days earlier. Her heart skipped a beat. There it was: a towering stack of Viader, seemingly untouched in its clear plastic wrap.

Viader sensed an opportunity. She turned around and quickly left the warehouse. She knew she needed to retrieve the wine that looked unscathed. It was only a matter of time before officials would exert greater control on who went in and out of the burned building. She had to act fast.

Viader got into her car, pulled out of the warehouse parking lot and hit the accelerator when she reached the highway. The trip back to her winery took about a half hour. Once there, she ordered her entire crew—grape pickers, wine blenders, cellar rats, interns, about fourteen workers—to return with trucks to Wines Central. Viader was determined to take out some of the wine before unscrupulous people carried it off to sell on the gray market. She felt her reputation depended on it.

By late afternoon, Viader was a dripping mess, her jeans soaked with wine, water, and foam and smelling of smoke. But she and her crew had rescued enough wine with the labels intact to fit inside the back of a small pickup truck and an SUV. They had to squat in the muck and pull bottles from the bottom of a mound of wine to do it, but they had succeeded.

The rest of her wine, Viader realized, must lie under the pile of charred and broken bottles.

Dick Ward was unlucky. Saintsbury's library of wines had been on the wooden mezzanine level of the warehouse, just a few storage bays away from the space rented by Anderson and right near the ignition point where damage was greatest. The fire had eaten away at the wide plank floorboards and support beams, sending parts of the mezzanine cascading down onto the main floor. There was little that was recognizable in the rubble.

When Ward was finally allowed to go into the warehouse, he peered up in the mezzanine level. Nothing remained. The boxes holding Saintsbury's library of wines had been burned completely. The only remains of 3,000 cases and 200 large-format bottles from vintages stretching back to 1984 were small pieces of glass. A wave of sadness poured over him. The library wines represented his life's work, years of cultivating grapes in the vineyard, tinkering with wines in the barrel, and rejoicing when the flavors soared. He had wanted to taste those bottles as they aged to see how his wine evolved. Now that would not happen.

Ward took out his camera and took photos of the collapsed pallets and burned support beams, but felt so shell-shocked and emotionally drained that his gestures were almost automatic. In the days to come, as Ward replayed the scene at the warehouse over and over in his mind, he would remember how spooky and eerie the warehouse felt. The smoky smell lingered on his clothes long after.

When the consulting winemaker for Long Meadow Ranch, Cathy Corison, heard that the fire had ruined the winery's entire 2002 vintage, some of the 2001, and numerous large-format bottles from other years, she went into shock. Words virtually left her. For three days she mourned in near-silence, torn apart inside by the realization that the wine she had labored over for so long had essentially been evaporated. Long Meadow Ranch had stored its wine almost directly below the spot where Anderson had his wines. So the winery's shrink-wrapped pallets had been among the first to collapse in on themselves, shattering bottles and leaking red wine out onto the cement floor.

The conversation Ted Hall had with Miranda Heller, the woman who had entrusted about 175 bottles of the wine made by her great-great-grandfather in 1875 into his care, was not easy. Hall had met Heller when they both served on the board of a private elementary school in Marin County that their children had attended. They also shared a love for the San Francisco Symphony. Heller had turned to Hall as an expert she could trust, and he had the feeling that he had let her down. While Heller hadn't made the wine that burned, hadn't personally toiled to blend it, she nonetheless felt a strong kinship to the destroyed Port and Angelica. The wine had sat for decades in Heller's grandmother's house in Atherton on the San Francisco peninsula. Heller had taken possession of the dozens of wooden cases upon her death. She had sent them to Hall to be examined, and he and Fritz Hatton, a consultant and the auctioneer for the Napa Valley auction, determined that the wine was sound. They thought it should be drunk soon, though. They recommended that Heller create wooden cases that would appeal to collectors interested in historic wines. They suggested packaging six bottles to a box: three bottles of Port and three bottles of Angelica, a sweet, fortified white wine. At recent auctions, similar bottles of Heller's ancestor's wine had sold for more than $400 each.

It was ironic that, in looking to protect the old wine, Heller had sent it to Hall. That move from family wine cellar to professionally managed wine warehouse had led to its destruction. To Heller, the 130-year old wine symbolized her family's legacy and the bounty of California. If only she had left it alone. Now it was gone.

As the weeks passed, word spread about what the fire had destroyed. Most of the ninety-five wineries affected by the fire had been small, family-owned operations that produced fewer than 10,000 cases a year. A few, though, only made a few hundred cases a year. A number of large corporate wineries also lost wine. Most of the wineries were located in Napa or Sonoma counties, but there was also wine from Paso Robles in central California, and the states of Washington and Oregon.

Some of the wine filled a niche market, like Marilyn Wines, which put a picture of Marilyn Monroe on every bottle. Their wines had been on the mezzanine level. There were celebrity wineries, like one owned by the Italian racecar driver Mario Andretti. Realm Cellars, which had only released three hundred cases in 2003 from one of Napa's most storied vineyards, To Kalon, saw its entire production destroyed.

Saintsbury was not the only winery that had lost its library wines and its history. ZD Wines, owned by the deLueze family, lost its library, including a 1969 pinot noir, which many regarded as the first commercial Pinot Noir to ever come out of the Carneros region. Now there were no liquid records left of those early days. Signorello Estate, which started making wines from its vineyards off the Silverado Trail in 1985, also saw its earliest vintages destroyed.

Numerous small wineries that had just been getting their start suddenly found themselves with nothing to sell. Poorly capitalized, they couldn't even struggle to stay afloat. Many of them discovered that they did not have insurance. Many insurance companies declared that the wine at Wines Central was "in transit," moving from the winery to restaurants, and thus was not insured. While companies insured wine at the wineries, the policies didn't cover wine on the move.

Before the fire, Allen Christensen had been rejoicing that Amazon Ranch, his brand new winery, had just gotten a positive review in a major magazine. He hoped that would impress the name of his fledgling label into the mind of wine aficionados. Christensen soon found that his insurance company would not pay for the 141 cases burned beyond recognition. Gary Lipp and Brooks Painter had just started Coho Wines, named for the "salmon of knowledge," which focused on making cool climate wines. They lost 988 of the winery's 1,000 cases of the 2003 vintage. The sale of the remaining twelve cases would not sustain them. Insurance would not cover their losses either. Sterling Vineyards, one of Napa's oldest wineries, now owned by the multinational Diageo, was also uninsured. It lost about $37 million in wine in the fire.[9]

Sean Thackrey wasn't insured, either, but the maverick art dealer turned winemaker tried to be creative with his damaged wine. He wasn't the kind of man to pay close attention to convention anyway. Thackrey, with a wild head of gray hair that he rarely combed, had set up his winery in a redwood barn in Bolinas, a small coastal town in Marin County that was only accessible by an unmarked windy road. It was more than an hour's drive to Napa, where Thackrey sourced his Zinfandel grapes from a vineyard that had been planted in 1905. Thackrey was famous for his collection of more than 800 ancient texts that informed his approach to making wine. Instead of crushing grapes and letting their juices ferment, like most winemakers, Thackrey had been known to let the fruit sit intact for days, sometimes under the stars (the reason his wines are named after the constellations) while the sugars converted to alcohol. Only then did he press out the juice. It was a technique written about by the Greek poet Hesiod in 8 BCE.

When Thackrey found out that he was not insured for the 4,000 cases he had stored in Wines Central, he swore at his agent, and then got to work. Thackrey decided to see what he could salvage. He tested some of his wine that had been at the edges of the warehouse and decided it tasted fine. There was no hint of char, no off flavors. So he slapped on a new label and sold the wine. That way he could bring in income without damaging his brand.

Other winemakers did the same thing. John Caldwell, who was widely known for smuggling French vine cuttings in from Canada in 1983 at a time when the U.S. banned foreign vine imports, bought back his scorched wine from his insurance company. Caldwell thought the wine made from grapes from the Coombsville section east of the city of Napa tasted all right. He relabeled it. The wine had originally been called Rocket Science. The new title was Reentry.

Julie Johnson of Tres Sabores winery in Rutherford had stored close to 2,000 cases in Wines Central. She used some of the scorched wine to make a fire-roasted Zinfandel and pomegranate marinade that she called ¿Porqué No?, or Why Not?, after one of the vintages that had been destroyed. It was so tasty that Johnson not only sold the sauce in her tasting room, but in boutique shops like the Oakville Grocery. Her favorite way to enjoy it was as a marinade for a blue cheese and bacon hamburger.[10]

These winemakers refused to let the fire defeat them, a resilience they had used to make their way into the highly competitive California wine market.

CHAPTER FIVE

JOE SAUSALITO

M ark Anderson eased his vintage burgundy Cadillac into the garage of his apartment building in Sausalito, a town of 7,000 people seven miles across the bay from San Francisco. It had been a grueling and emotional few days. Anderson's father, James, was battling cancer, and appeared to be near the end of his fight. Anderson had driven to Yountville in the heart of the Napa Valley a few days earlier to see him at the Veteran's Home, a massive white building that was home to more than a thousand men who fought in America's wars. Anderson's father had been a merchant marine in World War II. The visit was a good-bye, although the elder Anderson would not die until right before Thanksgiving. It was also Anderson's alibi. "The last day I saw him alive was when I gripped his hand farewell, as he struggled to speak, writhing in pain, . . . in Yountville, October 12, 2005 at about 4:30 p.m., just about the time the fire was raging at Wines Central in Mare Island," Anderson wrote me years later. "My thoughts were on family matters, not business or wine."

Anderson had ignored the urgent phone calls that had come in the last few days from the various police agencies requesting an interview. The Vallejo Police Department, the fire department, the ATF—they all wanted to talk to him about the Wines Central warehouse fire. Anderson had graduated from San Francisco Law School, although he had never passed the California bar, and knew he wasn't legally obligated to answer any questions. He was an expert at the non-answering answer, something he had learned in the last year as civil and criminal complaints had piled up. He regarded delay as a powerful tactic.

So on October 16, 2005, four days after the fire, Anderson heaved his large body out of his car and started the climb up to his third-story apartment. The older and heavier he had gotten, the more difficult the ascent. At fifty-six, with a bad back and other ailments, walking up that steep flight of stairs could be downright painful.

But Anderson didn't consider moving. The apartment at 895 Bridge-way offered unobstructed views of the Sausalito harbor. Every time he looked out his picture windows, Anderson could see sailboat masts bob up and down with the changing tide. Harbor seals sunned themselves on the docks and pelicans and black cormorants swooped up and down. The view of Richardson Bay had enchanted him ever since he had moved in twenty years earlier. It still gave him pleasure.

Anderson lived in the apartment with Cynthia Witten, his girlfriend of more than ten years. The two had met in 1978 when both of them were working in Japan and had started dating a decade later. Witten, originally from Oregon, had pale skin and raven hair. She had worked in real estate in Japan, but was working at the time at Pegasus Leathers on Princess Street in the tourist section of the town.

Sausalito, the first city across the Golden Gate Bridge from San Francisco, was a small enclave noted for its views, artistic community, and bohemian ways. Sally Stanford, who ran one of San Francisco's most notorious bordellos in the 1940s, was elected mayor in 1975, just one of many alternative lifestyle seekers who settled in the bayside town. They were drawn to the water, with its whimsical collection of houseboats, or to the hills with houses that offered spectacular views of San Francisco and the bay. Thousands of tourists strolled the city's water-front promenade lined with eclectic shops and art galleries each year.

When Anderson first moved to Sausalito in 1967, he had come, like so many before him, seeking freedom and creative expression. Anderson had been born in Berkeley in 1948 during a time when that city was more Republican than radical. His family was well-to-do (the 1944 marriage ceremony of his parents, James and Patricia, at the St. Clement's Episcopal Church in Berkeley had been featured in the local newspaper) and he grew up on Brookside Avenue in a wealthy enclave near the Claremont Hotel, a 1915 building that served as a local landmark. Mark and his brother, Steven, who was born in 1953, had the kind of idyllic childhood that involved flattening pennies on the trolley tracks and sneaking into the hotel to ride down the circular slides that served as the building's fire escapes. Anderson attended John Muir Elementary School and was a member of the junior traffic patrol, which helped students cross the street. In 1957, Anderson won the citywide fishing derby off the Berkeley pier.

When Anderson was eleven, his family joined the growing exodus of people moving to the suburbs. Orinda, just over the hill from Berkeley in rapidly growing Contra Costa County, was a town with curving streets and cul-de-sacs, large oak trees, and much warmer summers. Anderson's father took advantage of the growth; he built a successful mortgage brokerage that catered to the new arrivals.

Anderson's involvement with a pipe bomb two years later may have been a reflection of his boredom or of his cleverness and love of tinkering. When he was thirteen he brought home a pipe bomb (he later said a classmate gave it to him) and hid it in a closet that separated his bedroom from his brother Steven's bedroom. The bomb exploded one night, ripping a six-inch hole in the wall and shooting shrapnel near where Steven was sleeping. The fire marshal who came to inspect the damage said the blast could have been fatal. That incident may be when the fissure between the two brothers appeared, a crack that would grow so wide that they eventually stopped talking to each other. Steven Anderson clearly never forgot the incident; he kept newspaper stories about the blast for forty-five years and later presented copies to a reporter.[11]

Anderson moved to Sausalito in 1967, when he was nineteen. It was the height of the hippie era, and Anderson had grown his hair long and had spent time wandering Telegraph Avenue near the UC Berkeley campus, where street vendors burned incense and sold leather bracelets and decorative candles.

Anderson was attracted to the Sausalito waterfront, a picturesque community of more than 200 boats, tugs, ferries, and old submarine chasers that had been transformed into fanciful and ornamental floating homes. There was a bohemian feel to the community, with people gathering for communal dinners, sharing their possessions, walking around nude, or painting on a dock. The vibe was laid-back, the rent was free, and the sense of being an outlaw from a restrictive society was strong. In 1967, Otis Redding wrote an ode to the scene, "Dock of the Bay," while on a houseboat.

"People lived here because they could afford it," recalls one old-timer who bought his first boat in 1967. "You could find an old lifeboat hull to build on, and there was always stuff to recycle because of the shipyards. Whatever you wanted. If you needed a beam of wood ten feet long by one foot wide, one would come floating up."[12]

Anderson was handy and within a few years he had constructed a thirty-six-foot long A-frame houseboat on fiberglass pontoons for about $3,000. When he sat on his dock, holding a glass of wine, he could look out over the water and see sea lions basking in the sun on the docks, or pelicans swooping down to catch fish.

Almost forty years later, Anderson was entrenched in the town's establishment. He was a member of the Rotary Club and served on the board of the Chamber of Commerce. He had been appointed to the Parks and Recreation Commission and the Arts Commission, and was almost single-handedly running Sausalito's Sister City commission. But for all his civic engagements, in the food-obsessed Sausalito he was best known for his love of sushi.

Anderson's fame stemmed from his patronage of Sushi Ran, a Japanese restaurant on a small street on the edge of Sausalito's downtown. Sushi Ran had sort of sneaked up on the residents of Sausalito. For years the top restaurant in town had been the Trident, a bayside restaurant started by the music group the Kingston Trio in the 1960s. The Trident had tapped into the cultural zeitgeist with its natural food and creative cocktails and had attracted celebrities like Janis Joplin, Jerry Garcia, and Joan Baez. The Trident got really famous when concert promoter Bill Graham threw two private parties for The Rolling Stones there in the early 1970s.

Yoshi Tome took over a nondescript Japanese place in 1986 with the goal of transforming it into a top-notch restaurant that would attract politicians, business people, and Sausalito's artists so often that they would come to regard Sushi Ran as a second home. Tome hit upon the idea of launching the Sushi Lovers' Club, with a Hall of Fame for the most loyal patrons. Those who racked up dozens of visits could have their photos prominently displayed on the restaurant's front wall.

From the start, the Sushi Lovers' Club was a hit. People who might have visited just a few times a year started coming frequently. They wanted to see their photo on the wall. "The competition was unbelievable," said Tome.

It helped that Tome had brought in a talented chef who wowed patrons with his intricately sculptured towers of sushi, tempura, and sashimi. Tome imported the freshest fish from the famed Tsukiji Market in Tokyo and stocked his cellar with one of the best collections of sake around. The food earned glowing reviews—and three stars—from the *San Francisco Chronicle* and was anointed one of the best restaurants in the Bay Area by both Michelin and Zagat. Sushi Ran soon felt exactly how Tome had hoped—a hometown draw.

Anderson soon became a regular, often walking the four blocks from his apartment "to the Ran" for lunch. His favorite dish was Ten-Tama Soba: buckwheat soba noodle soup with a raw egg cracked over the broth and a few pieces of shrimp tempura piled on top. He often stopped by late at night as well to drink wine or sake and share gossip with Tome at the bar. The pair became close friends.

Many people still carry images in their head of Anderson at Sushi Ran—laughing, telling jokes, hanging out with Sausalito's politicians and civic leaders. Martin Brown met Anderson at Sushi Ran around 1992—and found him "really witty, really enchanting." Brown had just started a new alternative weekly newspaper called *The Signal* and he invited Anderson to contribute after he saw him doodle amazing illustrations on a napkin. Anderson eventually started to write a column about the town's politics and culture under the pen name "Joe Sausalito."

All those visits earned Anderson a spot on the Sushi Lovers' Hall of Fame wall. His photo first went up in 1987 after he had made 100 visits, the fourth most of any customer. In 1994, he won the number one spot, visiting 211 times. He won again in 1996 after visiting 195 times. His biggest competitors were his friends, other food-oriented people like Jack Rubyn, the chair of the Marin Food and Wine Society. In 1995, Rubyn took the number one spot after he ate at Sushi Ran 458 times. Anderson came in second that year by eating at the restaurant 192 times. All together, Anderson ate at Sushi Ran more than 2,000 times.

"Mark turned it into an absurd competition," said Tom Stern, a Sausalito journalist. "He would go there every day. For three years, he had more than 365 visits. He wanted to be number one. He would go there and order a glass of wine and that would count as a visit."

All that eating and drinking took a toll: Anderson was in his late thirties and slim and strong from playing tennis and other sports when he first visited the restaurant; over the years he ballooned to more than three hundred pounds.

It's funny what having your photo on the wall of a popular restaurant can do. That's what people would remember Mark Anderson for years later, after news broke that he was charged with wine theft and arson. Anderson may have been lauded by the Sausalito mayor for his civic involvement and the column he started to write for the region's big weekly, the *Marin Scope*, in 1999, but it was his Sushi Ran meals that won him the most attention.

Despite his high profile, Anderson remained a mystery to many people. How, for example, did he earn a living? Martin Brown assumed he was an "estate baby" who lived off inherited income. There were lots of those in Sausalito.

Anderson was deliberately vague about his income. But he constantly dropped hints about how famous and accomplished he was, hints that at the time no one had reason to disbelieve. He told people that he had invented voice mail. He said he had managed the rock and roll band Iron Butterfly. He claimed to have been a spokesman for SRI, the Stanford Research Institute. He would later tell me that he crossed the Sahara desert with a tribe of Toureg nomads he met in Timbuktu. They sold him a wife, Fatima, for eight dollars. The camel for the trip cost seventy-five dollars. Then there was the time he had lunch with Chairman Mao. It's not clear if that was before or after Anderson became an Israeli spy.

It was only after Anderson's arrest that people started to dissect the tales that characterized him as a dashing, successful businessman and traveler. One of the members of Iron Butterfly said he had never heard of Anderson. The human resources department at SRI told me it had no record of Anderson's employment.

But the most damning exposé came from Anderson's younger brother, Steven. He grew so frustrated by his sibling's tales that he created an entire website devoted to debunking his brother's various assertions. He named it *Corpulent Raider*. "Among his many incredible claims is that along the line somewhere he helped to 'Invent and Develop Voice Mail,'" posted Steven Anderson. "eeee . . . yah. Right. He worked as a salesman for one of the first voicemail companies that was forming back in the 70's. For about 6 months. They . . . brought out the 7-League boot." (Translation: they kicked him out of the company.)

It takes a certain kind of personality to tell so many lies with a straight face. I didn't meet Mark until 2010, decades after he regaled his friends in Sausalito with his stories, but for about two years we spoke regularly on the phone and exchanged letters. Even as he sat in a jail cell, even as he faced the prospect of years in prison, he still twisted the truth. As Debbie Polverino, the manager of Wines Central, noted, Mark's stories were rarely linear. Nor did they always make sense. He would launch into an explanation, for instance, of why he could not have set fire to the warehouse and within minutes his explanation was so tortured and complex that I couldn't follow along. His stories would always contain something that seemed to be a kernel of truth so you couldn't dismiss them outright. One of his attorneys even had a psychiatrist evaluate Anderson for narcissism.

Why did Anderson spin so many tales about his supposed accomplishments? He clearly loved to hear himself talk. Many other people enjoyed his stories and his corny jokes. Perhaps it covered up a deep insecurity, for Anderson was smart, but thwarted professionally. He had attended school through his forties, but never ended up with a permanent paying profession. Anderson enrolled at more than nine institutions, earning an AA degree, two bachelor's degrees, including one from the University of California at Berkeley, a master's in economics, and two law degrees.[13] But he never passed the bar. "I have more degrees than a thermometer," Anderson would joke.

The one professional constant in Anderson's life was photography. He started snapping photos of houses for his father's mortgage company when he was a teenager. In the early 1970s, Anderson traveled to the Sahara Desert and Ethiopia to take pictures, and in the late 1970s he shot film in Afghanistan, Iran, and Iraq—or so he says. When he eventually settled permanently in Sausalito, Anderson did portraits of family and friends and shot large-format photos of flowers and landscapes. Anderson sometimes hand-colored sepia-toned prints and rephotographed them. His work was respected; his clients included a mayor of Sausalito, a number of influential local businessmen, and Tome, the owner of Sushi Ran. He said his work had been shown in Parisian and Japanese galleries. Anderson may have been exaggerating. Eric Johnson, a successful artist who served with Anderson on the arts commission and considered him a friend, said his photographs were never particularly memorable. I looked in vain for proof that Anderson had risen to the top of his profession, as he claimed, but never found any examples of his work online or in the archives of stock photo agencies.

Then one hot August day I was browsing in an antique store in

Healdsburg, California, a town in northern Sonoma County wine country. A framed photograph caught my eye. It was of three red tomatoes. They sat on a ledge, in front of a window covered by a slatted blind. Dappled specks of sun shone on the tomatoes. I looked more closely at the photo and saw it was signed "Mark Christian Anderson." An inscription on the back said the photo was taken in 1992 but printed in 1994. I couldn't believe it. Here at last was a photo of Mark's!

The price tag said forty dollars. I thought that was too much for the photo, which was pleasing, but nothing special. But how could I pass up buying a photo made by Anderson? It offered concrete proof that he was a photographer, that he actually did something he said he did. I bought the picture. It now sits on a counter in my office.

The day Rosie the arson dog nodded her head up and down while sitting in Mark Anderson's storage bay at Wines Central, ATF forensic chemists brought the propane torch, bits of cardboard, cloth, and charred wood from the scene to the forensics science lab in Walnut Creek, about twenty-five miles east of San Francisco. The lab, tucked innocuously in a business park, is one of only three ATF labs in the country to specialize in examining evidence from fires and explosions. It handles cases on the West Coast from California, Oregon, and Washington stretching east to Montana and south toward Texas. The ATF technician used an analytic technique called gas chromatography mass spectroscopy (GC/MS) to determine if any of the material from the wine warehouse had accelerants. The technician dissolved some of the cloth into a solvent and then injected a tiny bit into the gas chromatography machine. The machine separated the sample's components and sorted them by volatility and mass, allowing the technician to see the chemical's identity. During the next step, the mass spectroscopy machine blasted the sample with electrons, and then produced a computer analysis of what was on the cloth.

By October 17, five days after the Wines Central fire, the technicians had finished their tests. They had found traces of gasoline in the evidence, proof that the fire had been deliberately set. And by that point the police only had one suspect: Anderson.

No one investigating the fire had yet talked to him. He had been ignoring their calls requesting an interview. It was time to go get him.

On October 18, 2005, two days after Anderson returned home from visiting his father, he sat down at his computer. Anderson was a bit of a computer geek, an early adopter. In high school in the mid-1960s, he was a member of the electronics club and stayed after school to build radios and primitive computers. Business associates remember him as an early advocate of Google, back in the time most people were using Altavista or Yahoo as their search engines Anderson would surf the web to find funny jokes and websites, and send the links to friends.

Anderson typed in www.federalcrimes.com. It was a website that detailed possible prison times for various federal crimes. What Anderson saw could not have been reassuring.

The next morning, as Anderson lay in bed next to Cynthia, he heard a loud banging on the door. It was a contingent of cops from Vallejo and the ATF, many of whom were dressed in white t-shirts with their logo in large letters on the back. A few carried large guns. Within seconds, police were swarming through the apartment. "The ATF came crashing in my back door with assault rifles locked and loaded in S.W.A.T. gear, with bomb-sniffing dogs—waking me up at 6 a.m. with guns pressed against my head," Anderson later recalled.[14]

ATF agent Brian Parker handed Anderson a search warrant authorizing the police to take Anderson's computers, BlackBerry, passport, and electronic records and search his Cadillac and Audi. Just the day before, the ATF had named Parker head investigator on the case, the biggest he had led in his five years as an agent. Parker had an unusually strong grounding in the forensics aspect of his job, as he had worked as a chemist in the ATF lab in Walnut Creek for a few years before deciding his true calling was in fieldwork. He had always loved architecture and engineering while growing up in Livermore on the eastern edge of the Bay Area, figuring out how something fit together and came apart. He brought that same attitude to his job as special agent. "I love digging through fire scenes. It's like opening up a new puzzle every time you go out to the scene." Parker would soon be consumed with tracking down a connection between Anderson and the plumber's blowtorch recovered from his storage bay.

Anderson stood there trying not to let his face reveal any emotion as the agents tore through his apartment, picked apart his life, and carried the pieces to the fleet of waiting police cars parked outside, in full view of his neighbors and commuters driving by on Sausalito's busiest street. It would have been hard to miss the sight of Rosie, the yellow Labrador arson dog, sniffing the seats and trunk of Anderson's cars.

PART TWO

INVENTION

CHAPTER SIX

THE BEGINNING OF RANCHO CUCAMONGA

The grapevines were scraggly. They pushed their way out of the ground with barely enough enthusiasm to crawl up the metal stakes meant to hold them. Some had a few bright green leaves and twisting tendrils emerging from a winter sleep, but a significant number were gray and barren.

As I stood under the warm April sky and looked at the vines, I found it hard to believe that this spot was once home to one of the most admired vineyards in California, lauded for its wine, Port and sweet Angelica. Weary travelers on their way to the gold mines had exulted in the liquid made from its grapes, and judges at nineteenth-century state fairs had given the wines top awards.

But Rancho Cucamonga, forty miles east of Los Angeles, was now a city of strip malls, chain restaurants, and hotels, indistinguishable from surrounding towns. Three highways cut through the once-verdant area. Lines of houses crawled all the way to the base of the nearby San Gabriel Mountains, which were often obscured by smog wafting east from Los Angeles.

I had come to Rancho Cucamonga to see if I could find any reminders of the 1875 wine that had been destroyed in the Wines Central warehouse fire. Ever since I had heard that my cousin, Miranda Heller, had stored our great-great-grandfather's wine in the warehouse and it had boiled in its bottles, I wanted to know more about its creation. I couldn't find any reference to that specific vintage in the forty boxes of my great-great-grandfather's papers stored at the California Historical Society. No family letters about the wine remained. The only clue I had to the origin of the wine was the label on one of the green oversized bottles that had not burned up. "Private Stock, Isaias W. Hellman" was printed at the top, under what looked like a cattle brand with the initials "IWH." "Port wine, Cucamonga Vineyard, San Bernardino County, California" was spelled out below in ornate script. "Vintage 1875. Bottled from wood 1921" was under that.

So I traveled to where the wine had its beginnings. I knew that Hellman was only one of a long string of stewards of the vineyard that yielded the grapes for the 1875 bottle of wine. I had traveled 400 miles from Berkeley to see if I could reconstruct that lineage and chain of ownership, a task that would take months of searching through county deeds, court cases, and history books. Who had planted the grapes, I wondered. Who had made the wine? I eventually would follow the path the wine took from its inception in 1839 to its creation in 1875 to its destruction in 2005. The story was, in many ways, a reflection of the history of wine in California. The bottles were connected to the early days of the wine business in Los Angeles, when it couldn't even be characterized as an industry, to winemakers' attempts to capture the attention of East Coast drinkers, to battles for market domination that raged until Prohibition.

That's how I found myself standing near one of the few remaining vineyards—if it could be called that—in the area. It was just a small patch of grapevines in front of a historic home that belonged to one of the early owners of Rancho Cucamonga. Clearly it was not well tended. Right after World War II, there had been 32,000 acres of grapes[15] around Rancho Cucamonga, making western San Bernardino County the largest grape-growing region in America—larger than Napa and Sonoma combined. Urban development wiped that away. Now, there was little to remind me of what the land had been like during that era, let alone in 1839 when the first cultivated grapes went in the ground.

The first man to plant grapes on Rancho Cucamonga was Tiburcio Tapia, a Mexican soldier and descendant of one of the earliest Spanish settlers in California. When he was fifty, Tapia lived in Los Angeles, a tiny pueblo of fewer than 1,000 residents who lived in adobe houses centered around a central plaza. The biggest building in town was a white chapel constructed in 1784. Tapia lived in a large home nearby. He was a prosperous merchant and served as *alcalde*, a type of mayor, who was noted for his "strict integrity." But his financial success came, in part, because he broke the law. California, then part of Mexico, required all ships coming to trade to anchor first at Monterey and pay taxes on the goods they wanted to sell. Tapia bypassed those extra costs by convincing the captains to bring their cloth, furniture, and tools directly into caves he owned along the coast near present-day Malibu. Tapia was then able to sell the smuggled goods at a reduced price, and undercut his competitors. He became very successful. "We stopped by the house of Don Tiburcio Tapia, the '*alcalde Constitucional*,' of the town, once a soldier in very moderate circumstances, but who by honest and industrious labor had amassed so much of this world's goods, as to make him one of the wealthiest inhabitants of this place," wrote the Yankee adventurer Alfred Robinson. "He was the principal merchant and the only native one in El Pueblo de los Angeles."

California was in transition in 1839, and Tapia, ever the shrewd businessman, aspired for more than a store on the plaza.

When Spain colonized Alta California in 1769, it created a rigid, three-pronged system of control. At the top were the presidios, which were garrisons stocked with soldiers, horses, and guns. Then came the missions, where Franciscan fathers built a chain of churches from San Diego to Sonoma and forcibly converted thousands of Indians to Christianity. The neophytes, as the Native Americans were called, grew the wheat, corn, grapes, and vegetables that fed themselves, their religious overlords, and the soldiers in the presidios. Then there were the pueblos, small towns of inhabitants who relied on the presidios and missions, but lived independently.

The Spanish exerted tight control over California, even prohibiting most ships from other countries to trade with those living in the state. Very few people possessed property; the missions controlled huge swaths of land where the fathers pastured their sheep and cattle. Spain only awarded twenty large land grants during its fifty-three-year rule.

When Mexico took over California from Spain in 1821, it abolished the restrictions on land ownership and, eventually, the mission system. Suddenly, California's pastureland, rolling hills, and oceanfront property were up for grabs. In the next twenty-seven years, the various governors of California would give out seven hundred land grants of more than eight million acres, ushering in the ranchero era of *vaqueros*, cattle, *haciendas*, and legendary *Californio* hospitality.

Tapia wanted to make sure he got a piece of the land rush sweeping California. In late January 1839, he mounted his horse, left his adobe home in Los Angeles, and rode ninety-five miles up the coast through wind and rain to Santa Barbara to petition Governor Juan B. Alvarado for more land. There was nothing extraordinary about Tapia's application. He could have bragged about his military exploits or how he was a descendant of Felipe Santiago Tapia, who rode with the De Anza mission on its 1775 exploration of California, six years before Los Angeles was founded. Instead Tapia simply mentioned that he was constrained by having to share grazing land with his brothers. Cattle stock "suffer untold prejudice by reason of being kept on lands of inheritance," he told Alvarado.

If there was one thing Governor Alvarado understood, it was cattle ranching, California's main source of revenue. There was no official paper money or coin, although a few paid with Spanish *reales* or *piastres*. Commerce was done by barter. The main "currency" of the state came from the cattle that roamed the hills: bags of tallow that were used to make soap and candles and cattle hides that were used to make shoes and machine belts. Clipper ships from around the world, free from the restrictions placed on them by Spain, pulled into the harbors of San

Diego or Santa Barbara to pick up the stiff hides, often referred to as "California dollars." The captains would trade calico or furniture for the skins. Alvarado knew it took a lot of land to raise cattle, particularly in arid southern California. The conventional measurement was one cow per acre.

It's hard to imagine a California like this, so sparsely settled that one could ride for days on horseback and only see cattle grazing on the hills. The state was, relatively speaking, a wilderness, miles away geographically and culturally from the growing cities of New York, Philadelphia, and Boston. While waltzes and balls were common on the East Coast, fandangos and bullfights were popular in the West. There were only around 10,000 non-native settlers in California in the 1830s and about 100,000 Native Americans.

When Tapia appeared before the governor, he handed him a simple map showing the parameters of the land he wanted, "*El Paraje llamado* Cucamonga," or "The Stopping Place Called Cucamonga." It covered three leagues of land—a swath of approximately 13,000 acres about forty miles east of the pueblo of Los Angeles. Maps didn't need to be precise back then. They just needed a few obvious landmarks to delineate boundaries. Tapia's map had a sketch of a mountain range at the top, a dotted line in the center which he marked "*Camino que va a San Bernardino*," or "The road that goes to San Bernardino," and a few lines depicting a hill and some creeks. Tapia asked that the governor grant his request quickly because "it was the season to commence a tillage and other business of the plains."

I found this 185-year-old map archived in the Bancroft Library. The paper on which it is drawn is a faded yellow, but the lines are clear and well preserved. It is a simple sketch, done by hand. Tapia must have drawn it. I wonder, when he sat down at his desk to make the primitive map, if he imagined he was laying the groundwork for a storied vineyard and a future city.

On March 3, 1839, Governor Alvarado granted Tapia's request. There was no acknowledgment that this area belonged to the Kukamongo tribe, the nomadic Native American group that had wandered the area for hundreds of years. It was as if a people who had made their home roaming the mesa by the San Gabriel Mountains didn't exist.

Tapia had to survey the land, but like many rancheros, he was only obligated to designate boundaries by naming significant natural markers, like a big sycamore tree or a creek. A year after visiting the governor, Tapia performed a Mexican ceremony that spiritually bound him to the land. He took the paper proclamation granting him Rancho Cucamonga, set it on the ground, and walked over it with his boots. He then picked up stones and pulled up grasses, held them in his hands, and then flung them into the wind. The stones dropped and the wind scattered the grasses in all directions, like the four winds of heaven. In March 1840, Rancho Cucamonga was his.[16]

Tapia had picked an extraordinary spot, an oasis in the middle of an arid plateau. The new rancho nestled up against Mount San Antonio, the highest peak of the San Gabriel Mountains. Three creeks tumbled down from the hills, forming a marshy area filled with stands of sycamore, alder, cottonwood, and drooping willow trees at the base of a red hillock. Wild grapevines curled up the trunks and around the branches, offering a cooling green canopy for travelers. Tulle grasses pushed their way out of the boggiest patches.

Mexican law required that Tapia construct a house on his new rancho and inhabit it within a year. Despite the legal edict, it is not clear if Tapia ever seriously considered moving permanently from Los Angeles to Rancho Cucamonga. The place was so isolated, so exposed to the bands of marauding Indians who stole horses and cows to fight against the encroaching settlements, that it might not have been safe enough. Instead, Tapia hired the domesticated Indian laborers whose world had been turned upside down when the mission system had been dissolved. They built him a large, fortress-like adobe home on top of Red Hill. The house had a commanding view, one that looked south over the mesa and north to the mountains. Tapia moved his cattle from near Los Angeles to the rolling hills of Rancho Cucamonga. He also made a decision that would have repercussions that resonated well into the twenty-first century: to plant grapevines and make wine.

The Los Angeles region in 1839 had a small yet vibrant wine economy. Winemaking had started with the Franciscan fathers who arrived in Alta California in 1769 to set up a string of missions. For a number of years, the fathers relied on ships from Mexico or Baja California to bring them wine for use in the sacrament. The ships came so infrequently, however, that there often wasn't wine for religious ceremonies. There were wild grapevines in abundance in parts of California, but the grapes were small and bitter, and not usable for wine. Seeing the wild vines twist their way high up into the branches of trees gave Father Junipero Serra, the force behind the construction of the mission system, hope that grapes might thrive in California one day. After all, the soil in parts was rich, the sun was warm and constant, and there was ample winter rain. So in 1777, Serra wrote to the viceroy of Mexico, Antonio María de Bucareli, and requested that he send some grapevines up to their newest colony. "Some improvements could easily be introduced from [Baja] California," wrote Serra. "For instance fig and pomegranate trees and grapevines."

A year later, on a bright day in May 1778, the Spanish clipper ship the *San Antonio* sailed into a cove along the Pacific Coast in an area that would one day be known as Orange County. The ship had spent sixty-nine days at sea, difficult days where the crew subsisted on dried beef and water and little else. But it had finally reached its destination.[17]

The ship carried precious cargo: grape cuttings from vineyards from the missions in Baja California. The Indian neophytes carefully carried the grapevines that had journeyed so far to their new home at Mission San Juan Capistrano, about ten miles inland. The cuttings thrived. Green shoots soon appeared from the once-dormant vines. Then the Franciscan fathers made an unexpected decision: the mission would have to relocate. So in the summer of 1778, the padres and their Native American followers moved to a new location.

Father Serra and the other Franciscans didn't want to leave the grapes behind. They had waited too long, had thirsted too much, to abandon the grapes that might produce a steady supply of sacramental wine. Yet the season in which to plant the grapes had already passed. So they left the vines in the ground over winter. "Snow is plentiful, wherefore, until the severe cold moderates and the floods subside, the vine cuttings, which at your request were sent to us from the lower country, have been buried," Father Pablo de Mugártegui wrote to Father Serra on March 15, 1779. The next spring, when the ground had warmed, the vines were uprooted and replanted.

It takes a number of years for grapevines to bear fruit, and the shortage of sacramental wine continued to plague the Franciscans. In 1781, Father Serra wrote to a padre at San Juan Capistrano expressing dismay at his dwindling wine supply. "I hope . . . that your vines will survive and bear fruit," Serra wrote on December 8, 1781. "The lack of wine for Mass is becoming unbearable."

It is not possible to pinpoint the date of the first vintage in California. No records remain detailing that significant event. But it probably happened in 1782.[18] When Pablo de Mugártegui wrote his biography of the recently deceased Father Serra in 1784, he mentioned that the vines "have already produced wine, not only for use at Mass but also for the table."

In a few decades, winemaking was an integral part of the mission system. All but four of the twenty-one missions produced wine for their own tables and for sacramental purposes. A few missions made enough wine to sell to soldiers or those living on the ranchos that soon spread out across California.

Wine grapes flourished particularly well at Mission San Gabriel, the fourth mission founded by Father Serra, which was nestled at the base of the San Gabriel Mountains, about ten miles east of present-day Los Angeles and thirty miles west of Rancho Cucamonga. Under the guidance of Father José María de Zalvidea and the padres who succeeded him, Mission San Gabriel developed 170 acres of some of the most productive vineyards in Alta California. It was known as *La Vina Madre,* or the mother vineyard. By 1829, the mission may have been producing from 400 to 600 barrels of wine a year.[19]

The Native Americans living at Mission San Gabriel did virtually all the work to make the wine. They cleared the ground of shrub and chaparral. They planted Mission grapes and tended the vines. They picked the grapes and carried them to the wine house, where they crushed them. The Indians fastened a cowhide, the hair side down, to four poles, leaving some sag in the middle. They put the grapes in the center and climbed inside to crush them by foot. The grape juice flowed into a tub where it fermented over a period of a few weeks.[20] Some of that wine was later distilled in copper vats into brandy.

None of this work was voluntary. Many Native Americans first interacted with the Franciscans fathers because they were curious about their tools and the weapons carried by soldiers. The padres talked to them about Christianity and convinced the Indians to join them at the missions. Once baptized, however, the Native Americans suddenly found they had entered a contract of sorts, a contract they could not break. The Franciscan fathers regarded the neophytes as inferior, childlike beings. The Native Americans had no rights: they couldn't live independently, they were sequestered into same-sex, often squalid, dormitories, and they were prohibited from riding horses or practicing their traditional ceremonies. They could not leave the mission. They were treated like slaves.

Life for the hundreds of Indians at Mission San Gabriel, and other missions around California, was rigid. They were summoned from activity to activity by ringing bells. "Field hands worked, played, prayed, ate, slept, married, and were even born and buried according to a system of bells," noted one historian of California field laborers.[21] Visitors to the mission in the eighteenth and nineteenth centuries noted that the Native Americans looked unhappy. They rarely smiled or laughed and they lived in degrading conditions. The threat of punishment hovered. "They are kept in great fear, and for the least offense they are corrected," one visitor to the San Gabriel mission noted in 1826. "They are . . . complete slaves in every sense of the word."[22]

The Mexican government secularized the missions in 1833, and it led to the eventual disintegration of the winemaking operations at Mission San Gabriel. Before long, the small pueblo of Los Angeles was the center of winemaking in the state. Americans and Europeans who had come to Los Angeles after Mexico loosened Spain's restrictive policies on immigration joined *Californios* in planting vines. The banks of the Los Angeles River were soon dotted with thousands of grapevines, forming a bright green, cooling swath.

The wine made was mostly drunk at home or traded locally. Los Angeles was still extremely isolated. Clipper ships only pulled into San Pedro, thirty miles away, a few times a month. The wine and brandy were not particularly good, either, as the men making it did not have much experience. In 1827, the French captain Auguste Bernard Duhaut-Cilly, who spent a year traveling up and down the Pacific Coast on the ship *Héros*, noted its inferiority. "The vine succeeds very well; but wine and brandy extracted from it are very inferior to the exquisite taste of the grape used for it, and I think the inferiority is to be attributed to the making rather than the growth."[23]

It took a French immigrant named Jean-Louis Vignes (pronounced "vines") to recognize that there was a market for wine outside of the Los Angeles area. Vignes is credited with being the first commercial winemaker in the state. His nephews would also play a large role in developing the California wine industry. They also would be instrumental in elevating the reputation of the Rancho Cucamonga vineyard.

Vignes, a rotund man with graying muttonchops, was an itinerant Frenchman who landed in Los Angeles around 1831. He had been born in 1779 in Béguey, near Cadillac, right in the heart of the Gironde, the wine-growing region of Bordeaux, and grew up surrounded by vineyards and *vignerons* making wine. Vignes's father was a cooper and taught his son the art of making barrels. At the age of twenty-two, Vignes married, and he and his wife had four children. They were Catholic and very religious. Why, then, did Vignes leave them all behind when he was forty-seven? Was it wanderlust? Economic uncertainty? No one is quite sure, but a letter written by a friend with whom Vignes traveled provides some clues. "Vignes had been forced into exile as a result of troubles caused by his loyalty, his misplaced tenderness and his over-zealous desire to be of service."[24]

Vignes boarded a French merchant ship traveling to the Sandwich

Islands, now known as Hawaii, as part of a crew on its way to China. He ended up staying in the islands for a few years, earning a living by raising cattle and managing a rum distillery. When that closed, Vignes decided that better economic opportunities lay in California.

Vignes was fifty-two or so when he traveled from Monterey down to Los Angeles in 1831. Most men that age would be looking to slow down, to enjoy the remaining years of life. Not Vignes. He saw how well grapes grew along the banks of the Los Angeles River and in the vineyards that spread out from the water. The weather was perfect—warm, sunny, with good rain in the winter, but no frost. The terrain must have reminded Vignes of his home in Bordeaux, where vineyards covered the hills and fields, and life was centered on the seasons of the grape. Vignes soon knew he could make a living as a winemaker.

With the money he had made in Hawaii, Vignes purchased 104 acres on the west side of the Los Angeles River, right near the main road leading to San Bernardino. (The land is now home to Union Station.) The distinguishing landmark of his property was an ancient sycamore tree towering more than sixty feet high that could be seen from miles around. The tree's branches spread out 200 feet in diameter, creating a welcome umbrella of shade. Vignes built his wine cellar right near the tree. His vineyard was soon known as El Aliso, which is Spanish for sycamore. Vignes became known as Don Luis del Aliso.

Within a few years, the vineyards and Vignes's home became a gathering place for Los Angeles, a place people enjoyed visiting for parties and meals. The centerpiece of the estate was a quarter-mile-long arbor draped in grapevines. Thirty-five acres of grapes extended along the river, along with orchards of oranges, lemons, pomegranates, and other fruit trees. "Mr. V's vineyard is doubtless a model of its kind," said one visitor in 1847. "It was a delightful recreation to stroll through it."[25]

By 1840, Vignes had more than 40,000 vines in production. He stored the wine in oak casks he had made by hand.[26] The wine was widely regarded as the best around, the result, perhaps, of Vignes's lifelong exposure to winemaking. "We drank today the wine of the country, manufactured by Don Luis Vignes, a Frenchman," Lt. W. H. Emory, an

American, wrote in 1847 when he was part of the group of soldiers oc-
cupying Los Angeles during the Mexican War. "It was truly delicious,
resembling more the best description of Hock (a German white wine)
than any other wine."[27]

Thirteen years after Vignes left France, his family sent one of his
nephews, Pierre Sainsevain, to see if he was still alive. Sainsevain, twenty,
arrived in Los Angeles in 1839, and was the first in a long string of
Vignes's relatives who would immigrate to Los Angeles and form the
core of a vibrant French community.

With another set of hands to rely on, Vignes decided to sell his wine
in other parts of the state. California was still sparsely settled, so trade
between the small pueblos was limited. Vignes sent young Sainsevain
on a mission to sell wine up north. "In 1840, I started out on the ship
'Moosoon' with a cargo of his wines and brandies, for the ports of Santa
Barbara, Monterey and San Francisco, and sold them at the good price
of $2.00 per gallon for the whites, and $4.00 for the brandies," Sainsevain recalled years later.[28] Historians consider this the first commercial sale of wine in California.

Vignes's wine may also have been the first California vintage to be
destroyed in a fire. In 1842, Vignes presented a barrel of his wine to the
French sea captain Duflot de Mofras and asked that it be delivered to
King Louis Philippe of France to show what a Frenchman could do with
California grapes. Mofras agreed to transport the barrel. He brought it
as far as Hamburg, Germany. He left the wine there for storage. A short
time later, a fire destroyed the warehouse and with it Vignes's hopes to
show off California wine.

So when Tapia planted the first vines at Rancho Cucamonga in 1839,
winemaking was already established in southern California. He could
probably see that immigration was increasing. As settlers built homes and
raised families, demand for wine would increase. With his businessman's
eye, Tapia may have regarded wine as a prudent investment.

Tapia used Native American laborers to clear about an acre of land
of chaparral, chamise, sagebrush, and manzanita. They then planted about
565 vines. They used Mission grapes, the hardy, high-yielding, long-

living vines that the Franciscan fathers had been using for decades. The vine was resistant to disease, grew well in hot weather, and thrived in the sandy, loamy soil of Rancho Cucamonga.

The grapes planted by Tapia that year on the fertile fields in Rancho Cucamonga were the basis of a wine lineage that would last more than seventy-five years.

No evidence remains of Tapia's presence on Rancho Cucamonga's Red Hill. One cool fall day, I drove to the top of the hill—really a knoll—to find the plaque that marks the site of his adobe home. Tapia certainly knew his real estate. Red Hill is now one of the nicer neighborhoods in Rancho Cucamonga, which has about 170,000 residents. Comfortable one-story older homes (the city is mostly full of newish tract development) sit on large lots with lawns. Cedar and maple trees dapple the sunlight. Some of the houses overlooking the valley have sweeping views of the mountains to the south. The person who had told me about the marker wasn't sure of its whereabouts, so I drove around looking for it. I walked up and down driveways and pushed back bushes and flowers. Nothing. It seemed like all marks of Tapia's home were gone.

Months later I learned that the plaque, an official California historical marker, was actually located a half mile away in a less residential section of town. I never located it personally, but the picture online showed that it read: "The large adobe house was abandoned in 1858 when his heirs sold the rancho. The adobe soon disintegrated into its native earth."

Reminders of Tapia's winemaking were easier to find. People in the area believe that a long rectangular building located in a strip mall off the old Route 66, near the intersection of Foothill Boulevard and Vineyard Avenue, is the site of Tapia's original winemaking operation, although the historical documentation proving that is scant. Hugh and Ida Thomas, a local winemaking family, acquired the property in 1920. The original vines had been dug up three years earlier and the Thomases replanted the area with grapes that produced "Old Rancho" wine. Longtime residents described the Thomas Winery as both a park and a museum. Orange groves, rosebushes, sycamore, and avocado trees created a lush landscape, while old wine barrels, bottles, presses, and other winemaking gear scattered around lent a historical twist. The Thomas Winery flourished for almost fifty years, eventually passing into the hands of the Filippi family.[29] Then in January 1969, after a spate of heavy rain, Cucamonga Creek spilled over its banks. A wall of water six feet high came through the winery's back door, pushing boulders, brush, and stacked wine barrels through the fragile adobe walls.

The building was repaired, but hardly any of the original adobe material remained. In 1980, a developer acquired the land and built a small strip mall he named the Thomas Winery Plaza. There are modern restaurants and shops, and thousands of cars whiz by daily. While there are no vineyards nearby, reminders that this was once the center of an important wine-growing region dot the mall. Huge pockmarked redwood barrels that came around Cape Horn in the middle of the nineteenth century (or so a sign claims) decorate the plaza. Smaller barrels sit on top of a wagon. An old rusting tower remains, as well as a large round brass vessel once used to distill brandy. There is a retail wine shop where visitors can taste wine made elsewhere. Customers can even blend their own vintages to order.

Most interesting is a sign painted on the side of a barrel, not far from Vineyard Road. It reads "California's oldest commercial winery." Since winemaking began in southern California and all the vineyards of Los Angeles have long been paved over, history buffs and boosters claim that the rectangular building covered in vines in the Thomas Winery Plaza may be the closest we now have to the one of the birthplaces of California's $24.6 billion wine industry.

CHAPTER SEVEN

WINE FEVER

The travelers couldn't believe the sight before them.

For three months they had been trekking across deserts and mountains, exhausted and half starved. They had killed off their horses and mules one by one for food, and stuck their heads in tiny pockets in the ground to drink up drops of moisture. The plan, to take the southern route to the California gold fields, had seemed like a good idea when they left Provo, Utah, three months earlier.

Now it was Christmas Day in 1849 and the twenty-five would-be gold miners were nearly spent, their clothes in rags, their boots worn down, their spirits low. They had come out of the mountains hours earlier and had made their way to Rancho Cucamonga, a welcoming spot of green after days in the desert. They thought the place was called the Pokamongo Ranch.

The men were still about five hundred miles from the gold mines, but the sight that greeted them, the first sign of civilization they had seen in months, promised riches of another kind. Two naked Indians stood on a platform made from a cowhide stretched between four poles. In the center sat a pile of fermenting grapes. The Indians trod up and down, squishing the grapes into a bright red liquid that flowed out of a hole in the bottom of the hide.

The travelers grabbed their tin cups and filled them with the young wine, as the superintendent of the rancho, a dark-skinned man, looked on with amusement. "We went at the wine, caught it in our tin cups, as we all had one apiece," one traveler recorded in his diary. "We drank it as fast as the Indians could tramp it for awhile. The old negro after awhile said 'Gentlemen, you have had a hard time of it, I know, but de first ting you know you will know nothing. You are welcome to it.'"

The travelers drank draught after draught of the young wine until they collapsed on the ground in a stupor. They fell asleep right where they lay. "Now this spree was on Christmas day. In the morning when we all got up we felt pretty good but awfully hungry."[30]

The travelers hadn't hit the gold fields yet, but they had stumbled upon what would one day be another of the state's riches: purple gold. Rancho Cucamonga was the first settled place many gold seekers taking a southern route into the mines would find as they came out of the mountains. It became a regular stop. And word spread that the wine from the vineyard was worth seeking out.

When Tapia died in 1845, he passed his property on to his daughter and her French husband, a grape grower who had vineyards near the coast. Their main abode was in Los Angeles, and although they traveled back and forth for a time, it appears they neglected the rancho. A member of a U.S. surveying expedition who visited in 1854 described abject working conditions for the Indians. The vineyard belongs to "a Californian, living at a great distance off, who had placed these people here to look after it. They were evidently very poor, and lived in rude log huts . . . and who, in their scanty ragged clothing appeared the picture of misery. They stand much in the position of serfs."

In 1858, Tapia's daughter and son-in-law sold Rancho Cucamonga's 13,000 acres to an American Confederate supporter. California had become a territory of the United States in 1848 and a state in 1850. As the country geared up for Civil War, southern California was dominated by people who supported the Southern cause.

The buyer, John Rains, considered himself a modern man, someone with a vision. The old *Californio* way of life, with its vast ranchos, giant herds of cattle, and focus on family life rather than commerce, was rapidly disappearing now that California was part of the United States. Americans and Europeans had flocked to San Francisco and the foothills of the Sierra Nevada during the Gold Rush. Some found their way south, to escape the arduousness of the mines, or to set up small businesses, or to escape a criminal past.

Rains straddled the American and old Spanish-Mexican lifestyles. He had come to California from Alabama in 1847 after a stint with the Texas Rangers. From the time he had arrived, he had lived by his wits and his willingness to try his hand at almost any type of business. He had herded thousands of head of sheep and cattle across the unforgiving Mojave Desert, fought off Indians, and even run unsuccessfully for sheriff.

In October 1854, Rains made his smartest move yet: he signed on to look after 1,000 head of cattle belonging to Isaac Williams, a Pennsylvania native and cattle baron who had made a fortune selling tallow and hides to the ships that arrived at the port at San Pedro. Taking that job at Rancho Santa Ana del Chino in modern San Bernardino County put Rains in close proximity to Williams's young daughter, Maria Merced. With his dark hair, full beard, and heavy eyebrows, Rains was a handsome man. He wasn't well educated, but resourcefulness counted more than school learning on the western frontier. Before long, Merced was smitten. She may have been seeking a protector as well because her father was ill in bed with heart disease. The fifty-seven-year-old Williams never recovered. He died on September 13, 1856. Three days later, the twenty-seven-year old Rains and the sixteen-year-old Merced were married by Reverend Padre Raho at the Catholic church on Los Angeles's main plaza.[31]

The union thrust Rains into the upper echelons of society, for Doña Merced was *Californio* royalty. Merced was a descendant of some of the first Spanish settlers in California and her maternal grandfather had been one of the few granted land by Spain. Her father acquired even more. When he died, Merced inherited half of one of the most beautiful ranchos in the region, the 35,000-acre Rancho Santa Ana del Chino, near present-day Chino, among other land holdings, and huge herds of stock. Her total dowry was worth around $70,000.[32] Rains only brought about $1,850 to the union, all of it in cattle and sheep.

Rains immediately started to invest his wife's money. Perhaps he was thinking of his father-in-law, whom one observer thought combined the best of American ingenuity with the best attributes of the *Californios*. Rains bought land in San Bernardino. He invested in the Bella Union Hotel on Main Street in Los Angeles. And two years after the wedding, after selling his wife's stake in the Chino rancho, he used the proceeds to purchase Rancho Cucamonga for $8,500. Rains had to pay another $8,000 to convince a longtime tenant to relinquish claim on the land.

Rains had big plans for the property. Although Tapia's home still stood on top of Red Hill, Rains dreamed of a modern house, one that would announce to the world that the Rains family was important. Impermanent adobe was the predominant building material of the time, but Rains aspired to build a home of fired red brick. He found five Ohio brick makers living in Los Angeles and hired them to move to Rancho Cucamonga and construct close to 300,000 bricks by hand.

The finished house was a marvel. It was U-shaped, with a round brick fountain in the patio. Flumes from a canyon stream filled the fountain and funneled water beneath the house, cooling it during the hot days of summer. The rooms had twelve-foot-high ceilings, wide plank floors, fireplaces, and large windows to let in the light. Elegant wood furnishings brought around the horn from Boston probably decorated the home. The home was large enough to accommodate the Rains's growing family, and Merced's three younger siblings.

Rains's attention then turned to Tapia's vineyard, which spread out over 100 acres right near the new house. The Cucamonga region had proved well suited to grape growing: its sandy, loamy soil was loose and porous; and the climate was ideal. While temperatures could reach over one hundred degrees in the summer, it never dipped to freezing in the winter. Moreover, the area sat over a water table, which encouraged the vines to send out roots deep into the ground.

In October 1858, Rains laid out another 100,000 new vines on 160 acres. He set the vines in a grid pattern and planted rows of sycamore trees around the vineyard's perimeter to break the wind that often whipped through the area. Rains interspersed orange hedges between the trees, forming a natural fence to keep out animals. The scent of the blossoms mixed with the earthy smell of grapes.

Rains planted mostly Mission grapes, the most widely planted strain of grapes in the state. But he also used some "foreign" varieties of *vitis vinifera*, too. Winemakers had begun to realize that the wine made from Mission grapes was inferior and some were experimenting with varieties imported from Europe. Grapes offered for sale in local nurseries included Black Hamburgh grapes, which one newspaper ad described as "luscious," and "an immense bearer," and Large Rose of Peru, touted as "a large and very superior white grape, very prolific very large."[33] It would take decades, and much trial and error, to discover which grapes worked best in California.

Rains, like most southern California winemakers, made red and white wine. He distilled brandy in large copper vats. He also produced two types of fortified wine, Port and a sweet white wine called Angelica, which was made by mixing one part grape brandy to three parts wine.[34] Bottled Angelica created a small sparkle—which delighted the tongue but could produce a terrific hangover. When Paul Revere's nephew Joseph Warren Revere came to Los Angeles in 1847 and tasted Angelica, he was transfixed. "A most delicious cordial is likewise made, called Angelica, and if the Olympian gods could get a drop of it, they would soon vote nectar a bore, and old Jupiter would instantly order Master Ganymede to change his goblet and change it with the new tipple to the brim," wrote Revere.[35]

Because summer temperatures got so high in Rancho Cucamonga, the wines had a high alcohol content—as high as 14 to 18 percent. They were also sweet, which imbibers at the time preferred. "The wine made here is the most celebrated in the country, on account of its peculiar, rich flavor, being some twenty percent above Los Angeles wine in saccharine matter," one visitor wrote about Rains's wine in 1861.[36]

Rains sold most of his product in Los Angeles or San Bernardino or to whomever came to the rancho. He sent some to San Francisco as well. By 1862, the value of his wine operations topped $50,000. For a man who came to California with practically nothing, that must have felt like a great accomplishment.

One reason Rains expanded his vineyard was that California was caught up in a wine fever.

The state had seen a huge influx of people after gold was discovered in the American River in 1848. People from around the world had responded to the promise of easy money. They dropped their farm implements, left their villages in Germany, Austria, France, Chile, Argentina, and China, and got on clipper ships and steamers to make their way to the foothills of the Sierra Nevada Mountains.

San Francisco's population soared from fewer than 450 people in 1847 to almost 56,000 by 1860. Thousands more lived in the foothills where the gold was concentrated. These people needed to be fed and clothed and in the early years of the Gold Rush the dons of southern California were in an excellent position to do that. The boom brought tremendous prosperity to the area. Cattle that had sold for three dollars in 1847 were selling for seventy-five dollars a few years later. Fresh fruit commanded record prices. For a few years the streets of Los Angeles were full of newly rich *caballeros* riding horses bedecked in silver.

Ambitious businessmen looked for ways other than panning for gold to earn money. Increasingly they saw it in grapes. Fresh grapes commanded huge sums in San Francisco. The newspapers also touted grape growing as a surefire method to get rich, particularly for those exhausted by the arduousness of the gold fields. "The yield of grapes is immense, and the profits per acre much greater than the tillage of the soil for any other kind of fruit or produce," claimed the *California Farmer and Journal of Useful Sciences* in 1856. Growers could make $200 per acre by growing grapes, according to the article.[37]

The promise of easy money led to a rush to plant grapes. In 1855, there were about 324,234 grapevines in the state. By 1858, around the time Rains expanded his vineyard, there were 4 million vines. One year later, there were 6 million grapevines in California.[38] The California Legislature exempted growers from paying any tax on vines until they were four years old, thus providing another incentive to plant.[39]

"Nearly every land owner caught the wine fever, entertaining the idea that the planting of a few thousand vines would make him rich and vineyards sprang up, as if by magic all over California," wrote Charles Kohler, one of the nineteenth-century businessmen who did grow rich by making and selling wine.[40]

Miners turned farmers planted grapes all over California, including near the gold diggings in El Dorado and Sutter counties. Most of the grape growing in northern California was concentrated in Sonoma County, with Alameda, Contra Costa, and Napa counties not far behind. The bulk of the vineyards, however, were in southern California, as they had been during the Mission era. Los Angeles was the center of the wine trade, with at least seventy-five vineyards within the town's borders—most along the west side of the river—and another twenty-five nearby. By 1859, there were twenty-three commercial wine producers. The road leading from the port of San Pedro to Los Angeles became known as "Vineyard Lane," because it was lined so heavily with vineyards and fruit orchards. Los Angeles was soon referred to as the "City of Vines."[41] Wine was abundant and cheap and was served free at every meal.[42] There were also vineyards in Anaheim, south of the city, and the San Gabriel Valley, about ten miles east.

The increase in wine production created an acute labor shortage. Most white and Mexican men had left the pueblos to try their hand at gold mining, leaving Native Americans to do the bulk of the planting, pruning, and harvesting of the grapes. It was a situation ripe for exploitation and the vineyardists took full advantage of it.

The Indians who had been recruited into the Mission system had never recovered from its secularization in 1833. They couldn't return to their ancestral lifestyles, as they were several generations removed from that world and knew little of its rhythms. They gravitated instead to Los

Angeles and other pueblos seeking homes and work. Freed from the strict restrictions of the Franciscan fathers and the security offered by the missions, they faltered. In Los Angeles, many became addicted to *aguardiente*, a type of brandy with 18 to 20 percent alcohol. (The Franciscans had not permitted them to drink alcohol.) Many Native Americans found irresistible the lure of a short street right off the plaza named Calle de los Negros. The one-story adobe buildings that lined the street were filled with saloons, houses of prostitution, and gambling parlors where disputes over monte and faro were resolved with guns and knives, not words. The temptations proved too much for many Indians (and others) who often could be found passed out drunk in the street or in doorways.

When California became a state in 1850, it immediately legalized a practice of short-term indentured servitude for the Native Americans, a practice of which winemakers took advantage. One of the first acts passed by the California Legislature was a law nicknamed the Indian Indenture Act. It stripped Native Americans of most of their rights, including the right to vote or testify against whites in court. The law also made it easy for vineyardists and farmers to use the pretext of vagrancy to obtain cheap Indian labor. Any Indian who appeared to be drunk or loitering, or was seen in a place where liquor was sold, could be arrested. Sometimes just the word of a white man could lead to an arrest. A justice of the peace could order that the Indian be hired out for up to four months to the highest bidder to pay off his fine.

Los Angeles adopted its own, stricter, version of this law on August 16, 1850, one of the most vicious in the state. It allowed Indians to be arrested for not working. Around sundown on Sundays, the town marshal would roam Calle de los Negros and other nearby streets looking for inebriated Indians. The marshal would drag them to a corral to sleep off the liquor. On Monday morning, he would put the Indians up for sale for a week to whomever would pay the most. The price was generally from one to three dollars. At the end of the week, the vineyardists or farmers would pay two thirds of the fine to the city and the rest to the Indian worker—in high-alcohol *aguardiente*, therefore assuring the cycle would be repeated.[43]

"Los Angeles had a slave mart as well as New Orleans and Constantinople—only the slave at Los Angeles was sold fifty-two times a year as long as he lived, which generally did not exceed one, two, or three years under the new dispensation," wrote one observer. "Those thousands of honest useful people were absolutely destroyed in this way."[44]

The sight of the Native Americans toiling in the fields made a strong impression on whoever saw them. "Stripped to the skin, and wearing only loin-cloths, they tramped with ceaseless tread from morn till night, pressing from the luscious fruit of the vineyard the juice so soon to ferment into wine," wrote one observer. "These Indians were employed in early fall, the season of the year when wine is made and when the thermometer as a rule, in southern California, reaches its highest point; and this temperature coupled with incessant toil caused the perspiration to drip from their swarthy bodies into the wine product, the sight of which in no wise increased my appetite for California wine."[45]

CHAPTER EIGHT

BLOOD ON THE LAND

The troubles of Rancho Cucamonga started on November 17, 1862. Rains got up early that chilly fall day to ride into Los Angeles, a trip of about forty miles. It was a journey he took often, steering his horse across the mesa covered in chaparral, sagebrush, and manzanita and past the great Chino and San Antonio ranchos. Rains, in fact, had just returned a few days earlier from the pueblo where new two- and three-story brick buildings were replacing traditional one-story adobes. He was reluctant to leave his wife, Merced, and their four young children so soon again, particularly since the twenty-three-year-old was pregnant. But business was pressing. Debts were closing in on him.

As he prepared to depart from Rancho Cucamonga, Rains, thirty-four, entered his bedroom and walked over to the bureau where he stored his pistols. They were not there. Puzzled, Rains asked his wife if she had seen them. She had not, nor had anyone else in the household. Rains was concerned about traveling without a gun—few did that in the turbulent days of the Civil War—but he decided not to postpone the trip.

Around noon, Rains went out the corral behind his house, the one that looked down on his fruit orchards and vineyard spreading to the south. The vines were increasingly barren, dropping their leaves as winter advanced. But Rains must have had a sense of satisfaction, tinged with worry, as he looked over his property. It was prospering, producing high-quality grapes and wines, pears, apples and other fruits, even though it was heavily mortgaged. He had come a long way from his childhood in Alabama. He was now a land baron, owner of thousands of acres of prime ranch land in southern California, a man to be respected. Rains ordered his horses to be hitched to his wagon and began what he expected to be a six-hour journey west.

He never got there.

Two days after Rains departed, the horses he had hitched to the wagon turned up at Rancho Cucamonga. They were covered with sweat. They had no harnesses. They had no riders. But for some reason, the unaccompanied horses did not raise alarm.

In Los Angeles, Rains missed the appointments he had scheduled. The room set aside for Rains at the Bella Union Hotel on Main Street was never occupied. On Friday, five days after Rains left his home, Dr. Winston, one of the people who had expected to see Rains in Los Angeles, knocked on Doña Merced's door in Rancho Cucamonga. He was traveling from Los Angeles on his way to the Colorado River and he decided to inquire about his missing friend. Rains's wife, caught up caring for her young children and the three half siblings also in her care, had not thought hard about the whereabouts of her husband. But the unexpected visit from Dr. Winston made her realize something was amiss. She sent word to her brother-in-law, Robert Carlisle, at the nearby Rancho Chino: Rains was missing.

By the next day, a Saturday, scores of men led by Carlisle and Sheriff Tomás Avila Sánchez were combing the roads and trails between Rancho Cucamonga and Los Angeles. They rode their horses into washes, traveled up arroyos, and looked for freshly overturned soil. Nothing.

On Sunday, the search party fanned out in a hilly area that lay between the road to Los Angeles and one that cut away north to the old Mission San Gabriel. Someone spotted a hat hidden away in the brush. It was identified as Rains's.

The next couple of hours were brutal ones as the searchers made their way up a sandy arroyo. Finally, as the sun was setting and dusk was descending, a searcher discovered Rains's wagon at the bottom of a steep ravine, tucked into bushes to hide it from the road.

After a night of heavy rain, the search resumed on Monday. Rains's harness, neatly folded, was found high in a sycamore tree. His overcoat was discovered a half mile away near a Honolulu newspaper that Rains had carried from home. It was soaked in blood. But no body was discovered.

"The melancholy fact that he has been murdered, in broad daylight, on the open road can no longer be doubted," reported the *Los Angeles Star*. "The deed was the result of a deliberate plan, carried out more successfully than any ever heretofore attempted in this section of the State."

The paper held out little hope for Rains, whom it characterized as a man who had a "courage that knew no danger." Although Rains was "impulsive," he was "of a most generous nature and we do not believe harbored ill will of anyone," read the article.

Finally, on Friday, November 28, eleven days after Rains had left home, searchers, including Carlisle and A. J. King, an undersheriff for Los Angeles, spotted Rains's body. It had been hidden in a cactus patch about 400 feet from the main road. The sight was not pretty. Rains had been murdered. The assailants had lassoed Rains's right arm and tugged him off the wagon, pulling so hard they dislocated his shoulder. Then they shot him twice in the back, once in the chest, and once on the right side. His clothes were gone; all that remained was one boot. Coyotes had mutilated the corpse. Rains's face had started to decay; his rescuers identified him by his black beard.[46]

"The murder was not committed for the sake of plunder," wrote the *Star*. "It must have been the result of some slight, long brooded over by a black malignant heart, associating with itself others of like nature."

Rains was just the first in a long line of men who would die because of Rancho Cucamonga.

———

More than 150 years later, I was sitting in the light-filled reading room of the Bancroft Library at University of California at Berkeley, thumbing through a fragile diary. Before me was a calculation of assets and liabilities that Rains had written. It showed that he had borrowed large sums of money just five days before his death, using his rancho as collateral.

The lined blue paper was brittle, and crackled as I handled the edges, making me afraid it might tear. The fact that it was still around seemed miraculous. Benjamin Hayes, a lawyer and the sole judge for Los Angeles, San Diego, and San Bernardino counties in the early days of California's statehood, had preserved the paper. Hayes, who had come to Los Angeles in 1850, recognized he was living in the middle of a historic moment: California's transition from Mexican to American rule. As an educated man with a degree from St. Mary's University in Baltimore, Hayes decided to document the era. He amassed thousands of newspaper clippings about the region's climate, agriculture, people, and business, into 138 scrapbooks. They now reside at the Bancroft.

I looked at the figures Rains had written down more than 150 years earlier.

"Amount due me from the government: $15,000," Rains had written at the top. "Amount due me from wine: $3,500," read the line below. And then, "Amount due me from other parties: $2,500. Wine on hand in San Francisco: $3,000." In total, Rains was expecting $24,000 in income.

Then Rains listed his liabilities. They totaled $14,600 and most came from loans he had taken out from various Los Angeles merchants, all of whom happened to be Jewish. He owed Bachman and Fleishman and Sichel $5,000; Helman & Co. [sic] $2,000; Fleishman by himself $1,300; Lazard and Co. $500 and Kalisher & Co. $1,300. He also owed $2,500 for the Bella Union Hotel and $2,000 to others.[47] Rains also noted that he had 6,000 head of cattle, horses, mares, rents due, and land totaling $184,000.

I was a bit in awe as I looked at Rains's mathematical notations. It was if I was looking at a piece of evidence, a clue to a long-ago event that shattered lives and led to enormous changes in the ownership of

Rancho Cucamonga and its famed vineyard. The paper connected to my life, too. My ancestor, Isaias Hellman, eventually took over that land. The grapes Rains planted had probably been used to make the wine that was destroyed in the Vallejo warehouse fire.

I wondered why Rains had been murdered. He was a wealthy and influential man, the kind who usually didn't get gunned down in broad daylight. He may have had enemies, but he had many more friends, and they were the leading businessmen and merchants of the day. He had a beautiful and well-connected wife, one whose roots extended to the earliest days of Spain's domination of Alta California. Who would want him dead?

Hayes soon found himself obsessed with that exact question. Hayes only knew Rains and his wife slightly before the murder. He had seen the couple a month after their marriage, when he visited one of the region's ranchos. He noted their meeting in a diary entry, referring to Merced as the "rich heiress."[48] But as the region's judge, Hayes found himself drawn into the search for Rains's body and the hunt for the killer. He signed arrest warrants and held hearings for the various suspects. Hayes eventually became so absorbed with Rains's death and the fate of his vineyard that he became the lawyer for his widow. He lent her money and got the Cucamonga Vineyard as collateral. He recorded his observations and growing involvement in the case in a section of a scrapbook titled "The Cucamonga Papers." The notes and articles present a horrifying picture of death, vengeance, revenge, and betrayal. The murder and the hunt for the killer set off a reign of terror in southern California and deepened the distrust between the *Californios* and Americans. In total, five men would die because of struggles surrounding Rancho Cucamonga.

The mud was thick and water pooled in the carriage tracks on Main Street in Los Angeles as the group of Masons followed John Rains's casket to the Bella Union Hotel. It was ten a.m. on November 30, 1862, two days after Rains's body had been found under a cactus patch, and

hundreds of people had come to pay their respects. After some brief remarks by the priest, a procession of mourners walked behind the hearse
to the cemetery. A band playing somber music accompanied the procession. It was "one of the most sad and impressive spectacles which has
ever been witnessed in our midst," noted the *Los Angeles Star*.

Rains's death threw his wife, Doña Merced, into a panic. She was
only twenty-three and had always lived under the protection of a man—
first her wealthy and generous father and then, scarcely three days after
her father's death, her husband. She was now a widow with four children
under four and another one on the way. Merced, who had deep brown
eyes and who piled her hair into an elaborate chignon on her head, had
been raised to be a genteel woman, skilled in the arts of beauty, dance,
and hospitality. She didn't know how to run a rancho or vineyard, and
hadn't the vaguest clue how to navigate a changing economy where the
unhurried ways of the *Californios* were giving way to a landscape ruled
by commerce and competition.

It soon became apparent to Doña Merced that her husband, the man
she had considered her gallant protector, had put her in a difficult situation. He hadn't written a will. He had left significant debts. Most om-
inously, Rains had not put his wife's name on any of the deeds securing
Rancho Cucamonga or other large parcels of land in San Diego and Los
Angeles counties, or on the papers that brought him partial ownership
of the Bella Union Hotel. Rains had used Doña Merced's inheritance
to become a land baron, but had not ensured her legal right to the
property. "He fraudulently contrived and intended to deprive her of
her separate property and convert it to his own use," Hayes wrote in his
scrapbook.

To the men surrounding Doña Merced, she must have seemed like
easy prey. She was young, she was isolated at Rancho Cucamonga, she
had small children and sisters to care for, and she was naïve in the ways
of the world. How else to explain their actions on March 14, 1863?

Doña Merced had just finished her breakfast and was bustling around
her home when there was a knock at the front door. Standing in the
entryway were six men, including three who were close to Merced—

Stephen C. Foster, her forty-two-year old uncle and the first American mayor of Los Angeles under U.S. military rule; Robert Carlisle, who was married to her sister, Francisca; and Elijah K. Dunlap, the vineyard manager and administrator of her husband's estate. Three others joined them.

A day earlier, Judge Hayes had ruled that all the land Rains had purchased also belonged to his wife, even though he hadn't recorded her name on the deeds. As soon as the judge signed the order, Merced's attorney rushed to the clerk's office in San Bernardino and registered half of Rancho Cucamonga in her name and half in her children's names. When Merced greeted her visitors, she was one of the largest female landowners in the state. All her landholdings in San Bernardino County, Los Angeles County, and San Diego County were worth more than $150,000.

Merced invited the men to her parlor, a room in the front of the house far from the noisy patio and kitchen. As they settled onto the silk-covered horsehair settee and dark wood chairs drawn close to a crackling fireplace, the men delivered a sobering message: Merced wasn't capable of navigating the world of business, of raising grapes and making wine, or managing cattle. They told Merced that Rains had taken out close to $14,600 in mortgages secured against Rancho Cucamonga (about $5 million in 2013 dollars), and it would take expert management to pay off the debt. How could a woman with five young children know the best way to proceed?

The discussion continued for hours, through lunch, past the deepening winter afternoon, and into the evening. By the time the meeting was over, an exhausted and defeated Merced had signed a power of attorney giving control over all her land and her possessions to Carlisle. Her brother-in-law would now make the decisions for Merced and her children. He could buy, sell, lease, or mortgage her lands. He could collect all the income from the vineyard, cattle sales, and rent from the Bella Union Hotel. He could decide how much to send to Doña Merced and her children for living expenses.

The legal document, written in English, a language with which Merced was not entirely comfortable, made the transfer of power irrevocable.

It was a decision Merced would soon come to regret.

Carlisle and Rains had worked closely together when settling up their father-in-law's huge estate, so it seemed to make sense that he would take over Doña Merced's affairs. But Doña Merced soon became convinced that her brother-in-law was focused more on his own interests than hers. He rarely sent her spending money, leaving her so poor that she and her three half sisters started doing the laundry and ironing for the vineyard workers to buy enough food and provisions for the family. Carlisle and his wife did not visit Rancho Cucamonga for a five-month stretch from October 1863 until February 1864, even though Doña Merced was at home with five young children, including a newborn, and her siblings. Nor did Carlisle and her sister, Francisca, invite Merced to their rancho in Chino. Doña Merced's modern brick marvel, once the expression of hope for the future, had become her prison. At one point Merced pleaded for help: "Judge Hayes, please to send me $30 to $40 if you can [spare] them for I have not a dollar in the house."

While Merced was desperate for cash, Carlisle was busy selling off her assets and pocketing the funds. He sold fifty head of her cattle for $5,000. He sold the 1862 wine vintage to a local wine dealer for $2,665. He collected more than $2,025 in rents from the Bella Union Hotel. But he did not use one penny of the money to pay down the $14,600 in mortgages on Rancho Cucamonga.[49]

Then on February 13, 1864, the San Bernardino probate court approved the sale of Merced's half-interest in one of her properties, Rancho Valle de San Jose, a 17,000-acre tract in San Diego County. Rains had purchased the land in July 1861 for $3,450. The new buyer? Robert Carlisle. The sale price? Three hundred dollars.

Carlisle's actions infuriated Doña Merced and Benjamin Hayes, who had become so involved with the case that he regarded himself as

Merced's protector. Carlisle had gotten her land for a pittance, a fraction of what it should have commanded. It seemed clear that he was intent on enriching himself at her expense. By not paying interest on the mortgages either, Carlisle appeared to want to deliberately put Rancho Cucamonga in jeopardy. In a March 5, 1864, notice in the *Los Angeles Star*, Merced announced she was revoking Carlisle's power of attorney. It had, she said, been obtained from her "without consideration and by fraud."

The *Star* was the most widely read English-language newspaper of the day and many of Carlisle's colleagues, the town's merchants, farmers, and politicians, would have seen the insulting notice. Carlisle couldn't let that slight go unchallenged. Four days later he ran his own notice in the newspaper. He denied all the charges and blamed the vitriolic ad on Hayes. "I declare such notice totally false in every respect and pronounce Hayes a low-lived nullifier, liar, and coward."

Sides had been drawn for a new battle over the fate of Rancho Cucamonga. The consequences would be bloody.

Rains's murder stirred up unease. Roads that were once considered safe were suspect. People feared that "dangerous characters were prowling around the city and surrounding country," according to an article in the *Los Angeles Star*. The killing put everyone on edge.

It's not that killing was unusual. Violence was a way of life in southern California. A murder a day was common in Los Angeles, as the gamblers resolved disputes with guns and bandits pushed out from San Francisco by the vigilantes preyed on travelers in the hills. "There is no country where . . . human life is of such little account," wrote the editor of the *Los Angeles Star*. "Men hack one another in pieces with pistols and other cutlery."[50]

Tensions were high in the region in 1862. The Civil War was raging, and although the battles were thousands of miles away, California also was divided between the North and the South. San Francisco and Sacramento were firmly behind President Lincoln. Many in the southern part of the state, including Rains, sympathized with the Southern cause. Rains's Bella Union Hotel had become the center of anti-Union organizing. On the wall of the dining room there was a picture of the famous Confederate general P. G. T. Beauregard, who had defeated the Union Army at the Battle of Bull Run. California's governor was so concerned that the southern part of the state might secede that he sent in troops to protect order.

But the more immediate tension was racial, and Rains's murder unmasked long-simmering hostility between the *Californios* and Anglos. The influx of settlers from the United States was squeezing out the Mexican-born natives who had long dominated California's culture, language, and economy. *Californios* regarded whites as invaders and, eventually, conquerors. The white newcomers were disdainful of the languid way of life of their predecessors. "The men are thriftless, proud, extravagant, and very much given to gambling; the women have but little education . . . And their morality, of course, is none of the best," one observer wrote.[51] In the span of a few decades, the *Californios* would see their ranchos lost to debt and trickery and would go from ruling the state to being ruled.

Deadly clashes between the two groups were frequent. Just a few years earlier, in 1857, the Los Angeles sheriff, James Barton, and three members of a posse were killed in the mountains near Los Angeles while chasing a gang of bandits led by Juan Flores.

From the time Rains's disappearance was first noted, rumors swirled that *Californios* had killed him. And in a lawless region like southern California, rumors were dangerous. Even though Sheriff Sánchez ostensibly was leading the investigation, his authority was so weak that vigilante justice was common—and accepted. Just days after Rains's murder, Carlisle, his brother-in-law, had vowed to go "out tomorrow on a rampage, that is, in search of the murderers, and to seek a clue to this great crime."[52]

Speculation about the killer or killers started almost immediately and whispers and innuendo soon were interpreted as facts. Suspicion landed early on Ramón Carrillo, a descendant of an old *Californio* family who became Rains's majordomo in 1861. Carrillo represented everything

Americans respected and feared. He was a renowned *vaquero*, or horseman, and expert lassoer, able to cast a rope over a steer from a long distance. He was one of the area's leading bear wrestlers. But he had also fought against the Americans during the Mexican-American War, earning special recognition for his role in what was known as the Battle of Chino. In September 1846, Carrillo had led a group of fifty *Californios* who captured twenty-four Americans who were hiding in Isaac Williams's adobe at Rancho Chino. The *Californios* marched their prisoners twelve miles to the eastern side of Los Angeles, where they were eventually released. The skirmish was militarily insignificant, but it embarrassed the Americans, who never quite forgave Carrillo.

Soon people were gossiping that Carrillo and Doña Merced were in love—and that Carrillo paid a group of men to murder Rains. There were also rumors that Rains had fired Carrillo after the pair exchanged "high words."[53]

Within days of Rains's funeral, Judge Hayes issued a warrant for Carrillo's arrest and set bail at $13,000. Carrillo appeared before Hayes, who let him go after Carrillo presented proof that he had been in Los Angeles on the day of Rains's murder.

But that explanation did not satisfy Carlisle and other men who were out for vengeance. They kept insisting, despite the lack of proof, that Carrillo was the mastermind behind Rains's death. The rumors got so loud that the *Los Angeles Star* printed articles declaring that Carrillo had ordered his gang to kill Rains. "Justice will eventually overtake these murderers and rid the earth of such fiends in human shape," an article in the paper noted on February 20, 1863.

Names of other of Rains's suspected assailants began to circulate, leading Judge Hayes to issue an arrest warrant for Manuel Ceredel, a field hand and laborer and a low-level outlaw, who had frequently been charged, but never convicted, of stealing horses, bridles, and saddles. As soon as the warrant was issued, Carlisle and his posse, not the sheriff, went looking for Ceredel. They had heard he was hiding in El Monte, a Confederate stronghold about twelve miles east of Los Angeles known for its lawless and violent ways. In mid-December 1862, just before some of the heaviest rains in California history would deluge the state and two weeks after Rains's murder, Carlisle rode to El Monte, but Ceredel was nowhere to be found.

Ceredel was finally captured in February 1863 and was led to the county jail. He was very sick—sallow, wheezing, and weak, and believed he was about to die of tuberculosis. He confessed to authorities that he and four other men had been hired by Carrillo to kill Rains, although the only proof was his word. "It appears Mr. Rains was met on the road by five men, whose names are given," an article in the *Los Angeles Star* on Feb. 14, 1863 noted. "One of them asked where he was going; he replied, to town. 'I think not, we have got you now,' said the assassin, or words to that effect."

Men like Carlisle and his friends continued to insist that Carrillo had been involved. In September 1863, responding to another warrant for his arrest, Carrillo appeared in a Los Angeles courtroom. He was allowed to leave after the district attorney "stated the people of California had no complaint against Carrillo and the District Attorney didn't know of any such testimony against him," according to the newspaper.

But the findings of two courts that Carrillo had nothing to do with Rains's murder did little to assuage those convinced he was involved. The legal decision stirred up even more anti-*Californio* sentiment and prompted a group of men to vow to capture Carrillo. The papers also began to report that Carrillo and a group of fifteen to thirty men had banded together and taken to the hills to rob and kill Americans. "Ramón Carrillo, it is stated, is the leader of this band of cut-throats . . . It was, without a doubt, some of this band who murdered John Rains."[54]

Ceredel went on trial in this atmosphere of distrust and suspicion. He had not been charged with killing Rains, but for attacking the sheriff who came to arrest him for Rains's murder. After a brief trial on December 5, 1863, Ceredel was convicted and sentenced to ten years' confinement at San Quentin state prison near San Francisco.

The vigilantes wanted blood for Rains's murder and the fact Ceredel had not been convicted of that crime infuriated them. Here, they thought, was one of the region's most prosperous citizens, cut down in broad daylight. Yet his murder went unavenged.

On December 9, 1863, Sheriff Sánchez and his undersheriff, A. J. King, brought a group of prisoners out to the new port in Wilmington to take them to San Quentin. The harbor was too shallow for steamboats to come to shore, so lighters, ferries, and tugboats met passengers at the dock and ferried them out to deeper waters. The sheriff and his prisoners boarded the tugboat *Crickett* for the trip to the steamer *The Senator*. Dozens of others crammed on board, some to go to the boat and some just to take a ride for pleasure on the water.

When the *Crickett* had pulled away from the dock and was chugging toward the larger boat, a group of men approached Sánchez and his prisoners. At a prearranged signal, the men, vigilantes who had disguised themselves as tourists, grabbed Ceredel and pulled him away from the sheriff. They brought out a noose, twisted it around his neck, and strung it on the yardarm hanging off the boat. Ceredel must have struggled and swung his legs in a frenzied attempt to find traction, any traction to stop the asphyxiation, but after twenty minutes it was over. He was dead. His body hung limply over the water. The vigilantes reached into their pockets and pouches and brought out rocks they had carried from the shore. They loaded them into Ceredel's pockets and threw him overboard to sink into the water, making him the second man with connections to Rancho Cucamonga to die.

The lynching of Ceredel did little to relieve the vigilantes' distrust of Carrillo, whom many suspected was the ringleader of the ambush.

Carrillo felt like a marked man. He knew that the white hostility against him in a region where impulse and prejudice carried more weight than facts and justice meant he might not live long. He came to believe that Carlisle was responsible for the spread of false rumors and accusations against him. Carlisle was eager to get rid of Carrillo, who had influence with Dõna Merced, so he could maintain control of Dõna Merced's fortune. "The person who has always persecuted me is a man by the name of Bob Carlisle," Carrillo wrote his brother Julio on April 16, 1864. "He does not do it personally, but through others paid by him. The reason for this continued abuse is because I did not abandon my place as superintendent of the stock at the time of John Rains' death, and that I still hold the position. . . . Carlisle . . . cannot conduct the business with as much liberty as he could if I was out of the way. He is trying to get the power which I have from the widow herself, who is the absolute owner of the property.

"Now I will tell you that if by bad luck I should happen to disappear, Bob Carlisle will know and he will be the cause of my disappearance and he is the one whom you should prosecute. I am satisfied that while awake he thinks of nothing else by a half chance to assassinate me so that he can do with the widow what he sees fit. I am resolved to protect her, if it cost me my life."[55]

Carrillo's words proved to be prophetic.

Around 8:30 a.m. on May 21, 1864, Doña Merced, her six-year-old daughter Cornelia, and her half sister Conchita left the brick house in Rancho Cucamonga and got into a carriage for a trip to visit an ill friend. The driver, a thirteen-year-old worker named Jesus, took up the reins and turned the carriage in a southeasterly direction toward the San Bernardino Road. Doña Merced must have been feeling relieved. A day earlier, her representatives had served papers on Carlisle informing him that he no longer had any jurisdiction over the affairs of Rancho Cucamonga.

Ramón Carrillo and another man, Santos Ruiz, rode their horses next to Doña Merced's group. Carrillo had been staying in Merced's house for the previous three weeks while he recovered from an injury to his arm. Jesus drove the carriage through the rancho's front gate and steered it across the creek. The vast Cucamonga vineyard lay south of the San Bernardino Road. In late May, the vines were covered with bright green leaves and the buds of grapes were just beginning to appear.

When the carriage had traveled about 300 feet on the road, a shot rang out from a clump of sycamore trees a short distance away. The whizzing bullet hit Carrillo. It entered his back and exited on the right side of his upper chest.

Carrillo dug his heels into his horse, which then galloped toward the carriage. "They have wounded me," he cried. As Carrillo started to slump, Doña Merced yelled out to Ruiz, "Don't let him fall! Oh God, what is this?" Ruiz quickly dismounted and ran up to Carrillo's horse just as the man was falling off. Ruiz set him on the ground. Blood gushed from the bullet wound. "Leave this place!" Ruiz shouted to Merced. The carriage carrying her and her family took off down the road, dust flying out behind it as it gathered speed. Ruiz, no hero, got back on his horse and galloped east as fast as he could, leaving the wounded Carrillo on the dusty road.

Carrillo managed to stagger down the road toward Rubottom's, a hotel and grocery store, clutching a handkerchief against his chest. Jose Ynocente Ybarra was sitting on the porch talking to Mrs. Rubottom when he saw Carillo approach. He ran over to assist. "They have wounded me," said Carrillo as Ybarra helped him over to the store.

"Who has wounded you?" asked Ybarra.

"Gillette and Viall [Gillette was the postmaster and Viall worked at the vineyard] and another person I did not recognize very well but I think he is Bob Carlisle," said Carrillo.

Carrillo thought his biggest fear had come true, that Carlisle, angered over losing control of Rancho Cucamonga, furious that a *Californio*, not a white man, had greater influence than he, had masterminded the ambush.

Carrillo lay inside the store for three hours, his breath growing shallower and his skin growing paler as time passed on. He repeated the name of his attackers to two other people. Ruiz returned and sat with him but could see recovery was futile. "During all the interval I stayed with him; his head generally in my lap, blood flowing freely from the wound all the time," Ruiz said in an affidavit.[56] "His countenance was much changed, very pale. He talked a good deal. About a minute before he died he complained of violent pain below the wound and almost immediately the blood came into his mouth. He spat it out, saw the blood and said '*Yo no soy muy bueno.*' Almost at the same moment he grasped my hand and said '*Adiós, amigos.*' And at once he died."

It was around three p.m., four hours after he had been shot. Carrillo was forty-one years old and the third man to die because of a dispute over Rancho Cucamonga.

"The narrative is short and simple," read an article in the *Los Angeles Star* on May 28, 1864. "The click of a trigger and a human being is hurried into the darkness of death and the silence of the grave."

The murder of Carrillo immediately put the *Californio* community even more on edge. "You have little idea of the quiet, deep-seated rage of the Californians on the subject," Hayes wrote after Carrillo's murder: "I think I understand them perfectly. They ask me continually if the authorities of San Bernardino are going to do something in relation to it. But in general they say little about it—so much the worse. If they were excited and passionate and clamorous, I should have less apprehension."[57]

Hayes was so fearful that a fight would break out that he pleaded with a Col. J. P. Curtis to send a group of mounted infantrymen known as Dragoons to protect Doña Merced at Rancho Cucamonga.

"The death of Ramón Carrillo caused a great excitement among the Mexican Californians & they threatened the whites with seceshion & all its bloody consequences, so Col Curtis, who is in command at Drum barracks, send 15 of us out here to keep the peace," wrote John W. Teal in his diary.

Doña Merced was terrified, and kept close to home. Yet another man to whom she was close had been murdered. She felt frightened and alone. "It is imposibel for me to be amongst so many theaves and murders," Doña Merced wrote to Hayes six days after Carrillo's murder. "I wish to cleir everybody out of this place. Receive a heart feeld with grief."

Merced was sufficiently scared that she hurried to align herself with another male protector, someone who could act as a shield between her and the world. A month after Carrillo's murder, she hastily married José Clemente Carrillo (no relation to Ramón Carrillo), the Los Angeles constable who had come to investigate the case.

About fourteen months after Merced and Carlisle paid for dueling news-paper notices, a judge cancelled Carlisle's power of attorney, effectively dismissing him from overseeing Merced's affairs. He ruled that Carlisle had obtained the power of attorney by fraud and deceit. The order meant that the power Carlisle had yielded the past two and half years, ever since that afternoon in the back parlor in the brick house on Rancho Cucamonga, was gone. He no longer had control over the 13,000-acre Rancho Cucamonga, the income from its vineyards, or the income from Doña Merced's other property. He could no longer enrich himself at his sister-in law's expense.

The judge appointed the thirty-one-year-old Los Angeles undersher-iff Andrew J. King, known as Jack, in Carlisle's stead. It proved to be a calamitous decision for all involved.

King and Carlisle were similar in many respects: they were both Southerners who had joined California militia units sympathetic to the Confederate cause. King had been born in Georgia in 1833 and had slowly moved across the continent with his family, arriving in the Los Angeles area in 1852. King had studied law, had been elected to the California Assembly in 1859, and had been appointed undersheriff in 1861. He had been on the boat when the vigilantes grabbed and murdered Ceredel.

King and his brothers—Samuel Houston King and Frank King—had a tough reputation. After their father was gunned down in El Monte, Samuel Houston King shot and killed the murderer in a gun duel. El Monte was a Secessionist hotbed east of Los Angeles and the home of many of the vigilantes who meted out frontier justice against the *Californios*. In 1862, King brought the huge portrait of Confederate General Beauregard to a cheering crowd at the Bella Union Hotel. The U.S. mar-shal, Henry Barrows, called King "one of the many dangerous seces-sionists living in our midst," and arranged to have him arrested and brought to Camp Drum. King was released after he agreed to swear al-legiance to the Union.

The appointment of King as receiver humiliated Carlisle, and served as a reminder that he had been called a thief and cheat. Carlisle began to focus on King as the source of his problems. It led to his undoing.

The fifth of July 1865 started off auspiciously enough. Robert Carlisle came into Los Angeles from Rancho Chino with his wife, Francisca. They had been invited to the wedding celebration of Caroline Newmark and Solomon Lazard. It was thought to be the social event of the season. Caroline was the daughter of Joseph Newmark, one of the earliest Jewish settlers in Los Angeles, a man who was instrumental in building the Jewish cemetery and leading worship services. Lazard, a Frenchman, had opened a dry goods store with his cousin Maurice Kremer, and was one of the handful of Europeans and Americans who were determined to transform Los Angeles from a dusty pueblo to a thriving American city.

The small marriage ceremony took place at the Newmark home. But the dinner and dance afterward were at the Bella Union Hotel, which had been decorated with summer flowers and greenery.

The guest list was filled with the old *Californio* elite, as well as the new guard of French, German, Basque, and American merchants. The Civil War—or the War of Northern Aggression, as many in Los Angeles referred to it—had ended a month earlier, which was another reason to celebrate.

At midnight, a drunken Carlisle walked into the bar at the Bella Union and spotted Andrew J. King standing there. King and his wife, Laura, were also guests at the wedding celebration.

Carlisle was infuriated at the mere sight of King. It reminded him of his public humiliation, his loss of control of Rancho Cucamonga. "Jack King is a g★★ d★★ s★★★ a★★," shouted Carlisle, grabbing the attention of other men in the bar.

King walked over to Carlisle and slapped his face. Carlisle returned the blow. The men hit one another until friends separated them. King then left the bar to return to the wedding celebration, but an enraged

Carlisle followed him. He pulled out a long dagger. Carlisle lurched to stab King, but missed his chest and plunged the knife into King's hand. Carlisle then took out his gun, but before he could fire a shot, King ran away. Right before he exited the bar, King pulled out his pistol and shot at Carlisle. The bullet missed.

When King's two brothers arrived in Los Angeles the next morning and heard about the fight, they vowed revenge. Carlisle had insulted the family's dignity; he must be forced to pay. Although A. J. King asked them to forget the slight, the two other King brothers saw the opportunity to resolve the bitterness festering between the family and Carlisle.

Houston and Frank King walked into the Bella Union around noon. They spotted Carlisle at a table with his friend, James H. Lander, the attorney who had helped persuade Merced years earlier to give a power of attorney to Carlisle. Frank King ran over to Carlisle, whipped out his pistol and started to beat Carlisle around the head, hammering his gun so many times he bent the trigger. Carlisle got out of his chair and grabbed Frank King. They fought their way out the front door. Frank King managed to shoot four bullets into Carlisle. Houston King also fired at Carlisle. Sheriff Sánchez arrived at that point and pulled apart the rivals. Carlisle fell to the ground, blood seeping from his wounds. Despite his injuries, he pulled out his gun and shot at Frank King. The bullet pierced King's heart, killing him instantly. He collapsed on the dusty street, his colorful Mexican serape falling over his face. Houston King had been shot in the chest, but the wound was not life threatening. Lander had been shot in the leg. A stray bullet had killed a horse standing on the street.

A group of men carried Carlisle to a billiard table inside the hotel where he lay in agony, blood rushing from his wounds. But he was still furious at the King brothers and repeated his threats to kill them. Just before he died three hours later, he told his friends "Good-bye, all."

Two more men had died because of their rivalry over Rancho Cucamonga.

Things didn't go much better for Merced. In 1870, a judge ordered a foreclosure on Rancho Cucamonga so Merced could pay back the $14,600 mortgage Rains had taken out on the property. The debt, with interest, had grown to almost $42,000. With taxes, court fees, and assessments, Merced's total bill was almost $49,000. There was no way she could pay.

More than 150 years have passed since John Rains died, but his unsolved murder is still remembered in Rancho Cucamonga. The killing has become one of the city's defining stories, told on the city's official website as an example of the violent past of a city now tamed.

Rains's brick house, the one he built with such anticipation for his family, still stands. It no longer sits in isolation, the only home around, right above the vineyard that brought the rancho such fame. Asphalt streets and stucco houses now surround his home. It sits close to the Thomas Winery shopping center.

Rains's house might have gone the way of Tapia's—"disintegrated into its native earth"—if it hadn't been for the efforts of a history teacher and her students. Dõna Merced moved out in 1876 and the house passed through a series of owners after that. For a long time it was a boarding-house. Laborers working in the vineyard also slept there. The last private family to live in Rains's old home sold the property in 1969 to a developer from Orange County. The population in the region was exploding and the emphasis was on the future, on a modern city, not on the past. The developer planned to tear down the house and install a trailer park. The location was prime because it sat between two major east-west freeways leading to Los Angeles and San Bernardino.

The brick house, with its links to the nineteenth century, began to fall apart. Vandals stole valuable historic artifacts. Hippies squatted and burned the wooden mantelpieces. The plumbing and electricity were ripped out. Taggers painted graffiti on the house's walls.

Maxine Strane, a social studies teacher at Cucamonga Junior High School, loved local history, particularly the sordid story of Rains's murder. She was always trying to show her students that history was all around them. All they had to do was look.

In April 1970, Strane brought one of her classes to the old house. As she and her students arrived, they had a shock: a bulldozer was tearing down an outbuilding. A demolition crew had already punched a hole in the north side of the Rains house and had ripped down a portico covering the brick patio. The bulldozer was preparing to knock down the entire building.

Strane rushed over to the foreman and pleaded with him to stop the demolition. She explained that the old brick house was a historic building constructed in the nineteenth century. She said she knew someone interested in buying it. The foreman turned off the engine to the bulldozer and agreed to postpone the demolition if Strane got the property owner's okay. Strane and two students rushed back to the school and hurriedly called the developer, who said he did not know the house was of historic importance. He agreed to postpone demolition and talk to the prospective buyer.

The interested buyer fell through. Strane didn't stop her campaign, though. She and her students flooded county and state officials with letters asking them to protect the historic home. They pointed out the house's virtues, its architectural distinctiveness, its important role in the development of Rancho Cucamonga. The students and Strane spent hours at the house as well, cleaning out debris and painting over graffiti.

Finally, on June 1, 1971, a county museum commission came to assess the old home. Strane and more than 250 students from the junior high school marched to the house carrying placards calling for the house's preservation. One student made a speech. Strane was so worried the students would be disruptive and interrupt the commission that she threatened to give an F to any student who spoke out of turn. She needn't have worried. The students were quiet. They were polite. They had developed a deep respect for the home.

After the museum commissioners toured the property, they voted to recommend that San Bernardino County buy the Rains house.[58] The county purchased the property in October 1971. It is now listed on the National Register of Historic Places.

I visited the Rains house a number of times. The scraggly grapevines that I first encountered while coming to Rancho Cucamonga are planted in front of Rains's house, a nod to the winemaking business that was begun in 1839 and continued by Rains and others. The entire house has been restored and decorated with furniture of the mid-nineteenth century. There are dark mahogany armoires, wooden beds with horsehair mattresses held up by ropes, and silk-covered settees and chairs.

As I wandered the house behind a tour guide, I noted the room that Doña Merced sat in when her brother-in-law Robert Carlisle and his cronies pushed her to sign that destructive power of attorney. I thought of Ramón Carrillo when I went out on to the patio, now decorated with historic implements like Native American mortars and pestles and an old carriage. His was a long, agonizing death. And what about John Rains? Did he know the men who ambushed him? Did he know why they wanted him to die? No one ever figured out who took his guns, weapons he might have used to defend himself.

Five men died in a battle for control of this house and its surrounding 13,000 acres. Three of those killings—of Rains, of Carrillo, of Ceredel, killed by vigilantes—are unsolved. So everything that came from this spot—the renowned wine, the historic home, the history—is drenched in blood, at least metaphorically. That violence would extend into the twenty-first century.

PART THREE

FABRICATION

CHAPTER NINE

SAUSALITO CELLARS

Mark Anderson stood in front of the ramshackle building and considered his options. The shack, with its peeling white paint, wasn't much to look at. The piercing salt air and fog that rolled in off Richardson Bay had weathered it and the other small storage sheds and bungalows in the shipyard. The structures were neglected and worn down. They looked like they hadn't been touched since the heady days of World War II when the area bustled with shipbuilders, steelworkers, and riveters.

But Anderson probably didn't focus on the front door, awkwardly positioned under a stairway, or the broken, potholed pavement. None of those defects mattered. Instead, Anderson must have thought of what was inside. Rather, what *would* soon be inside.

Anderson envisioned the space at 2350 Marinship Way in Sausalito as a state-of-the-art wine storage cellar. He imagined small collectors, wine clubs, even three-star restaurants storing their wine in a temperature-controlled environment, one that kept wine at precisely 55 degrees and 70 percent humidity. Wine is volatile, extremely sensitive to swings of hot and cold, and can get a cooked taste if it even reaches 85 degrees—which can happen if it is left in the trunk of a car on a hot day. So serious collectors, restaurants, and dealers store wine correctly to maintain its longevity.

The gap between Anderson's vision and reality was large in the late spring of 1999. The building he had selected for his new business, which he planned to name Sausalito Cellars, needed an overhaul before wine connoisseurs would find it appealing. So Anderson transformed the space. He hauled out the junk left by previous tenants. He swept out cobwebs and dust mites. He replaced lightbulbs. He stuffed silver-backed pink rolls of insulation between the wall studs. He added lights and sorting benches.

For the public face of his business, Anderson hired a designer to make an arresting website with a purple and blue color scheme. Bannered across the home page was the declaration: "Fine Wine Storage. Setting the Standard Nationally and Internationally."

Anderson also promised a number of other bells and whistles on the website, like an online inventory that was accessible by a password. In the late 1990s, the Internet was just becoming broadly popular and the idea of a computerized inventory system was novel. Anderson thought it would set his company apart. It would mean a client could check out his holdings from the comfort of his office or home, and see at a glance exactly what varietal and vintage he had.

There was just one problem: the computer program didn't exist. It never would exist.[59] Sausalito Cellars was built on a lie.

Anderson must have thought it was an auspicious time to open a new business. His reputation in Sausalito had never been better. Just a year earlier, after penning his "Joe Sausalito" column for years for *The Signal*, he made it into the big leagues, at least by Sausalito standards. Anderson had been invited to write a column for the *Marin Scope*, a weekly newspaper with broad circulation. He named the column "Mark My Words: A Marin Notebook." Anderson used a folksy style full of homilies and jokes to recount his adventures traveling around the world, eating his way through the better restaurants in the Bay Area, and rubbing shoulders with the town's A-list crowd. The prose could be dull and convoluted and Anderson sometimes repeated himself (and would eventually be accused of lifting from the Internet), but the column gave Anderson a prominent platform. And he wasn't shy about his accomplishments. "Mark C. Anderson is a longtime resident of Sausalito, a local artist and an internationally recognized expert on everything," read the short bio at the end of his first column in September 1998.

Anderson could be seen all over Sausalito. His chunky frame was a familiar sight, not only at lunch or late at night at Sushi Ran, but at meetings of the Sausalito Arts Commission, the Chamber of Commerce, and the Rotary Club. He was part of a group of businessmen who organized the Marin Technology Forum in 1998, Sausalito's attempt to lure technology companies to town.

Anderson was particularly proud of his involvement with Sausalito's Sister City Commission. For the last six years, he had been traveling with a group of high school students every other year to Sakaide, Japan, a city of about 70,000 people on the northern edge of Shikoku Island. The students would live with Japanese families, attend Kabuki theater, and tour the sights and museums. Japanese dignitaries would hold lengthy dinners and celebrations for their Sausalito visitors, which frequently included the mayor and other Marin County officials. Anderson was chair of the commission. He loved being at the center of all the activity and felt a special bond with his hosts.

Anderson had been fascinated with Japan ever since he was four, when his mother hired a Japanese caregiver in Berkeley to take care of him. The babysitter, Toshie, had come to the U.S. after World War II and barely spoke English, so Anderson picked up Japanese from her. During the six years she watched over Anderson, Toshie told the young boy tales about her life in Japan, recounted Japanese folktales and myths, and spun stories about the Japanese woodblock prints that hung on the walls of Anderson's home. "She taught me how to see things," said Anderson.[60]

Anderson had moved Hong Kong in his late twenties, and then spent five years in Japan, working for a bank in Tokyo. He enjoyed walking through the old parts of Tokyo, past shrines and houses. He even joined a sumo-wrestling club in an old part of the city called Sumida-Ku and competed using the stage name "Arase," which means "the strength of the power of the ocean's waves striking the rocks during a storm."

Anderson relished any opportunity to return to Japan and revisit his favorite Shinto shrines and eat authentic Japanese food. Some of the other members of the Sausalito Sister City Commission thought Anderson was too fond of Japanese culture. They said he would ditch the students as soon as he arrived in Sakaide to indulge his passions.

But none of those tensions were apparent on a clear and pleasant fall day in October 1998. It was the tenth anniversary of the Sausalito-Sakaide sister city relationship and a group of thirty-three Japanese dignitaries, including the mayor, had come to Sausalito to celebrate.

The Sister City Commission threw a huge party for the visiting Japanese delegation in a converted church rectory on the top of a hill facing out over Sausalito and the bay. The views from the house were spectacular; standing on the deck the guests could see the blue water, the Golden Gate Bridge, and the San Francisco skyline with the Transamerica pyramid's distinctive triangular shape. Lots of important people were at the party, from the mayor and members of the city council to top businessmen. Guests chatted and snacked on sushi and sashimi from Sushi Ran and freshly shucked oysters from Hog Island Oyster Farm on Tomales Bay.

Anderson was in the center of the activity, dipping in and out of Japanese to talk to the visitors, offering quick translations for their American hosts. He was charming and funny, full of stories of past trips to Japan and the adventures he and others had gone on. As chair of the Sausalito Sister City Commission, he was the man of the moment, the orbiting moon to the stars from Japan.

The mayor of Sakaide had hosted a large reception for the Sausalito delegation a year earlier. Now it was the Americans' turn to show their visitors the sights of the Bay Area. The day after the party, Anderson took the Japanese delegation to the Napa Valley, which lay about an hour away. He had arranged for the group to tour Hess, a winery in the Mayacamas Mountain on the valley's western flank. The winery, started by

German businessman Donald Hess, not only made excellent red and white wines, it had an extensive modern art collection and beautiful gardens. The group spent the morning wine tasting and strolling the grounds, breathing in the rich scent of lavender and thyme crushed as they walked around the winery. They then headed to the Étoile restaurant at Domaine Chandon in Yountville for lunch, not far from where Anderson's father was living in the veteran's home. No doubt Anderson regaled the group with tales about his wine-tasting adventures and insights about what made a good Cabernet.

Anderson was a self-taught wine connoisseur. He loved wine. He loved the taste of it as it rolled over his tongue. He loved its scent as he swirled it in a glass, letting the fumes waft up to his nose. He loved the stories of how winemakers crafted a particular vintage. He loved the social cachet of bringing wine to events or ordering a special bottle off a wine list. He loved wine so much that he traveled regularly to Italy and France and spent much of his time eating and drinking. He also enjoyed taking friends out to dinner and surprising them with an excellent bottle of wine he had brought from home. "Mark was one of the most knowledgeable people about wine I ever met," said Tom Johnson, who became friends with Anderson from their work together at the Chamber of Commerce.

Anderson grew up in the 1950s and 1960s in an era when most Americans didn't drink wine, preferring beer or spirits instead. Wine was not associated with high culture or sophistication. Instead, Americans thought of it as something immigrants drank. "If the ordinary American had any notions about winemaking or winemakers in the 1950s, they were probably something like this: vineyards were native to Europe, where one might expect to meet brightly costumed natives singing and dancing at vintage time, especially if they were Italian; winemakers were sturdy peasants who might wear berets or lederhosen, according to the country in question," wrote the wine historian Thomas Pinney.[61]

The wine business had never really recovered from Prohibition; in fact, the number of vineyards in the state in 1960, twenty-seven years after repeal, was lower than in 1920, right at the start of Prohibition. Around 200 California wineries went out of business from 1952 to 1970.[62]

When Americans did drink, they preferred fortified, sweet, or flavored wines with names like Thunderbird, Ripple, or Boone's Farm Green Apple wine. A sweetened red jug wine, Paisano from E. & J. Gallo, was also popular. Americans might open a bottle of wine for a birthday dinner or wedding celebration. But it was not a beverage for every night at the dinner table.

It wasn't until 1967 that table wines, the wine we think of today, outsold sweet wines. The shift in American perception about wine involved many factors, including growing American affluence and an increase in jet travel. American travelers in Europe saw how people there consumed wine regularly. In 1961, Julia Child published her wildly successful *Mastering the Art of French Cooking*, which introduced ordinary Americans to the idea that good food and good wine should be a part of everyday life.

Over the next decade, as nonconformity became hip, Americans started to drink wine as a way to differentiate themselves from the conventionalism of the times—which led to the boom that transformed the Napa Valley. The number of acres planted to grapes doubled between 1966 and 1976. Zinfandel finally triumphed over Carignane—suitable for blending into jug wines—as the most widely planted grape.[63]

Anderson learned to appreciate wine just as the revolution for varietal wine was taking off. Anderson was a lanky teen when he started traveling regularly to Santa Rosa in Sonoma County to attend junior college. Over the years, he explored the back roads of the region. Wine tasting was almost a casual affair then. It wasn't necessary to make an appointment. A visitor could just go to a winery and ask to sample whatever was on hand.

Anderson used to like to visit the A. Pagani Winery, a 187-acre winery off Highway 12 in the Glen Ellen section of Sonoma County. The patriarch of the family, Felice Pagani, had planted his first grapes in 1912, and his son Louis (whom Anderson and others called Old Man Pagani in the 1960s) ran an informal tasting room. Visitors could pull in with an empty jug and Pagani would fill it from the barrel for fifty cents. The red wine was a field blend made from Petite Syrah, Alicante, Grand Noir, and Lenoir grapes. Sometimes Pagani would join Anderson and his friends for a picnic under the fruit trees that dotted the property.

The Paganis shut down the winery in 1969 and shifted toward selling their grapes. In 1997, *Wine Spectator* named a Ridge wine made from that same Pagani field blend one of the best wines in the world.

That same informal atmosphere existed in Napa Valley. While the Napa Valley Vintners Association, a trade group, had erected two large wood signs along Highway 29 in 1949 welcoming visitors to this "world famous wine growing region," the words weren't quite true then. A few wineries, like Charles Krug, had tasting rooms, but the tourist traffic wasn't heavy. A handful of new wineries had opened up, like Stony Hill, famous for its lean Chardonnay, but they were hidden in the hills. Wine tasting was elevated to a new level, however, when Robert Mondavi opened his winery along Highway 29 in 1966. Clifford May designed the winery to be reminiscent of the missions that once dotted the state. Its signature arch and tower would soon adorn the label of every bottle of Robert Mondavi wine.

Mondavi, determined to make great California wines and to encourage people to drink them frequently, was a visible presence at the winery. Anderson remembers seeing and talking to him when he visited the winery.

There was a sense of adventure, of new things happening in the world of wine, and Anderson jumped right in. When he first went wine tasting he didn't know much about what made a good wine, or even who the local winemakers were, but he soon found out. He had a feeling he was learning as the winemakers were learning to make premium wines, and Anderson liked the idea of that inside connection.

In 1976, after graduating from UC Berkeley with a degree in economics, Anderson moved to Asia, where he began to delve more deeply into wine. In Tokyo, he fell in with a group of older, affluent Japanese businessmen who were wine aficionados. They liked to meet at night in a European-style restaurant or Japanese-style inn in Tokyo or Osaka and drink bottle after bottle of sake or wine. They would eat, laugh, and drink, often into the wee hours of the morning. They called themselves the "Kansai Wine Club," after a southern-central region of the main island. "The format was fairly typical: select a three-star restaurant, work with the chef to design a stellar selection of entrées . . . and pair the food selections with the best wine available," said Anderson. The businessmen would fly in from all parts of the world for "a fabulous dinner, fellowship and the very best in wines, cigars, sharing tall tales and enjoying a weekend of trying new restaurants."

Despite the difference between his age and that of the majority of those in Kansai Wine Club, Anderson, who was then in his early thirties, felt right at home. They all shared an appreciation for the finer things in life. Perhaps the men enjoyed how thoroughly Anderson embraced Japanese culture. His Japanese was good—although he definitely understood more than he could speak—and he had an understanding of the way things worked.

Soon, Anderson began traveling with members of the Kansai Wine Club—or so he claims. They went to France, he says, where they explored the castles of Bordeaux and the small towns in Burgundy. They went to Italy to sip Chianti and taste Brunello di Montalcino. They tasted wine inside the Great Pyramid in Egypt. At a celebration on a small coral atoll near Bora Bora in the South Pacific on the eve of the 1996 New Year, Anderson dined with a group of rich Japanese businessmen on the beach under a night sky brilliantly lit by stars. They feasted on lobster, monkfish, and giant beluga, and washed it back with vintage Champagne.

Some of the tastings were decadent, such as the one Anderson did of 100-point wines of ten châteaux properties across Bordeaux. Or the "Belle Époque," tasting of five châteaux from five years of the nineteenth century.

What did Anderson learn from these outings? If you asked Debbie Polverino, the manager of Wines Central, not much about wine. She always thought he bluffed his way through his descriptions and didn't convey any deep understanding of what made a particular vintage bad or good. Then perhaps Anderson learned how wine was a portal, a way to lubricate relations between people who spoke different languages and who had wildly divergent living standards. Wine provided him access to a world whose door might otherwise be closed.

CHAPTER TEN

FOR THE LOVE OF WINE

S ausalito Cellars threw open its doors for business on August 15, 1999. Its shelves already held wine from unclaimed cases Anderson had purchased from two San Francisco wine storage facilities that had gone out of business. Anderson also had cases from friends from Japan and Hong Kong who had bought wine while visiting the vineyards of Napa and Sonoma. Import taxes on wine were high in both countries, so some friends chose to leave their wine behind to consume at a later date.

Ron Lussier, a web designer, became one of Anderson's early customers. Lussier, a stocky, bearded computer programmer with an easy laugh, had not been interested in wine as a young man; he had grown up in a teetotaling family. Alcohol was never served at their dinner table.

But Lussier had a wine epiphany at a romantic dinner in Washington, D.C. He and his boyfriend had gone to the capital to participate in a protest march. At a restaurant after the demonstration, they asked the sommelier for a bottle of wine. He brought them a bottle from a small winery in Santa Barbara called Sine Qua Non. The winery, founded in 1994 by Manfred Krankl, a high-profile Los Angeles restaurateur, makes extremely small batches of red Syrah-based blends with whimsical and colorful labels. Sine Qua Non means an essential condition, a thing that is absolutely necessary. From the first vintage, which yielded four and a half barrels, the wine has been a hit, widely coveted and difficult to obtain.

One sip changed Lussier's life. He could taste the earth, the sun, the sky, and the steady hand of the winemaker in that glass. The flavor lured him into a dimension he had never known existed. The wine enhanced the evening, turning a special occasion into an exceptional one.

From that point on, Lussier began to collect wine, with a special focus on Sine Qua Non, which was part of a new trend called the "Rhone Rangers," which used Syrah and Grenache rather than Cabernet Sauvignon as its main grapes. The wine was extremely difficult to find. Krankl only made small amounts and sold most of it through his winery mailing list. But there was a five-year wait to get on the list (now up to ten years) so Lussier had to search out the wine from people who resold their allotment. Lussier had a list of wine stores he kept on speed dial. He would telephone them on a rotating basis. If they had any Sine Qua Non, Lussier would rush out of work and drive to the store to buy it. Bottles cost as much as $350, but to Lussier, they were worth it.

When Lussier had too many cases stacked up in his San Francisco apartment, he went looking for wine storage. He found Sausalito Cellars listed online and was impressed. The cellar promised constant monitoring, online inventory control, and video monitoring. There was pickup and drop-off delivery, too.

Lussier got in his car and drove over the Golden Gate Bridge to check out Sausalito Cellars. The reality was different from the advertisement. The small storage unit in the Marinship area of the waterfront was so jammed with boxes that there was little room to navigate. The cases were stacked floor to ceiling and clients' wines were comingled. But Lussier, who bonds easily with others, was a trusting sort, so he didn't think badly of Anderson's obvious disorganization. Besides, he liked Anderson. They were both photographers and they talked about cameras. Anderson was also funny. So even though the storage cellar was a mess, Lussier moved in his cases.

Michael Bales, a Latin teacher from Toronto, and his wife, Margaret, also found their way to Sausalito Cellars. Bales was fascinated with Napa wine, particularly high-end Cabernet Sauvignon, and over the years had made his way onto the mailing lists of some of Napa Valley's most exclusive cult wineries. That meant he was permitted to buy a few bottles every year from Bond, Bryant Family Vineyards, and Dalla Valle—wine that sold on the secondary market for thousands of dollars a bottle. Bales even had a few bottles of what some people regarded as the most sought-after wine in the world: Screaming Eagle. The winery, then owned by Jean Phillips, only produced about 400 cases of wine each year from its fifty acres of Cabernet, Merlot, Petit Verdot, and Cabernet Franc grapes in Oakville. The winemaker was Heidi Peterson Barrett, considered one of the top winemakers of the valley. Many considered her to have a magic touch, balancing the lushness of Cabernet Sauvignon grapes with elegance.

Bales's previous wine storage facility had stopped accepting direct shipments from wineries, so Bales needed a new place, preferably one near Napa that he could visit easily when he came from Toronto. Anderson assured him he could pick up his wine at any time. With that promise, Bales signed a contract on February 21, 2001, and soon sent about eighteen cases to Sausalito Cellars.

In May 2001, Sausalito Cellars landed its biggest client yet: Bacchanal, a restaurant that had opened in 1999 in a $1 million space in the Metropolitan Hotel, just minutes from the San Francisco airport. The restaurant served classic American fare like Caesar salad and steaks, but, as its name suggested, it was best known for its wine. The menu listed more than 100 wines by the glass, with thousands of other bottles in its cellars. But Bacchanal had sputtered and filed for bankruptcy. One of its partners, Samuel Maslak, needed a place to store 756 cases of wine, around 9,000 bottles, while he and his partner sorted out the details of the restaurant's dissolution. He selected Sausalito Cellars and contracted to pay $600 a month for the service. By that time Anderson's storage unit was overflowing, so he rented an adjacent building, effectively doubling his business. He now had 800 square feet.

On the surface everything looked good for Anderson. In the summer of 2000, he went on an extended trip to France. Anderson loved to eat and he delighted in finding great restaurants and hotels in little-known locales. Anderson and his girlfriend Witten traveled to a small town near Tours in central France and stayed at La Croix de la Voulte, a country inn located in a fifteenth-century building. They ate at the best restaurant in nearby Saumur, Les Délices du Château, which overlooked the Loire River.

When Anderson returned from France, he wrote about his trip in one of his weekly columns for the *Marin Scope*. He started to travel so much around this time that the editor often included a note when his column did not appear. "Mark Anderson is on another adventure and was unable to find a modem or a fax. He'll be back next week."[64]

Perhaps it was the extended trip to France that caused financial troubles for Anderson. Or the visit to the truffle festival in Italy. Perhaps it was his notoriously sloppy bookkeeping, which meant he often neglected to charge clients their storage fees. Or perhaps it was just that he had finally tapped out his father and could no longer turn to him for a regular source of cash.

After his mother, Patricia Anderson, died of cancer in 1995, Anderson's father, James, sold their home in Orinda and moved into the Veteran's Home in Yountville. James Anderson evidently was a soft touch, eager to help his sons in whatever way possible. When Anderson needed money he asked his father. And asked again. And again. Anderson turned to his father for financial assistance so often that he eventually depleted his savings.[65]

Anderson's younger brother, Steven, who worked as a handyman in the northern Sonoma County town of Windsor, apparently couldn't prevent his father from repeatedly opening his checkbook for Mark. He grew incensed by his brother's exploitation of their father. He cut off communication with Anderson and then channeled his hostilities toward his brother on his "Corpulent Raider" website. He called Mark Anderson a narcissist and a phony, a crummy artist, and a poseur. He wrote and posted a number of poems and offered it up as "A Christmas Sampler" to his brother.

"Run" by my Brother
Sausalito Cellars.
Mark Christian Anderson
Paid for with someone else's money.
An Elder Person's Money.
Appropriation by Intimidation
Stolen, Really.

Steven Anderson exposed how his brother could pose as a wealthy man.

Just for Today
Mark would get checks once, twice
a month for $4K, $5k, and on.
In addition to the cards.
How did he manage this?
By phoning up the Elder Man and saying
if he didn't get the money Mark would be thrown
out of his Luxury Sausalito Apartment and
"would be Homeless." Mark would then say he
would have to "Jump Off the Golden Gate Bridge."
This would Scare the Elder Man.
So out comes the checkbook.
A check would be written.
And Mark runs off to yet another
$500 Lunch.
To celebrate with jaded local yups who think . . .
He is "Independently Wealthy"
or a "Successful Businessman."

Steven Anderson suggested that Mark was manipulating their father:

The Elder Man?
Our Father. James Anderson.
Our Mother Died.

And it crushed him.
Lost his judgment. And was afraid.
Of what Mark might Do.
If he didn't Play Ball.
But it didn't matter. Mark has him
where he wants him.
Alone.
In an Institutional Cage.

It is unclear at what point Anderson realized that he had a huge amount of capital—liquid capital—in his possession. And it wasn't money he collected from rents. It was wine, all those bottles of wine sitting in Sausalito Cellars, bottles of fancy Bordeaux and Burgundy, hard to find cult wines, and huge magnums of California Cabernet. They had cash value. If Sausalito Cellars wasn't bringing in lots of money, perhaps there was another way to liberate its resources?

CHAPTER ELEVEN

WINE FRAUD

In the dark evening hours of November 28, 2013, at a time when most Seattle residents were just finishing their Thanksgiving dinners of roast turkey and stuffing, two men drove a large black SUV and a van up to a warehouse on the city's south side. The industrial spaces, artists' lofts, and galleries that gave the neighborhood, nicknamed Soda, its character, were quiet.

The men smashed the locks on the door leading into the warehouse. They ignored the cavernous room at the front, and instead headed into a small utility closet in the rear of the building. They pulled out some tools to cut through the sheetrock. When they broke through the wall, they had gained entry into Esquin Wine & Spirits, one of Seattle's leading wine retailers and home to thousands of bottles of fine wine.

The burglars immediately made their way to a private wine storage area in Esquin's basement, where dozens of temperature-controlled wooden lockers lined the room. Then the burglars acted with the precision of characters in a *Mission: Impossible* movie.

The two men had prepared for the theft. The previous night they had visited the wine storage room right at closing time. While the staff wasn't watching, the men had thrown plastic bags over the motion detectors of the alarm system. Then they spray-painted the lenses of the surveillance cameras. The staff, eager to start their Thanksgiving holiday, didn't notice.

So when the men broke into the storage area on Thanksgiving night, their movements were invisible. They were not afraid of getting caught. They went to work and methodically emptied the area of some of its most precious contents. They unscrewed the doors of storage lockers they had identified as containing valuable wine. They removed dozens of wooden boxes, which they transferred to a black Cadillac SUV waiting outside.

Over the next fifteen hours, the two men made nine trips in and out of the Esquin storage room. They whisked away 200 cases of wine worth an estimated $650,000.

The thieves were not done yet. They needed to cover their tracks and had the brilliant idea of setting the warehouse on fire. So they punched numerous small holes in the gas lines in the large front room of the warehouse. Then they ignited the gas coming out of a heater mounted near the ceiling, forming an impromptu pilot light. The men hoped that once the leaking gas filled the space, the pilot light would ignite, causing a huge fire that would destroy all evidence. Then the men departed into the early morning light, as silently as they had arrived.

Hours later, around 11:30 a.m. on Friday, November 29, the owner of Esquin came to work. He smelled gas. By some miracle the gas leaking into the warehouse space had not ignited. For some reason, the flames never ignited the gas lines. Esquin's owner rushed to the building's turn-off valve and stopped the gas at its source. He then alerted the police.

The theft from Esquin's storage lockers, with its cloak-and-dagger techniques, was dramatic, but in no way unique. Wine theft is fairly common. Wine may not be as valuable as diamonds or gold nuggets, but some bottles are worth thousands of dollars, even tens of thousands of dollars. Wine is hard to trace, too, since producers make many bottles of each vintage. The rise of the Internet and the proliferation of websites selling or buying wine make purloined wine fairly easy to get rid of.

Wine storage facilities are natural targets. Many collectors park their wine in their temperature-controlled lockers and don't check their collections regularly. Often a collector doesn't notice a theft until long after a thief has sold his wine to an unsuspecting buyer.

That's what happened in a wine storage warehouse in the Orange County city of Irvine. Legend Cellars was located in an innocuous business park in the southern California city, but had a reputation for good service. Scott Osumi owned the business, and his father, George, managed it. Wine collectors could rent lockers that held as few as eight cases of wine or as many as 250 cases. One of the business's selling points was that the 15,000-square-foot facility was monitored by video cameras twenty-four hours a day.[66]

Since George Osumi managed Legend Cellars, he often helped new clients move into their lockers or assisted them when they brought in more cases. That gave him the chance to scope out who had rare and expensive wines and who only visited the place irregularly. That knowledge proved too valuable for Osumi to resist.

George Osumi had two ways of stealing wine: by stealth, or out in the open. Sometimes at night he entered the warehouse wearing latex gloves. He had hired a locksmith to make keys that fit the private padlocks on some of the locker doors. Osumi would enter and break open wooden wine storage boxes. He would remove expensive bottles of French and California wine and replace them with cheap bottles. Then he would nail up the boxes and place them back exactly as he found them. On other occasions, Osumi would order subordinates to enter the lockers and remove wine.

Over a five-year period from 2008 to 2012, Osumi stole about $2.7 million in wine, including bottles from a friend who had recently died. He stole 1,200 bottles from another collector. Osumi then asked his girlfriend to approach the Belmont Wine Exchange near the San Francisco airport and consign wines through them. She sold about $280,000 of wine during a one-month period in 2008. Osumi gave her a portion of the sales. Osumi also sold wine over the Internet. He pocketed a total of $311,000. Police later determined that neither Osumi's girlfriend nor the store knew the wine had been stolen. Osumi's son, Scott, was also ignorant of his father's theft.

Osumi was caught after a client of Legend Cellars noticed that the contents of his wooden box that was supposed to contain six bottles of white wine from Domaine Leflaive, worth about $370 each, had been replaced with bottles of Chardonnay worth six dollars each. He went to the police. A jury found George Osumi, sixty-four, guilty of theft in 2013. He was sentenced to six years in prison.

There's a pattern to many wine thefts. In May 2011, six thieves broke into an east London wine storage facility in Bethnal Green, disabled the alarm and CCTV cameras, and then used a forklift to place about 400 cases of wine on a pallet. They then carted the wine, worth an estimated $1.63 million, away in two white vans and a brown truck. They have never been caught.

Private collections are also at risk. On Christmas Day, 2014, thieves broke into the French Laundry, chef Thomas Keller's storied restaurant in Yountville. It had just closed for a six-month renovation. The thief or thieves knew what they were after. They jimmied the door of the un-marked wine cellar and nabbed seventy-six bottles of top French wine, including vertical collections of Burgundies from Domaine de la Romanée-Conti and Dom Perignon Champagne worth an approximate $300,000. Most of the bottles were recovered a few weeks later at the home of a collector in Greensboro, North Carolina.

There are no firm numbers on how much wine has been stolen in recent years, but the numbers certainly reach into the millions of dollars. It's a tough crime to track, as criminals often sell the stolen goods online case by case or bottle by bottle. Unlike art or antiquities, there is no centralized registry for stolen wine, making it difficult to connect any specific bottle to one that is missing.

A thief has numerous ways to get rid of stolen wine. He or she can put it up for sale on websites like eBay, Craigslist, or Alibaba, a Chinese e-commerce site. He can approach a wine broker who buys old cellars or collections and sells them to wine stores. Or he can approach any one of a number of wine retailers who sell their products over the Internet.

And some restaurants have been known to buy wine sold to them for much less than the wholesale price, which suggests they may realize they are buying stolen goods.

In turn, there often is little scrutiny of the wines offered for sale or consignment. Few retail stores or brokers expect sellers to have receipts for their wine, particularly older vintages. They assume that the wine was purchased long ago, has sat for a decade or more in a cellar, and the receipts are lost. This courteous attitude may reflect the gentlemanly origins of wine collecting, when it was an avocation of just an elite few. There is a camaraderie between those who revere wine, a brotherhood, and a sense that too much crass commercialism and scrutiny of a wine buyer taints the process. When I called numerous merchants around the country to ask about this dark side of wine, few were willing to talk about the underbelly of the wine world. None wanted their names attached to their remarks. "We don't want any bad publicity," one said.

Wine merchants do try to check to see if a seller is legitimate, but they rarely delve deeply into someone's background. One retailer told me he puts the name of any potential seller into Google, and if there is any whiff of wrongdoing he immediately aborts the transaction. But if nothing turns up, he makes the sale. Another online retailer who deals in expensive French, Italian, and California wines asks potential sellers for photos of their cellars or refrigerated spaces. On occasion, he will visit. To cut down on the possibility of buying stolen wine (which has happened, he confessed), he won't pay cash for wine. He will only pay by check to establish a paper trail.

When Mark Anderson approached various wine houses around the Bay Area to see if they would be interested in purchasing wine, none of them asked for proof that he owned the bottles. All Anderson did—and all that was required—was offer verbal assurance that he had the legal right to sell the wine. It was not until years later, after newspaper articles appeared detailing Anderson's crimes, that the wine merchants cut off relations with him. Even then, Anderson managed to circumvent the obstacles and sell wine under a fake name.

Given this lack of scrutiny and how difficult it is to track down stolen wine over the Internet, happenstance can often play a large role in catching criminals.

It was sheer luck that authorities uncovered a wine theft ring in Sonoma County in 2008. A group of men, led by a customer sales representative working inside a distribution center for Jackson Family wines, the umbrella organization for the dozens of wineries owned by the late Jess Jackson, the lawyer-turned-wine magnate, managed to steal about $200,000 of wine by falsifying internal records. The sales rep set up shipments of wine to phony customers and then reported the wine as lost so it wouldn't be traced. He and two accomplices then sold the bottles of red Bordeaux-like wine, valued at $150 to $175 a bottle, on eBay. They also sold some to online wine retailers. They got caught when they sold some wine that hadn't yet been released to the public. A company official noticed, realized that the theft must be an inside job, and contacted authorities.

In fact, stupidity may be the police's best friend. The two men who stole 200 cases from the Seattle wine store never got the chance to dispose of the wine. They made several mistakes during their cloak-and-dagger burglary that ultimately led to their arrest. When they spray-painted the lenses of the security cameras, they neglected to cover them completely. An employee of the wine store reviewed the security tapes and was able to identify one of the thieves as a customer who had rented a basement storage locker just a few weeks earlier. When police went to his apartment, they found a black gym bag with lists of wine and descriptions of wine in it, along with emails to a San Francisco wine broker offering to sell about $100,000 worth of wine. Inside the glove compartment of the SUV, police found a notebook that had "The Plan" written on the title page. It included a step-by-step to-do list for the wine theft, including what tools to buy, how to destroy evidence, and how to escape to another country.

Within days, the Seattle police department had arrested two men in connection with the crime. The stolen wine was also recovered, in a temperature-controlled facility less than a mile from where it was taken. When the two men pleaded guilty in July 2014, the prosecutor called it "the poorest execution of the greatest heist of wine."[67] The man who tried to set the fire was sentenced to nine years in prison; his accomplice got six years.

The problem of wine theft is small, however, compared to that of wine fraud, which has been going on for millennia. Pliny the Elder, who lived from about 23 BCE to 79 ACE, complained that much of the wine passed off as fine Roman wine during his time was actually fake.[68]

The most coveted wine was Falernum, a sweet white wine that turned deep amber as it aged. The wine was praised by nobles, coveted by everyone, available to just a few. But amphorae supposedly containing Falernum were ubiquitous, according to Pliny, even though the grapes for Falernum wine only came from three vineyards high on the slopes Mount Falernus, north of Naples, Italy. There was hardly enough to be as abundant as claimed.

One of the largest cases of wine fraud in the United States happened in 1987, and Steven Lapham, who would prosecute Mark Anderson twenty years later, was the assistant U.S. attorney spearheading the case. Interest in California wine had exploded in the late 1970s when a young winemaker named Bob Trinchero accidentally created a sweet, light pink wine he called white Zinfandel. Trinchero had been pushing his father Mario, the owner of Sutter Home winery in St. Helena, to plant more Zinfandel grapes. Zinfandel had once been one of California's most popular varieties, but had fallen out of favor after Prohibition. Trinchero was one of a new group of young winemakers who saw potential in the grape. He loved its dense, fruity flavor. But Mario was skeptical, and only grudgingly allowed his son to proceed.

Ridge Vineyards and Mayacamas Vineyards had also gone into Zinfandel in a big way and Trinchero wanted to make a wine that was better than theirs. In an attempt to enhance his Zinfandel, in 1972 Trinchero crushed the grapes and drew off some of the juice before the wine started to ferment. The French call this process *saignée*. It intensifies the color, body, and flavor of wine by decreasing the amount of juice relative to the amount of skins. The process worked: the Sutter Home 1972 Zinfandel was a rich, flavorful wine with a deep red color.

Trinchero was left with 550 gallons of light blush liquid. He fermented it into wine and sold it, with mild success, in the Sutter Home tasting room along Highway 29 in St. Helena.

But in 1975, the saignée juice pulled off the Zinfandel got "stuck." During fermentation, the sugar in grapes turns to alcohol, but conversion stalled that year. No matter what he tried, Trinchero could not get his wine to complete fermentation. The resulting wine was sweeter than usual, with a 2 percent sugar level. Trinchero bottled it anyway.[69]

The slightly pink wine was a hit. Consumers loved its sweetness. People who rarely drank wine were soon regular buyers of white Zinfandel. In 1980, Sutter Home produced more than 25,000 cases of the wine. By 1987, the winery was selling two million cases of white Zin, as it was affectionately called.[70]

Soon, around 125 wineries around the state were selling their own versions of white Zinfandel, including some of the larger winemakers like E. & J. Gallo, Beringer, and Robert Mondavi.

The new popularity of the blush wine meant there was a rush to buy Zinfandel grapes. Demand soon outstripped supply. Prices soared. Zinfandel grapes, which had been selling for $100 a ton in the early 1980s, sold for $900 a ton a few years later.[71] That was about $750 more a ton than other varietals like Carignane or Barbera.

To a number of grape growers in the Central Valley, the shortage of Zinfandel presented an opportunity—but not a legal one. Why not, some reasoned, pass off cheaper varietals as Zinfandel? After all, to the casual observer Barbera grapes looked much like Zinfandel grapes—big, red, and fat. How about going a step further, too, and selling French Colombard grapes as Sauvignon Blanc grapes or Thompson seedless as Chardonnay?

Why not give it a try?

In the predawn darkness of the San Joaquin Valley, the men began to arrive slowly. Some came by car, others by truck. Engines rumbled, doors slammed, and soon the sounds of Spanish rang out across the hundreds of acres of grapevines that stretched far into the horizon. The men, most from Mexico and Central America, donned their heavy work gloves, picked up their shears and got to work.

Harvesting grapes is an art form of sorts, a balance of speed and delicacy. Temperatures in California's vast Central Valley in late summer can easily reach 100 degrees by noon, so a worker has to pick quickly before the heat affects the fruit, but handle the grapes gently enough not to split their skins. The laborers that day worked at a rapid pace, clipping off the red, fat clusters and dropping the grapes into plastic crates at their feet. They moved from vine to vine and when the crates were full, they dumped the grapes into the back of a tractor-trailer narrow enough to navigate between the rows.

The pickers were probably too busy to notice the two men parked a few hundred feet down the road. The men had gotten to the vineyard even earlier than the workers and grabbed a spot under a large shade tree. It takes a long time to fill up a truck with twenty tons of grapes. The men in the American sedan had to blink off sleep and keep up a constant banter to stay alert over the course of the morning. They tried to be innocuous, too, by parking their car facing away from the vineyard. That let them monitor the harvest through the rearview mirror. But the men had gotten good at spying, their instincts honed after staking out a dozen vineyards over a six-week period. They had been working for almost a year to uncover one of the biggest wine frauds in California history, and the season of proof had finally arrived.

As the sun inched up higher into the sky, a truck loaded with glistening grapes pulled away from the vineyard. The two men watched it drive off, then did a U-turn, hoping the managers and workers in the vineyard didn't notice them. The men followed the truck over back roads and watched it pull into a large winemaking facility. They noted the truck's license plate, the time it left the vineyard, the time it arrived at the winery, and where the grapes came from.

They had snared their prey.[72]

The trucks laden with grapes had pulled into Delicato Vineyards in Manteca, about seventy miles east of San Francisco. In the late 1980s, Delicato was the largest maker of bulk white Zinfandel wine in California, producing it for Sutter Home and other wineries that sold it under their own labels. Delicato got many of its grapes from Michael Liccardi, a prominent wine broker from Stockton. Liccardi provided so many grapes that Delicato had given him unprecedented—and unsupervised—twenty-four-hour access to their wine production facility. Liccardi even had his own office in the Delicato complex where he could schedule and oversee the grape deliveries.

With a seemingly bottomless market for Zinfandel grapes, Liccardi needed to figure out a way to increase his supply. So he recruited two grape growers, the brothers Frank and Nick Bavaro, to help with a scheme he concocted. The Bavaro brothers would harvest Carignane and Valdepena grapes and pass the thick, red-skinned grapes off as white Zinfandel grapes.

To make sure the falsification was not detected, the Bavaro brothers had their farmworkers pick grapes in the cool of the night and deliver them to Delicato anywhere from two a.m. to four a.m.—when no one but Liccardi was around. Over a few years, Liccardi managed to broker the sale of 4,900 tons of grapes valued at $3.1 million that weren't what they purported to be. Those grapes produced 900,000 gallons of wine worth $18 million. The Bavaro brothers not only provided grapes to Delicato, but to unsuspecting wineries like Sebastiani Vineyards, Charles Krug Winery, and the Robert Mondavi winery.[73]

Another grape grower who sought a shortcut was Fred Franzia, the nephew of Ernest Gallo and the founder of Bronco Wines (which would eventually launch the world's best-selling brand, Charles Shaw, better known as Two-Buck Chuck). Franzia, a brash, loud man, thought most Napa Valley winemakers were snobs. Franzia disdained those "highfalutin" vintners because he believed good wine could be made inexpensively. He became particularly creative with the grapes he passed off as Zinfandel. His crew scattered leaves from Zinfandel vines on the top of other grape varieties to obscure their true origins. Franzia called this the "blessing of the loads," a reference to the practice of blessing the harvest. Franzia also passed off Carigne and Grenache grapes, which brought in about $196 a ton in 1992, as Cabernet grapes, which commanded about $387 a ton.

The growers and winemakers obscured the varietals by falsifying the tags accompanying the loads of grapes to the winemaking facilities. When grapes are harvested, the grower is supposed to fill out a field tag with the name and address of the grape grower, the grape variety, the date and time they were picked, the name of the trucking company delivering the grapes, and the license number of the trucks. The truck driver takes the field tag to the winery, which then uses the information to prepare a certificate for the California Department of Food and Agriculture. The winery also uses the information from the tag to file reports to the Bureau of Alcohol, Tobacco, Firearms, and Explosives. Often, a state inspector is on site to examine the grapes. The men taking shortcuts began falsifying the field tags to read "Zinfandel" rather than the true names of the grapes.

The money came rolling in. Some brazen grape growers bragged about the scam openly in coffee shops and diners. Word of their exploits spread around the San Joaquin Valley's tight-knit wine community. It angered a lot of grape growers who struggled to make an honest living. Some called up the California Department of Food and Agriculture to report the rumors. Others telephoned the ATF. Soon, the two agencies had agreed to work together to break open the counterfeit ring.

When the agents went into the wineries and asked to examine the field tags on file, they did not find anything suspicious. The paperwork was impeccable, disguising any evidence of fraud. So the agents dug up maps filed with the county that detailed what kind of grapes were grown in specific vineyards. Teams of agents staked out vineyards around the region to observe which grapes were picked and where they were delivered. At times, it was a twenty-four-hour job as the agents monitored the huge mechanical pickers that worked throughout the night, followed by the bands of laborers who arrived to pick at dawn.

By following the grapes from the field to the winery and comparing what was picked to the description on the field tags, the agents were able to document that some growers were passing cheap grapes off as more expensive varietals.

Steven Lapham had been working at the U.S. Attorney's office in Sacramento for four years when an ATF agent came in one cold day at the end of December in 1989 with a case he wanted to drop. It involved a grape scam and the agent didn't think he had enough evidence to go forward. Besides, the ATF "did guns and drugs," not wine. He needed Lapham's okay to stop the pursuit.

The federal government at that time had a spotty history prosecuting wine fraud. The cases it did pursue were relatively minor in scope. In 1974, Almaden Winery had misrepresented what was inside 28,000 cases of wine it sold to airlines to put in those tiny screw-top wine bottles. The winery was fined $250,000—at that time the largest fine ever levied.[74] In 1982, the bureau arrested a Sausalito man then living in New York, Louis A. Feliciano, who had commissioned wallpaper with the design of Château Mouton Rothschild labels. He cut out the labels and pasted them on forty cases of California wine.

As Lapham listened, he realized that the scale of the fraud the ATF agent was describing was huge. Lapham wasn't someone who thought wine drinkers were rich and snobbish and deserved whatever they got. Nor did he think falsifying wine or switching out one type of grape for another was a minor matter. The California wine industry brought millions of dollars into the state economy each year and employed thousands of people. Lapham thought that if government didn't clamp down hard on grape fraud, it would only grow in scope.

Lapham was a wine lover, and perhaps that perspective made him eager to pursue the case. It certainly helped him understand the seriousness of the fraud.

Lapham had a realization about wine in 1982 when he was thirty. He had been a casual wine drinker until then, never paying close attention to what he bought or what he drank. He was in Laguna Beach in southern California on Mother's Day, visiting his closest friend and his parents. His friend's father, a cardiac surgeon, brought a bottle of 1966 Château Lafite Rothschild to celebrate. Lapham still remembers his first taste of that famed wine. "It was like velvet. The tannins had all disappeared. It was flavorful, rich and full-bodied. I learned for the first time what good wine was supposed to taste like." He vowed then and there to only drink good wine—not Château Lafite–level good—but good California Cabernet.

Lapham recruited a more enthusiastic ATF agent to oversee the grape fraud case. Eight months later, agents started to stake out grape fields all over the Central Valley. In the early 1990s, Lapham and California state prosecutors brought more than twenty civil and criminal lawsuits against Delicato, its president, Anthony Indelicato, the Bavaro brothers, Michael Licciardi, Fred Franzia, Bronco Wines, D. Papagni Fruit Co., and others, charging that they had fraudulently sold $26 million of grapes and wines that were not what they professed to be. All of those charged either pleaded guilty or were convicted. Bronco Wines agreed to pay a $2.5 million fine for misrepresenting 5,000 tons of Grenache and Colombard grapes as Zinfandel. They had passed off one million gallons of wine worth approximately $5 million as white Zinfandel when it was made from other grape varietals. Franzia paid a $500,000 fine and was forced to step away from the company's presidency and the board for five years.

Lapham could have pushed to send Franzia to jail, as he did for the others convicted of fraud. But Franzia persuaded the prosecutor that the small town of Ceres, home to Bronco, would suffer financially if Franzia's imprisonment triggered the company's collapse. It was a concession that Lapham would regret years later as he watched Franzia and Bronco Wines grow in strength and financial stability while, it seemed to Lapham, skirting the edge of legality in other ways. Franzia's conviction has not slowed down his ability to turn Bronco into the fourth largest wine company in the U.S. He now refuses to talk about the conviction in interviews. It weighs on his mind, though. In 2008, he asked President George W. Bush for a presidential pardon. One reason he wanted it was because he wanted to own a gun, which he couldn't do as a convicted felon.[75] His application was denied.

In 2012, federal agents busted open the largest wine-counterfeiting scheme in the twenty-first century. What made the arrest so shocking, so singular, was that it involved the wine elite, the men who prided themselves on their sophisticated palates and bank accounts deep enough to acquire the most coveted wines in the world. Discovery of the fraud revealed how the pursuit of trophy wines by the rich eager to flaunt their wealth made them vulnerable to deceit and fraud. These men, ranging from young Turks on Wall Street to software founders to energy billionaires, were so intent on acquiring rare wine—and auction houses were equally focused on helping them—that they ignored signs they were being conned. The fraud put wine collecting in the worst light possible, exposing the greed, obsession, and hubris that can accompany a love of wine.

The groundwork for this fraud was set during the last twenty years with the rise in popularity of wine auctions. For many decades, the only wine auctions in the United States were held in San Francisco and Chicago. Other states outlawed them. London was the wine auction capital of the world. Then in 1994, New York State legalized wine auctions, which transformed the affairs formerly held in windowless rooms in auction houses like Sotheby's and Christie's and attended by a small group of collectors into raucous events. Wine auctions moved into elegant three-star New York restaurants where the wine poured at the tables rivaled that sold on the auction block. The lunches held to showcase the wines became Bacchanalian affairs where numerous bottles of high-priced wine washed down cuisine prepared by some of the world's top chefs.

Within a few years New York had overtaken London as the economic center of the fine wine world, led by newly aggressive auction firms like Acker Merrall & Condit and its young president, John Kapon. Young and wealthy Wall Street financiers with a love for rare Bordeaux and Burgundy wine, almost unlimited wealth, and the stamina to withstand days of heavy drinking became the new kings of the wine world. They gave themselves cowboy-like nicknames like "Big Boy" and "King Angry." It was common for them to throw around tens of thousands of dollars on a bottle of wine. It became "my bottle is bigger than your bottle," noted one critic.[76]

Wine auction frenzy was ratcheted up to a new level when Hong Kong decided in February 2008 to eliminate its 40 percent import tax on wine. While the economic downturn dampened the economies of the U.S. and Europe, Asia thrived. Asian buyers were enthralled with Bordeaux, particularly Château Lafite Rothschild, and the prices they paid at auction continually set new records. In 2010, for example, three bottles of 1869 Lafite Rothschild were expected to sell for $8,000 apiece; instead the bottles sold for $232,692 each.[77] Auctions worldwide raised $92 million in 2000. By 2011, global auction sales soared to a record $478 million.[78]

The rush to acquire—and sell—rare and hard-to-find wine meant its provenance was not always scrutinized. "In the rare-wine world, doubts are endemic; murkiness is built into a product that is concealed by tinted glass and banded wooden cases and opaque provenance and the fog of history," wrote Benjamin Wallace, the author of *The Billionaire's Vinegar*, a book about one of the greatest wine frauds in history. "At the same time, the whole apparatus of the rare-wine market is about converting doubt into mystique. Most wealthy collectors want to spend big and drink famous labels, not necessarily ask questions or hear the answers."

It was in this world that Rudy Kurniawan thrived.

For more than a decade, Kurniawan was the boy wonder of the fine wine world. He was the kind of person who opened rare bottles of Château

Cheval Blanc and Mouton Rothschild at parties, who treated his friends to thousands of dollars of wine—often in a single dinner—and who spent as much as $1 million a month to acquire coveted vintages. His penchant for Domaine de la Romanée-Conti—considered the most prized Burgundy in the world—was so well known among his circle of high-spending, heavy-drinking friends that he earned the nickname of "Dr. Conti."

Kurniawan was a bit of a mystery when he first came to public attention in the early 2000s, but it didn't take long before he dazzled the world of wine collectors. He said he had been born in Indonesia to a wealthy ethnic Chinese family and his father had given him the last name of Kurniawan to protect his identity. He had come to California to attend Cal State Northridge. Kurniawan seemed to have endless amounts of cash, but was vague about its origins. He drove a Ferrari and a Bentley, dressed in custom Hermès suits, and had a collection of expensive watches.

Kurniawan had an epiphany about wine in 2000 when he had a glass of 1995 Opus One, a Napa Valley Cabernet made in a joint venture by Robert Mondavi and Baron Philippe de Rothschild. The wine was a revelation, and it sent Kurniawan on a journey to learn more. He soon became fixated on wine and joined three Los Angeles wine-tasting groups. All had provocative names. One was called the BurgWhores and focused on Burgundy wines. Another was titled Deaf, Dumb, and Blind, and a third was known as the Royal Order of the Purple Palate. Its members included Hollywood directors, movie producers, and business managers for A-list stars. He started to meet movie stars, like Will Smith and Jackie Chan, and treat them to gourmet dinners filled with special wines. Within a few years, Kurniawan had become one of the most high-profile wine collectors in the U.S.—or at least one of the most willing to make a show of the wines he bought and drank.

At one notorious dinner in New York in 2004, Kurniawan and John Kapon, the then thirty-two-year-old president of the New York auction house Acker Merrall & Condit, and some friends went on a four-day eating and drinking binge at Cru, a restaurant just north of Washington Square in New York famous for its 150,000-bottle wine list.

The guests consumed dozens and dozens of bottles, what wine writer Michael Steinberger called "a murderers' row of legendary wines." They included a 1945 Mouton Rothschild, a 1964 Romanée-Conti, and a 1971 La Tâche, wines so rare and expensive few had ever had the pleasure of drinking them.[79] The wine critic Robert Parker had dubbed the 1945 Mouton Rothschild "immortal," it was so good. At the end of the bacchanal, the bill came to $250,000. Kurniawan paid for all of it on his American Express Black card.

Kurniawan's largesse soon became legend and it immediately elevated him into the upper echelons of the wine world. But the evening also provided a glimpse into Kurniawan's baser instincts, although no one recognized it at the time. At the end of the evening, Kurniawan asked the restaurant to mail the empty bottles to his house near Los Angeles. It would only be years later that anyone understood the meaning behind the request.

The dinner cemented an increasingly close relationship between Kurniawan and Acker Merrall's president Kapon, a relationship that critics would later say made the wine auction house fail to do due diligence on wines Kurniawan offered up for sale. Their closeness was no surprise; they were both young, brash, loved to drink, and regarded old and rare wines as trophies worth spending lavishly on. Plus, they were both so rich price did not matter. And Kurniawan led the way, spending as much as $1 million a month on his wine habit.

In 2006, Kurniawan decided to sell bottles from his collection, which was stored at his house near Los Angeles. He turned to Kapon, who decided, for the first time in Acker Merrall & Condit's history, to hold an auction from just one wine cellar. In the glossy catalogue printed to promote the sale, Kapon extolled the collection, calling it "the greatest cellar in America," a cellar "beyond compare."

The wines were extraordinary—perhaps too extraordinary. They included six magnums of Domaine de la Romanée-Conti's 1971 Montrachet, six magnums of the mythic 1947 Château Cheval Blanc, a case of the 1961 Château Latour à Pomerol, a case of Armand Rousseau 1962 Chambertin, a case of 1947 Château Lafleur, and three bottles of 1921

Lafleur, among others. The availability of such a large collection of rare wine prompted a bidding frenzy. The auction, held over two days at Cru restaurant, brought in $10.6 million—making it the largest single-owner sale ever by an American collector.[80]

Then Kurniawan and Kapon outdid themselves. They held another auction called Cellar II (the January auction was named *The* Cellar) and topped previous sales. Eager customers spent $25.7 million. Together, the Cellar sales brought in $36.3 million.[81] Kurniawan instantly became known as one of the world's greatest collectors and Acker a major player in the auction world.

Two years later, at yet another Acker auction held at Cru restaurant, doubts about Kurniawan exploded into public view.

Once again, a number of the moneyed drinkers who called themselves The Angry Men had gathered to bid on bottles of Champagne from the cellar of Robert Rosania, the partner in a billion-dollar real estate company, whose collecting handle was "Big Boy." The crowd had been drinking for hours and raising their paddles time after time to bid on pristine bottles of bubbly. Never mind that Bear Stearns had collapsed a month earlier and the U.S. was on the brink of financial collapse. The men hooted and hollered during the telephone bidding war that broke out over two bottles of Moët & Chandon Dom Perignon Rose 1959, which had never been commercially released. The lot had been expected to sell for $5,000; it went for $84,700.[82]

At one point, Rosania stood on top of a table, told everyone to shut up and pay attention, and then used a saber to cut off the top of a $10,000 jeroboam of 1945 Bollinger Champagne.[83] It was a trick he had performed many times.

Kurniawan had consigned 268 bottles from three French Burgundy estates, Domaine Georges Roumier, Domaine Armand Rousseau, and Domaine Ponsot, for the auction. He and Kapon must have had high expectations for the bottles, considering the success of the previous auctions, and Kurniawan had flown in from Los Angeles to watch the bidding. But before the auction had started, the proprietor of one of those estates, Laurence Ponsot of Domaine Ponsot, called Kapon. Someone had notified Ponsot that there was a 1929 Ponsot Clos de la Roche for sale. Ponsot was immediately alarmed. That wine could not exist. The Ponsot family had not started producing wine under its own name until 1934.

Ponsot insisted to Kapon that the bottle must be a fake. He demanded that Acker withdraw all of the 97 bottles of Domain Ponsot that were listed in the catalogue.

Kapon, to his credit, gave Ponsot his assurances that the disputed bottles would be withdrawn. But the French winemaker boarded a jet to New York anyway to make sure that those wines were not auctioned off. His plane landed at four p.m. He rushed to Cru and arrived shortly after six p.m., right as the auction was getting going. Ponsot sat quietly in the back of the restaurant and watched as others drank and enjoyed themselves. Right at the point the Ponsot wines were supposed to have been sold, Kapon told the would-be bidders that the Domaine had requested that Acker Merrall yank the wines. "I guess there were a couple of inconsistencies there," Kapon told those assembled, "so we had to pull them."

The announcement surprised the crowd, and angered a few who had hoped to bid on the wines. It got people talking, too. While it isn't that uncommon for a few bottles to be pulled before an auction, Acker had just removed $1 million of wine. That was unusual. When a reporter later asked Kurniawan what happened, he downplayed any suggestion the wines were not authentic. "We try our best to get it right," Kurniawan told Peter Hellman of the *Wine Spectator*, "but it's Burgundy, and sometimes shit happens."

One of the collectors who had purchased wine from Kurniawan over the years was William I. Koch, a Florida energy magnate and brother of David and Charles Koch, who are well known for their financial support of conservative political causes. Koch is a great collector; his houses in Palm Beach, Florida, and on Cape Cod in Massachusetts are filled with paintings by Picasso, Monet, Degas, Modigliani, Homer, Chagall, and sculptures by Rodin and Botero. He loves to sail (he won the America's Cup in 1992), and has a large collection of maritime memorabilia, including paintings of ships and seascapes, model ships, and antique nautical instruments.

Koch also has one of the world's most impressive wine collections, with 43,000 bottles scattered across his two cellars. He has collected verticals of four of the world's greatest estates: 150 years of Château Lafite, 120 years of Château Mouton Rothschild, 100 years of Château Latour, and 90 years of Château Petrus.

Koch frequently buys at auction and in 2006 spent $77,925 at the Acker auction of Kurniawan's cellar. Koch paid $9,000 for a 1949 Château Lafleur and $30,000 for a 1947 Château Petrus, among others.[84] Over the next few years, Koch kept acquiring wine from Kurniawan; he eventually spent about $2.1 million on 219 bottles of his wine.

When Koch brought in an expert to authenticate his wines—including a number of bottles from the 1780s that supposedly belonged to Thomas Jefferson—he learned that about 421 of them, worth around $4.5 million, were faked. It was only 1.8 percent of Koch's collection, and for a man worth $4 billion, a small fraction of his net worth. But the discovery of the forgeries infuriated Koch. It sent him on a crusade. He hired former FBI agents, wine experts who used to work for Sotheby's auction house, glass historians, cork experts, adhesive specialists, and label experts to examine his collection—and pursue those who cheated him. He has spent $30 million to $40 million so far.

In 2009, Koch filed separate lawsuits against Acker Merrall & Condit and Kurniawan, alleging fraud. (He had filed a lawsuit in 2006 against Hardy Rodenstock, the man he believed faked the Jefferson bottles.) "I want to shine a bright light on this whole fraud to show how bad it is," said Koch.[85]

In the early morning hours of March 8, 2012, before the sun had fully risen over the San Gabriel Mountains in Los Angeles County, a group of FBI agents rang the doorbell of a beige and brick Mediterranean-style house in Arcadia. Kurniawan, a slight man with glasses, opened the door, still clad in his pajamas and bathrobe. As he stood there blinking at the sight of federal agents clustered on his doorstep in one of Los Angeles's suburban communities, he was informed he was under arrest.

After the agents led Kurniawan off in handcuffs, they searched the house he lived in with his sixty-four-year-old mother. It was a veritable wine-counterfeiting factory. There were hundreds of bottles stacked on the kitchen counters. Some lay casually on the floor. Hundreds of fake wine labels bearing names of the world's most prestigious wineries sat in drawers and on tables. There were forged Petrus labels, instantly recognizable to wine lovers, with its name printed in bright red against a beige background. There were labels from Domaine de la Romanée-Conti with its well-known black blocky lettering. There were labels from Château LaFleur and Screaming Eagle.

Kurniawan also had baskets filled with wine capsules that covered the tops of bottles, decorative stamps with the names of historic châteaux, stencils that could be used to make serial numbers, and sealing wax. Thousands of corks, both used and new, lay scattered about. Kurniawan had tacked aluminum foil over the windows so nosy neighbors couldn't peek in.

The arrest and raid answered the question that had consumed many members of the wine world: how had Kurniawan amassed hundreds of bottles of the rarest and most desired wine in the world?

As FBI agents swarmed through the house, the answer soon became clear. Kurniawan had been known in wine circles for his impeccable palate, his ability to remember the taste and feel of almost any wine he had ever sampled. He could pick up a glass, swirl it, smell it, taste it, and then name the type of wine, the region, the year, and often the grape. He had a sense memory that astounded those who had joined him at dinners where dozens of bottles of wine were poured in a single evening.

Kurniawan had used this special palate to forge wines. Agents found an area in the kitchen where Kurniawan mixed various wines together to imitate famous and rare vintages. The FBI agents found open bottles of Ridge Monte Bello Cabernet Sauvignon, reds from Charles Krug and Joel Gott, and newer French varietals as well. Investigators later determined that Kurniawan had mixed these newer California wines with batches of French wine from the 1970s he had purchased directly from a French négociant, or broker. One recipe for a fake 1945 Mouton Rothschild called for "one-half 1988 Pichon Melant; one-quarter oxidized Bordeaux; and one-quarter Napa Cab."[86]

None of the open bottles of wine were worth more than $100 to $250 a bottle, yet Kurniawan had convincingly blended them together to create wines that sold for tens of thousands of dollars a bottle.

The arrest shocked the world of fine wine, which for years had regarded Kurniawan as one of the most precocious and generous wine collectors around. It also vindicated some experts and wine collectors who had warned that the wine auction world was so caught up in its glass bubble of decadence and extravagant spending and drinking that it ignored obvious signs of fraud. In certain circles, drinking and buying large amounts of rare wine had become a competition played out on the world auction stage. Wine had always been a status symbol, but in recent years, with an increase in global wealth and the rising popularity of auctions, it had become obscene.

Many experts, and many of the young Turks who had so publicly celebrated with Kurniawan, were ashamed. His widespread fraud showed that people who considered themselves wine connoisseurs were as easily cheated as those who knew little about wine. They were so impressed by Kurniawan's palate, his fancy clothes, cars, and watches, and his unparalleled access to unusual wine, that they didn't bother to question the likelihood of one man owning bottles so rare that some had not been seen in the market for more than thirty years.

Kurniawan's ten-day trial in federal court in Manhattan drew reporters and camera crews from around the globe. Koch testified about his purchases, as did a number of other collectors who believed that Kurniawan had cheated them. In December 2013, the thirty-seven-year old Kurniawan was convicted of manufacturing and selling $1.3 million of fraudulent wine. Prosecutors believe that the number is much higher than that. They think that Kurniawan has sold more than $20 million in fake wines. Other specialists in wine forgery think the fraud may be as high as $100 million. But the prosecutors have not been able to get people who were defrauded by Kurniawan, except for a few like Koch, to step forward. Apparently they do not want to publicly admit they have fake wine, either to avoid embarrassment or to preserve their ability to quietly resell those fake bottles into the frenzied wine market to recoup their losses.

In August 2014, a seemingly contrite but stone-faced Kurniawan was brought back into court to be sentenced. Just a month earlier, he had settled the lawsuit brought against him by Koch. Kurniawan agreed to pay $3 million in restitution and tell Koch everything he knew about the world of wine fraud. Before the federal judge handed down the sentence, Kurniawan's lawyer suggested that his client should not get much jail time. After all, Kurniawan had swindled rich people of a luxury product, which hardly seemed a crime. One wine lover had even spent $231,000 for a single bottle of wine—which meant he had plenty of cash to spare. It was nothing like swindling someone of their life's savings, the lawyer argued. Nobody died.

The federal judge listened to Kurniawan's lawyer and then completely ignored the request. He sentenced Kurniawan to ten years in prison, fined him $20 million, and ordered him to pay $28.4 million to seven victims.

Why did Kurniawan do it? Why did he squander his family's fortune and its good name? In a revealing letter sent to the judge before sentencing, Kurniawan admitted that he became obsessed with rare wine because of the access it gave him to influential and wealthy people. He loved the attention he received when he swooped into a restaurant carrying some of the world's rarest (but fake) vintages. "Wine became my life and I lost myself in it," Kurniawan wrote. "This obsession attracted attention and I admit that I enjoyed it. I met a lot of interesting people who were very successful and intelligent. We shared a common interest in wine and my wines provided me with access to people and experiences I otherwise would not have enjoyed. I thought these people were my friends and I wanted to be accepted in their world."

Kurniawan's arrest and conviction has sparked a conversation about the amount of fraudulent wine in circulation. Koch and others, including Maureen Downey, a fraud expert who runs Chai Consulting in San Francisco and who helped the FBI with the Kurniawan case, have been stating loudly for years that some auction houses, brokers, and retail stores deliberately overlooked information about fakes because there was so much money to be made. The auction houses failed to thoroughly inspect the wines they sold, ignored troubling telltale signs like smudged labels, capsules with ages that didn't match the labels, or indistinct stamps. The auction houses and wine stores didn't want to alienate their customers (who are often those who consign wine) or shut down the auction party by questioning provenance. "It's a combination of laziness, greed and ego," said Downey. "They are lazy because they are not paying attention. They are greedy and therefore they don't choose to pay attention. The excuse I get time and time again is 'I've been in this business for thirty years . . . who are you to question me?'" Downey was referring in particular to John Kapon and Acker Merrall & Condit, even though prosecutors have never implicated the firm and its director in fraud, nor suggested they knew that Kurniawan was falsifying wine.

Even after 2008, when there was broad-based suspicion of the provenance of Kurniawan's wines (Acker Merrall & Condit distanced itself from Kurniawan after the Domaine Ponsot fiasco and stopped selling his wine), numerous places chose to disregard the warning signs. Sommeliers at Cru and other restaurants continued to mail empty bottles of rare wine back to Kurniawan. Although the sommeliers probably didn't know what Kurniawan wanted to do with the bottles, their assistance allowed him to refill the bottles with fake wine and repeat the cycle of fraud. In 2009, Christie's offered Kurniawan's wine at three separate auctions. In February 2012, just a month before Kurniawan's arrest, Spectrum Wine Auctions of Los Angeles and London's Vanquish offered up a number of large-format bottles of Domaine de la Romanée-Conti—the kind of rare large bottles that Kurniawan had often sold. A Los Angeles attorney named Don Cornwall did some research and learned that Kurniawan had used a proxy to consign the wines. But when Cornwall notified auction officials that Kurniawan was the true seller, they ignored him. Cornwall posted his suspicions on the wine bulletin board Berserkers, under the heading "Urgent Warning: Rudy Kurniawan Is Trying to Auction More Wine. Buyer Beware." His posts prompted a lively discussion that caught the attention of the wine press. Once reporters questioned the wines' provenance, they were pulled from the auction.

And what about of all the thousands of bottles of wine that went through Kurniawan's hands? Many of them now belong to private collectors, brokers, and wine stores. Many observers fear that those who were duped by Kurniawan might try to quietly sell their wine in China and other parts of Asia. Some say Kurniawan's deceit has tainted—perhaps irreparably—the rare wine auction market. Global auction sales of rare and fine wines dropped 19 percent in 2012 and another 13 percent in 2013, and some observers believe the doubts about provenance are partially to blame. Laurence Ponsot, whose wines Kurniawan faked and who embarked on a one-man mission to expose the fraud, estimates that as much as 80 percent of the pre-1980 wine for sale at auction may be counterfeit. Others believe the number is much lower than that.

The mailing address for the fine wine merchant Golden West Wines is located in an old Victorian building on San Francisco's tony Fillmore Street, not far from the Pacific Heights mansions with their breathtaking views of the bay and Golden Gate Bridge. Golden West sells high quality wines, but not through a storefront, and the address is just a post office box. Instead, Golden West lists its wines for sale online and sells to customers around the globe.

In late June 2001, Golden West's owner, William Mazer, got a routine request: Would his company be interested in purchasing a case of 1989 Château Palmer? The wine, from a respected producer, was a red Bordeaux made from grapes grown on gravel hillocks. Some critics thought the 1989 vintage was the best of the decade. Mazer said yes and paid the seller $95 a bottle for a total of $1,140.

Two weeks later, the same seller sent Golden West another inquiry. This time he offered eight bottles of Château Ducru Beaucaillou from the small Bordeaux town of St. Julien in France. Golden West paid the seller $105 a bottle for a total of $840.

Two months later, in late August, the seller offered the wine merchant a much larger selection: more than seven cases of outstanding French wine, including a 1982 bottle of Château Cheval-Blanc from the St.-Emilion section of Bordeaux, worth about $400, some Pichon Lalande, and a Pomerol from Château La Conseillante, among others. It was an excellent offering, one that Golden West's clients would be sure to snap up. Mazer offered $8,030 for the lot.

There was nothing unusual about the transactions. People who had wine to consign or sell routinely approached Golden West and similar auction houses. Interactions were often conducted by phone or email. The merchant usually asked if the seller had the right to sell the wine—but the inquiry into its provenance didn't usually go far.

In this case, the seller did not have the right to sell the wine, although he never informed Mazer and Golden West of this.

The seller was Mark Anderson. After two years of running Sausalito Cellars, he had finally figured out a way to make money on his business—although it wasn't legal. He sold his clients' wine.

Most of the clients at Sausalito Cellars did not actively manage their wine collections. They were collectors who wanted to age their wine, sometimes for decades, so they left it (safely, they thought) to sit in a cool and humid space. Some of the clients, like the International Society of Food and Wine or the Society of Medical Friends of Wine, were active, coming in every few months to pull out some bottles for an event or a tasting. But many of Anderson's far-flung clients almost never visited the cellar or came at most once or twice a year. And there was one client who was most unlikely to visit since his wine was caught up in bankruptcy proceedings: Bacchanal's Samuel Maslak, who had sent Anderson 756 cases of fine wine.

Over the next four years, Anderson would sell $279,418 worth of wine to Golden West.

That wasn't the only wine merchant Anderson sought out. In February 2002, Anderson approached Premier Cru in Emeryville, which had a retail store and an online market. Over the next two and a half years, Premier Cru would purchase $296,235 in wine from Anderson.

On the outside, everything looked normal at Sausalito Cellars. By the fall of 2002, the company had outgrown its small jerry-rigged place on Marinship Way. Anderson decided to move the storage facility a short way north to a class A building on Libertyship Way, right by the water. The new facility was located in a three-story peach-colored building owned by Orlando Lobos, a local businessman and property developer whom Anderson had gotten to know through the Chamber of Commerce. At 2,500 square feet, the new space was about three times larger than the original spot. The rent was $5,000 a month. Anderson installed steel shelves, rolling racks, and a video system so "each bottle is observed by no less than three high definition video cameras."[87] He once again offered a computerized inventory system and state-of-the-art cooling. He said on the Sausalito Cellars web page that the space was "setting the standard—nationally and internationally" and would keep the wine in "protected solitude."

There was one more thing promised on the website: security for clients' wine.

"Is Sausalito Cellars in the business of buying or selling wine?" Anderson wrote on the website. "No."

By the fall of 2003, Anderson had gotten into such a rhythm, was so unconcerned about his actions that he didn't even try to hide his illicit dealings from his employees. Anderson would pull out a box, strip off all signs of the client's name, and then hand the boxes over to a hired cellar worker to put in a van. Anderson and the worker would then cart the wine over to Premier Cru on the eastern side of the San Francisco Bay or to Golden West in the city. Anderson was so brazen that one of his employees, Elliot Brewer, made an annotation in his time card for the week of December 7–13, 2003. In the space where he was to note his activities, Brewer wrote: "Helped Destroy Evidence."[88]

PART FOUR

EXPANSION

CHAPTER TWELVE

THE STRUGGLE
FOR RECOGNITION

O n a warm day in June of 1862 a group of men gathered in a build-ing on lower Broadway in New York City. They were members of the American Institute of the City of New York, a civic organization formed by inventors in 1838 to promote agriculture and the mechanical arts. The men had come together south of Canal Street to sample California wine—considered an oddity at the time.

H. A. Graff of Brooklyn, who was "well acquainted with foreign wines,"[89] had brought six bottles to the meeting. The men, agriculture and horticulture enthusiasts, were part of the Farmers' Club, one of the institute's many committees. Each week, the members examined a different aspect of farming. Their topics were varied; they had recently discussed the cultivation of strawberries, the Hessian fly, and a new law about cattle on the highway.

Even though the Civil War was raging and recent battles in Virginia had claimed the lives of 12,000 men, the men's focus on agriculture was keen. None of them had ever tried California wine. It was a novelty product, difficult to find on the East Coast. California wine was just starting to be noticed in San Francisco—Virginia peach brandy, magnolia whiskey, Catawba wine from Ohio, and French Champagne were all more popular than California wine, so it is no surprise that hardly anyone in New York had sampled it.

California was so distant from New York that bringing wine there was a challenge. The transcontinental railroad hadn't been completed yet (that would happen in 1869) so the most common way to transport wine to New York or Boston was to ship it around Cape Horn. This voyage of 14,700 miles took six to seven months and added considerably to the price. But it had the advantage of allowing the wine stored in pipes, a kind of narrow barrel, to age, a practice few California wine-makers bothered with in those early years.

The first shipment of California wine to the East Coast occurred in October 1860, and was sufficiently significant that newspapers took note. "This commencement of the exportation of Californian wine will prove of much advantage to the State," commented an article. "Our natural market . . . will be in the Eastern States, where the climate is not favorable to the grape."[90]

The first exporters were Kohler & Frohling, a company formed by two German musicians in San Francisco who had given up their instruments to plant vineyards in southern California. The firm opened a New York store in 1860. A year later, Jean Louis and Pierre Sainsevain, the nephews of Los Angeles wine pioneer Jean-Louis Vignes, set up a shop on Broadway.

The members of the Farmers' Club were the type of people who sought out the new and unusual. So they must have been salivating as they picked up glasses of wine from the vintages of 1858 and 1860. There was white wine and Champagne from the El Aliso vineyard in Los Angeles, now owned by the Sainsevain brothers (which the note taker mistakenly called Alizo) and Port and Angelica from Kohler and Frohling.

The men tipped back the glasses one by one. They let the wine linger on their tongues and then swallowed. While not every man liked every wine, overall they were favorably impressed.

"These Alizo wines, particularly one of the vintage of 1858, is fully equal to the best Rhine wine or Sauterne," said James J. Mapes, a professor of chemistry and natural philosophy with an experimental farm in New Jersey. "These are very sound, possessing just spirit enough to preserve them, and have a fine, fruity flavor with a little of that pleasant bitter taste, that when once acquired is highly approved by those who use this class of wines."

Solon Robinson, a fifty-eight-year-old farmer and noted writer, said, "I think the samples shown today prove that America is capable of producing its own wine, and that we are really independent of the wine countries of Europe."[91]

These may have been the first tasting notes about California wine ever recorded in New York,[92] and they suggested a promising future for the beverage. Certainly the Sainsevains and Kohler and Frohling, who had invested heavily in the trade, hoped so.

But the enthusiastic reception of the men of the Farmers' Club would prove to be an anomaly. For the next thirty years, California vintners would fight their way into the eastern market, fending off slurs and competition from New York and Ohio winemakers and a strong bias in favor of French wine.

There were many obstacles to selling California wine on the East Coast: transportation costs, an unfamiliarity with the product, and America's penchant for beer, hard cider, coffee, and whiskey—anything other than wine. But most of all, California was its own worst enemy. Much of the wine sent to New York, Baltimore, New Orleans, and other places was awful.

The grape boom after the Gold Rush had attracted fortune seekers and speculators who didn't care about making fine wine. They were in the business for the money. They wanted to make wine, lots of it, and sell it off.

These winemakers often used shortcuts that degraded a wine's flavor. They relied on dirty, musty barrels. They would press plump, juicy grapes with grapes that were moldy, green, or sunburned, and they would neglect to remove the leaves and stems that could turn a wine bitter. One observer noted that some winemakers permitted the "cap" that forms on fermenting wine "to get white with mold and swarming with vinegar flies." He "then cheerfully stirs it under so as to thoroughly infect the wine with the germs of destruction." Winemakers also adulterated wine to make it darker or sweeter. Some added fuchsine, a magenta dye derived from coal tar, or natural vegetable dyes made from logwood and elderberry juice, or from the cochineal insect.[93] Sometimes the wine soured from heat while being shipped.

Part of the problem was the continued reliance on Mission grapes, which produced a bland wine. While enterprising farmers had started to plant other varietals in the late 1850s, it wouldn't be until the late 1870s that grape growers experimented widely, and tried grapes like Zinfandel or red or white Frontignan. In 1880, as much as 80 percent of the vineyards in California were still planted with Mission grapes. It wasn't until 1890 that the reverse was true.[94]

All of this contributed to California's bad reputation on the East Coast. "It is a notorious fact, that there is, and has been, a vast amount of adulterated and spurious Wines palmed off against the public," a California newspaper commented.[95]

Easterners also had a preference for French wine, which they equated with gentility and civilization. Most restaurants didn't even list California wine on their wine lists. This prompted unscrupulous merchants to take good California wine and slap on a French label when it was bottled. Only the cheapest and worst wine was sold as Californian, giving all of the state's products a bad reputation.

"Unfortunately for us, Americans are not a wine-drinking people," one newspaper lamented in 1875. "Their prejudices are so fixed in favor of Imported European Wines that our native wines remain unsold, unless placed before them with a foreign label attached during the transit from California to the American consumer via France and Germany."[96]

John Rains's family no longer owned Cucamonga Vineyard. Dõna Merced had been forced to give up the 13,000-acre Rancho Cucamonga when she couldn't pay the mortgage. The woman who had once been one of the largest landowners in southern California saw the San Bernardino County sheriff auction her land off on the courthouse steps to pay her debts. Isaias Hellman, my ancestor and a Jewish immigrant who had arrived in Los Angeles from Bavaria eleven years earlier, bought the land.

Hellman's purchase was emblematic of the changes sweeping California, where immigrants and Yankees bought old ranchos for pennies on the dollar. The end of the Civil War prompted a migration west and the new settlers flooding into the state were eager to own their own farms, prompting the wide-scale division of large tracts into smaller parcels. Hellman, a short man with brown hair and a bushy Vandyke beard, was just twenty-eight years old and the owner of a small bank in downtown Los Angeles, but he was already a wealthy man. He had been eyeing Rancho Cucamonga ever since he lent $5,352 to John Rains just two days before his murder in 1862.

On a cool Thursday in mid-November 1870, Hellman paid $49,200 to Sheriff Newton Noble for the rancho. When the title cleared on May 9, 1871, Hellman immediately flipped the property, selling 4,840 acres to a syndicate of San Francisco businessmen for $28,200[97] and the 580-acre vineyard to Joseph Garcia, a Portuguese sea captain, for $25,000, making a small profit.[98] He retained the other 7,600 acres to develop himself. In 1873, Hellman bought back the vineyard.

The vineyard had been the center of the rancho ever since Tiburcio Tapia oversaw the planting of the first grapes. By the early 1870s, however, it had a neglected air. The winery and cellar had not seen major repairs for close to a decade. In July 1870, a cloud of grasshoppers descended on the vineyard. Two hundred acres of green vines were decimated, the leaves chewed to nubs, the stems broken and bent. Half the vineyard was destroyed.[99] The vintage that year from the vineyard's 130,000 vines was a paltry 12,000 gallons, a small portion of its usual production of 60,000 gallons.[100] The grasshoppers came through again in 1871.

Jean Louis Sainsevain was the winemaker at Rancho Cucamonga at that point. He had started managing the property in 1867 when Doña Merced still controlled the vineyard. He and his brother had even owned it briefly. Hellman kept him on. Sainsevain had once been one of the most acclaimed wine merchants in the west, overseeing hundreds of acres of grapes and managing retail and wholesale stores in San Francisco and New York. Now he was a hired hand.

Sainsevain's downfall had been Champagne. After expanding their uncle's wine operation into a large commercial enterprise with retail and wholesale operations around the globe, including San Francisco, New York, and Mazatlan, Mexico, Jean Louis and his younger brother, Pierre, decided to produce Champagne, a risky proposition since sparkling wine had never been made commercially before in California. But it reflected the risk winemakers thought was necessary to solidify and grow the small wine industry. In 1856, Pierre Sainsevain returned to France and brought back Monsieur Debanne, a former Champagne maker for the widow Cliquot in Reims.[101]

The brothers leaped into the Champagne business. They made about 50,000 bottles of Champagne in 1857 relying on "a new process" in which they aged the Champagne for a year rather than the customary five to six years.[102] They called it "Sparkling California Champagne" and shipped bottles as far away as New York and Philadelphia.

At first, the project seemed to be a success. By 1859, the Sainsevains were selling three hundred cases of Champagne a month, worth about $3,600.[103] They sent some to President James Buchanan, who thanked them profusely in a note. The brothers turned around and used excerpts from the president's letter in newspaper advertisements. "Was the most agreeable wine I have ever drunk,"[104] the ads quoted Buchanan as stating. When the French government threw a party in 1860 to celebrate the opening of its consulate in Los Angeles, the Sainsevains' Champagne was served. It must have been a triumphal evening, one that showcased how French ingenuity had transformed the California wine industry.

But something was off about the Sainsevains' Champagne. About 20 percent of the bottles from the first vintage exploded while still in the Sainsevain cellars in San Francisco. Workers took to wearing masks to protect their faces from flying corks and shards of glass. Other bottles, once opened, had the unfortunate effect of making people gag. There was an unpleasant earthiness to the taste.[105] The brothers reportedly lost

$50,000 in the Champagne business in 1857—money they could not spare. More losses would follow.

The brothers shut down their Champagne operation in 1862 but by then they were on a downward financial spiral from which they never recovered. Vignes's children sued the brothers and accused them of underpaying for their father's vineyard. In January 1869, after losing their case in court, the Sainsevains were forced to sell the historic El Aliso vineyard with its towering sycamore tree and grapevine-draped arbor. They had other debts, which were satisfied when the sheriff of Los Angeles sold their possessions and stock of wine at public auction.

So Jean Louis Sainsevain became an itinerant winemaker. After Hellman took control of the vineyard, he brought in partners to finance improvements. Sainsevain oversaw the addition of fifty acres of new grapes. The partners also planted 5,000 orange, lemon, and walnut trees and erected new cellars and distilleries.[106] The vineyard, with a row of stately chestnut trees on one edge, the mountains rising to the north, and the sound of the gurgling Cucamonga Creek nearby, was a spectacular sight and garnered renewed attention.

"I have nowhere seen a vineyard which presented a finer appearance than Cucamonga," the noted travel writer Benjamin Truman wrote in 1874. "The foliage of the vines was just sufficiently advanced in growth to present an even surface of delicate green over the whole extensive area. Not a weed disfigured the ground, which careful cultivation had rendered almost as smooth and level as a ballroom floor."[107]

The vintage of 1875 was a difficult one. The last two weeks of October were hot in southern California, with afternoon temperatures reaching 100 degrees. The grapes dangling from the vines at Cucamonga Vineyard soaked up the sun. The purple, marble-sized orbs began to shrivel, almost like raisins, a sign that their sugars were intensifying. It was an encouraging development, as the season had started out with a deluge that dropped more than fourteen inches of rain in four days in mid-January, flooding parts of Los Angeles and drenching the vineyards of the region. In April, a frost killed about one third of the grapevines in the area. Winemakers were leaving the fruit on the vines as long as possible before harvest to make up for the early, miserable weather.

When the time came to harvest the grapes, groups of Chinese men went out into the fields with sharp knives and scissors. Chinese workers had been replacing Native American workers in southern California since 1869, when James De Barth Shorb, the owner of the nearby San Gabriel Winery, had hired them. Winemakers found the Chinese were more reliable than the Indians, for they didn't drink to excess and paid for their own room and board.

As Sainsevain stood in the middle of the vineyard to supervise the harvest, he could see the men in blue denim jackets and triangular grass hats squat down to pick the grapes off the low, umbrella-shaped vines. It was grueling, backbreaking work. Vines in those days were pruned to stay about a foot and a half off the ground. The pickers had to rest on their haunches, kneel, or bend over to pick the grapes. Then they carted baskets of grapes into the winery, where they were crushed with the new press and left to ferment.

The harvest was a success. Sainsevain still had his magic touch. A bottle of his 1875 sweet white wine won a first-place ribbon in the 1877 Southern California Horticultural Fair.[108]

Something strange happened with the wine made in 1875, though. The harvest came during a financial depression that had started in New York in 1873 with the failure of Jay Cooke and Company and had spread across the world, arriving in California in 1875. The downturn ripped apart the once-flourishing market for wine for the next five years, a cycle that would plague the California wine industry over and over again. Prices plummeted. Grapes soon sold for less than it cost to pick them. Some grape growers could not even find a market for their grapes, so they let hogs loose in their vineyards to gorge on the ripe fruit. Other desperate farmers ripped out their vines to plant oranges and peaches and walnuts—anything they thought would be more profitable than wine grapes. The number of wineries in California dropped from 139 in 1870 to 45 wineries in 1880.[109]

The depression may explain why at least two large barrels of the 1875 vintage from the Cucamonga Vineyard were never sold but sat in the wine cellar, untouched, for more than four decades. Maybe Hellman was too busy to deal with them. The downturn had presented a huge crisis for the Farmers and Merchants Bank, the bank Hellman founded in 1871. When a run on the bank at its downtown Los Angeles headquarters forced it to close its doors, Hellman had to cut short a vacation in Europe—the first time he had been back home since his emigration. Hellman rushed across half the world, traveling from Venice, Italy, to Los Angeles, a trip of 6,000 miles, in twenty-three days.[110] He stopped in New York and Los Angeles to borrow money to reopen his bank. Hellman had left his wife and young son behind in Europe, so perhaps there were more pressing matters on his mind than the two barrels of wine.

The Port and Angelica were finally bottled in 1921 and made their way into the cellars and basements of some of my family members. It was this wine—175 bottles of it—that was destroyed in the Wines Central warehouse fire 130 years after it was made.

The wine business recovered from the depression by the early 1880s and by the middle of the decade had reached new heights in southern California. Vineyards were scattered throughout the region, from Cucamonga and Pomona in San Bernardino County, west through the San Gabriel Valley to places like Alhambra and San Marino, all the way through Los Angeles and Orange counties. Large-scale producers like James De Barth Shorb of the San Gabriel Winery could ferment 1 million gallons at a time and store another 1.5 million gallons.[111] The Los Angeles Vineyard Company, which began as an agricultural cooperative in 1857, had lured dozens of German settlers from San Francisco to what eventually would be known as Anaheim. The industrious Germans had transformed 1,165 dry and sandy acres into lush vineyards and fifty distinct winemaking operations.[112] Benjamin Dreyfus, a partner in the Cucamonga Vineyard (and its manager after 1878[113]) had gotten his start in Anaheim in 1857 and had become the most important winemaker and merchant of the region. His B. Dreyfus & Co. sold the wine made by the Anaheim colonists, along with the state's first kosher wine. Before long the company was the largest wine wholesaler in the state. Dreyfus was so confident about the future of wine in southern California that he tore down the winery he constructed in the 1860s and in 1884 built a $40,000 cellar with a million-gallon capacity.[114] A longtime grower in Los Angeles, Matthew Keller, planted 170,000 vines on his property in Los Angeles in 1880 and announced his intent to plant an additional million vines on his ranch in Malibu.

Disaster struck in 1883. The winemakers in Anaheim noticed a strange, wavelike pattern appearing on grape leaves. The blight started on the outer edges of the leaves and moved inward until the afflicted leaves drooped and fell off. The grapes withered and did not ripen. Then the roots died.

The next year the affected vines were late in sending out shoots. When the leaves started to unfurl, they grew slowly and eventually developed the wave-patterned scalding. They died, and the vines died too.

A scourge had hit southern California that was quick and ruthless in its destruction of grapevines, even those that were fifty years old and had previously survived drought and flood. The rapidity and destruction of the disease took everyone by surprise. Anaheim Disease, as it was first called, hit hard and quick and was almost 100 percent fatal.

It killed off Dreyfus's personal 240-acre vineyard, and most of the acreage in Orange and Los Angeles counties and parts of the San Gabriel Valley. Old proud Mission vines, the backbone of California's wine economy, were reduced to leafless stalks poking out of the ground. A government report estimated the disease caused $10 million in losses to Los Angeles and Orange counties.

For some reason, Anaheim Disease (which would later be known as Pierce's Disease, after the scientist who first identified it) did not seriously affect the Mission grapes at the Cucamonga Vineyard. The soil there was sandy and porous, which apparently provided some protection. By 1890, the Cucamonga region was producing 279,000 gallons of wine a year, up from 48,000 gallons in 1870.[115]

Anaheim Disease, with its destructive and rapid rush through the vineyards, signaled the end of southern California's dominance in the wine industry. Winemakers shifted to oranges and other crops. Urbanization eventually took a toll, too, particularly after an influx of Midwesterners moved to the region during a boom in 1886. El Aliso, the vineyard planted by Jean-Louis Vignes in the 1830s and then taken over by his nephews, was subdivided into town plots.

The decline of the vineyards in southern California set the stage for the rise of northern California, which was better suited to growing grapes anyway. The terrain was more varied, with flat land and hills in Napa and Sonoma and plains in Santa Clara County. The climate was better, too. Southern California was very hot, which didn't allow the grapes to cool off at all, a process that contributes to their complexity. In the north, the cooling winds from the ocean and the summer fog modulated the temperature, creating temperate nights. By 1890, northern California produced almost eight times as many gallons as southern California.[116]

There was another significant change in the California wine business in the 1880s. Rich men looking to diversify their investments flooded the wine business. Today, it is Silicon Valley tech entrepreneurs and Japanese video game executives who buy trophy vineyards. In the late nineteenth century, it was men who had made their fortunes in the mines and railroads.

The new wine entrepreneurs included men like George Hearst, the U.S. senator from California who had made millions mining silver, gold, and copper in the west, and James Fair, the U.S. senator from Nevada, whose Virginia Consolidated silver mine yielded the largest silver strike in the world. (His family would eventually build San Francisco's Fairmont Hotel.) Hearst bought the Madrone Vineyard south of Glen Ellen in Sonoma County and Fair built a vineyard in the

Lakeview area of Sonoma County. In 1882, Hellman, former U.S. Senator F. G. Newlands and Senator William Gwin and a group of English businessmen invested $500,000 in the San Gabriel Winery, located in Alhambra, not far from Los Angeles.[117]

While mining interests had long dominated the west, smart men saw that agriculture was the future of California and they wanted part of the riches.

What set off the dollar signs in their eyes was the phylloxera devastation that had ripped through France's vineyards—and the potential opportunity it represented for California vintners. By the late 1880s, many of Europe's vineyards were dead. The grapevines that had covered the hills of Burgundy and Bordeaux had withered away, their green leafy vines turned into brown stumps by the insects that sucked the life out of the roots.

With phylloxera, California winemakers saw the opening they had been waiting for. They had long been convinced that California wines would one day equal the quality of French wines, although they had not yet been able to convince consumers of this. But with 40 percent of French vineyards decimated by phylloxera, imports had dropped. California winemakers were determined to replace the bottles of French wine that had long adorned the dining room and restaurant tables in New York and Boston with bottles from California.

Leland Stanford, the railroad baron and former California governor, was one of the many wealthy men who seized the opportunity. Stanford was a man who personified the West; he had grand visions, grand ambition, and a grand appetite. (Indeed, he weighed more than three hundred pounds.) Stanford had come to California during the Gold Rush and had opened a store to serve the miners. The open frontier and undeveloped landscape provided many business opportunities, and in 1861 Stanford and three other men, Collis Huntington, Mark Hopkins, and Charles Crocker, formed the Central Pacific Railway Company. Congress granted the company the right to build the western half of the transcontinental railroad in 1862. Tremendous riches and tremendous power followed.

Stanford had first gotten involved with wine in 1869 when he purchased land in Warm Springs, modern-day Fremont, in southern Alameda County. That winery, managed by his brother Josiah, made 50,000 gallons of wine in 1876.[118] But after he visited some of the great wine châteaux in Bordeaux during a trip to Europe in 1880, he announced plans to make California wine that would rival the greatest wine from France.[119]

In 1881, Stanford bought the remnants of an old rancho along the Sacramento River in Tehama and Butte counties in northern California. He named the 55,000-acre parcel Vina Ranch and he dreamed of creating the largest vineyard in the world, a place that produced huge quantities of fine wine and brandy that would be savored at homes and elegant dining establishments from San Francisco to London. It was a daunting undertaking: while there were seventy-five acres of old grapevines on the property, most of the land was grass dotted with sprawling ancient oak trees. Stanford spent $300,000 in the first year alone to transform the estate. Laborers blasted through 900 feet of rock and dug a two-mile long irrigation ditch to bring water from the Eagle River. (Workers would eventually build fifty miles of ditches, canals, and dams.[120]) They ripped out the massive oaks and blasted the trunks with a powder composed of nitroglycerine and a substance called kieselguhr. By the time they were done, the fields were flat and level.

Stanford then imported thousands of grapevines from San Bernardino County by rail car, bringing north Mission, Charbonneau, Burger, Zinfandel, Blau Elben, and Malroisie vines. The vines were treated gingerly. Workers were allowed to remove only five plants at a time, which they set out on top of the rail tracks until they could be transplanted into the ground. Stanford planted 1,200 acres of grapes in the winter of 1881–1882. Over the next few years, Stanford would expand the vineyard to 3,825 acres, making it the largest vineyard and winery in the world. At one point he had one million vines in production. He eventually added a massive winery with a steam-powered crusher and press and elevators to carry the grapes to the third floor.[121] He even added electric lights so work could be carried on at night during the harvest and crush.

From the start, Stanford hired both white and Chinese laborers to transform the massive property. At times, there were several hundred Chinese workers on the ranch. Almost immediately, his use of Chinese laborers became a flash point for anti-Chinese agitators, even though Chinese laborers had farmed the land for the previous owner, Henry Gerke.[122] While the Chinese had started coming to California in large numbers in the 1850s and had long been critical to the state's agricultural economy, they were derided as strange and different and given derogatory names like "coolie" or "Celestial," which conveyed their foreignness. While the state was still in the grip of gold fever, and for many decades after, there was a shortage of white labor. So the Chinese, widely regarded as reliable, stepped in as the Native Americans had done before them.

There was racial trouble almost from the start of Stanford's venture. The Chico *Enterprise* newspaper reported in April 1881 that the ranch's foreman had fired seventy-five white workers who were earning a dollar a day, plus board. He had replaced them with 135 Chinese men who earned the same amount but who fed themselves.[123] In 1886, a similar rumor swirled, leading the *Red Bluff Sentinel* to write: "it is greatly to be hoped that the heathen will have to shoulder their bamboo poles and skedaddle this time."[124]

A group called the State Executive Committee of the Anti-Chinese Association threatened to boycott Stanford's products in 1886, prompting Stanford to say that it was only his "humanitarianism" that led him to employ Chinese men. His "race prejudice," however, inclined him to employ white men, he said. When the poet Joaquin Miller came to the ranch, he noted the presence of several hundred Chinese workers—and the ill feelings directed toward them. "If only those men who run about making trouble over the presence of the Chinese were as steady and industrious," he wrote.

In 1887, Stanford started the first in a series of efforts to increase the number of white workers at the harvest. Vina contracted with a Mr. Hagden of San Francisco to bring up "city boys" (aka white) who might benefit from the fresh air and hard work. The newspapers speculated that they would also "stay out of trouble." But the experiment proved to be a failure. A group of about forty boys rode the train up to Vina in mid-August, at a time when the temperatures generally soared over 100 degrees, a much different climate than San Francisco's foggy summer weather. The boys arrived and were shown to their bunkhouses. Then were introduced to their boss, who was Chinese, "which did not suit them, nor did they like the food set before them," according to a newspaper report. The boys departed quickly.[125]

The next year, Stanford, who still maintained a large interest in the Southern Pacific Railroad, tried a different tactic. The railroad advertised that it would cut fares in half for white boys and girls who "desire to take a hand in gathering the fruit in interior orchards and vineyards in the coming autumn." The Chinese, of course, would still have to pay full fare.

Stanford would continue to rely on Chinese labor but he managed to get a steady supply of white workers in 1887 when he convinced a large group of French men and women from Bordeaux to come and work the harvest. The French took over some of the living spaces once occupied by the Chinese workers.

Stanford's hopes for Vina Ranch were never realized. It lost money and the wine was not particularly good. The area was too hot to produce good quality clarets and white wine. (Thomas Pinney, the wine historian, compared the climate of Vina Ranch to that of Algeria.) But Vina's sweet Angelica wine and its brandy were highly praised. Perhaps the ranch would have had more success if Stanford had not died suddenly in June 1893, leaving the property in the hands of his wife, Jane, and Stanford University officials. The school's first president, David Starr Jordan, was a Prohibitionist. Mrs. Stanford cut back on the winemaking operation and switched emphasis to wheat and other crops; the last of the grapevines were dug up in 1915.

By 1890, California had become the most important producer of wine in the United States despite Anaheim Disease and an outbreak of phylloxera in Sonoma County. It had finally surpassed Ohio, Virginia, and New York. By 1890, there were 200,000 acres of grapes planted in the state—only 175 acres fewer than the combined acreage in the rest of the United States.[126] California had taken over as the center of wine-making in the United States; a position it would never relinquish.

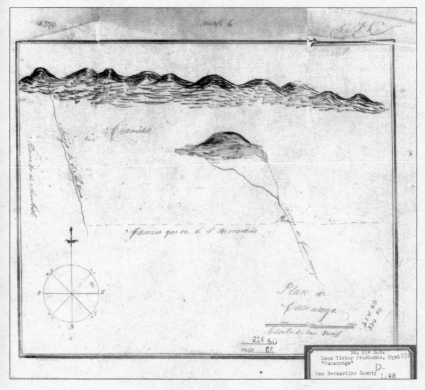

Tiburcio Tapia was awarded the 13,000-acre Rancho Cucamonga in 1839 after he presented this map to the Mexican governor of California. The area was so sparsely settled that Tapia, a former soldier and Los Angeles merchant, only had to sketch out general landmarks such as the San Gabriel Mountains to establish the rancho's boundaries. Tapia moved his herds of cattle to the land. He was the first to plant grapes there. (*Photo courtesy of the Bancroft Library*)

In 1858, John Rains, a former cattle driver and Confederate sympathizer, used funds from his wife, Maria Merced Williams de Rains, to purchase Rancho Cucamonga for $16,500. He expanded and improved the vineyard. Rains's murder in 1862 sparked a series of killings that terrorized the Los Angeles region. *(Photo courtesy of the Model Colony Room of the Ontario City Library)*

Maria Merced Williams de Rains was *Californio* royalty and was born into great wealth and privilege. When her husband John Rains died in 1862 she was ill equipped to deal with his debts, and the deceit of those around her led to her losing her beloved Rancho Cucamonga.

In 1870, Isaias W. Hellman, a twenty-eight-year-old German Jew who opened one of the city's first banks, bought Rancho Cucamonga at a sheriff's sale for $49,200. Hellman sold off pieces of the rancho and brought in business partners to expand and improve the vineyard. He owned the vineyard and Rains's old house for forty-seven years. Hellman, the author's great-great-grandfather, was president of the Wells Fargo Bank when he died in 1920. *(Photo courtesy of the Heller family collection)*

Jean Louis Sainsevain came to Los Angeles from France in 1853 to join his uncle, Jean-Louis Vignes (pronounced "vines"), whose 104-acre El Aliso vineyard was the centerpiece of winemaking in southern California. Sainsevain and his brother Pierre bought the vineyard in 1855 and their firm, Sainsevain Brothers, was soon selling California wine around the world. After a series of financial reversals, Sainsevain became the winemaker at the Cucamonga Vineyard. 175 bottles of Port and Angelica he made in 1875 were destroyed in the 2005 Vallejo warehouse fire. *(Photo courtesy of UCLA Department of Special Collections)*

Painting of the Cucamonga winery by Henry Chapman Ford. In 1874, Isaias W. Hellman and his business partners, former California governor John Downey and Anaheim wine merchant Benjamin Dreyfus, poured money into the Cucamonga Vineyard and winery to increase its production. The artist probably painted this undated picture in the late 1880s. *(Photo courtesy of the Huntington Library)*

Workers picking grapes at the Cucamonga vineyard in the late 1880s. *(Photo courtesy of the Early California Wine Trade Archive)*

The Mission grapes that the Franciscan fathers imported in 1778 to make sacramental wine thrived in the hot sun of southern California. The vines could live for more than fifty years and grow several feet around and six feet tall. The table wine made from Mission grapes was not very good, though, which complicated California's attempts to penetrate the New York City market. The grapes, however, produced excellent fortified wines such as Port and the sweet white Angelica. In this 1884 photo, a young girl stands under a forty-eight-year-old Mission grapevine in Montecito in Santa Barbara County. *(Photo courtesy of the Bancroft Library)*

CALIFORNIA
BIG TREE WINE EXHIBIT.
HORTICULTURAL HALL.

In 1893, in one of many attempts to elevate the reputation of California wine, four wine merchants created the "Big Tree Wine" exhibit for the Chicago Columbian Exposition. A statue of "Viti-culture," along with one of a Franciscan friar and an Indian woman holding a basket of grapes, stood in front of a forty-foot-tall, hollow replica of a redwood tree. Inside, fair revelers could marvel at displays of California wine. *(Photo courtesy of the Early California Wine Trade Archive)*

In 1894, the California wine industry was in disarray, caused by a glut of grapes, low prices, and fierce competition among the wine merchants of San Francisco. Percy Morgan, an English accountant, was instrumental in the creation of the California Wine Association, which brought together seven large wine houses and stabilized the industry. Within twenty years, the CWA monopolized the wine industry, controlling 80 percent of the production and sale of wine in the state. *(Photo courtesy of the Gail Unzelman collection)*

KOHLER & FROHLING'S WINE CELLARS.

The California Wine Association established its headquarters in 1894 in the former Kohler & Frohling building on Second and Folsom Streets. San Francisco was the center of the wine world in that era, as grape growers and winemakers shipped their products there to be blended, aged, and sold.

Everything the California Wine Association did was on a massive scale. Wines in the latter part of the nineteenth century were not aged, but blended and shipped around the world in barrels. S. Lachman & Co., one of the original members of the CWA, had the world's largest oak storage tank at its headquarters on Brannan Street in San Francisco. It held 80,000 gallons of wine. *(Photo courtesy of the Bancroft Library)*

The 1906 San Francisco earthquake and fire destroyed many of the buildings owned by the California Wine Association, including its headquarters, and ruined 10 million gallons of its wine. Percy Morgan, the company's president, is one of the men standing in front of the rubble. *(Photo courtesy of the California Historical Society)*

In 1906, after the earthquake, the California Wine Association built Winehaven, near the city of Richmond on the eastern shore of San Francisco Bay. It was the largest winemaking facility in the world until Prohibition. Many of the original buildings, including a crenellated brick building that resembles a medieval castle, are still standing, although they are disintegrating. *(Photo courtesy of Willie Agnew, caretaker, Point Molate)*

The arson fire that ripped through the Wines Central warehouse in Vallejo on October 12, 2005, destroyed around 4.5 million bottles of wine worth at least $250 million, making it the largest crime involving wine in history. It took more than a year to clean up the building and remove all the debris. *(Photo courtesy of the Bureau of Alcohol, Tobacco, Firearms, and Explosives)*

Mark C. Anderson started a wine storage business in Sausalito in 1999 and was charged a few years later with embezzling 8,000 bottles of wine worth more than $1.1 million from his clients. Federal officials believe Anderson set fire to the Wines Central warehouse to cover his tracks. In this 2006 photo, Anderson is at the Marin County courthouse for an embezzlement hearing. *(Photo courtesy of Jeff Vendsel/Marin Independent Journal)*

ATF investigator Brian O. Parker holds the propane torch that was used to start the Wines Central warehouse fire. An arson canine discovered it in Anderson's storage bay on the mezzanine level. Parker spent ten years working on the Anderson case, from the 2005 fire to Anderson's 2007 arrest to his 2012 conviction and subsequent appeal. The case lasted so long that Parker had three children during that time. *(Photo courtesy of the author)*

Steven Lapham was the assistant U.S. attorney who prosecuted Mark Anderson. A specialist in arson, white-collar crime, and wine fraud, Lapham handled many high-profile cases, including that of the Unabomber. He is shown at left being interviewed by a camera crew outside the federal courthouse in Sacramento. *(Photo courtesy of the author)*

Dick Ward, who cofounded Saintsbury, in the Carneros region of the Napa Valley, stands by boxes of wine that were scorched, but not destroyed, in the warehouse fire. Ward has stacked the boxes in the back of his barrel room, a constant reminder of the fire that destroyed his winery's library of wine on the eve of its twenty-fifth anniversary. *(Photo courtesy of the author)*

Delia Viader, who started Viader Vineyards on Howell Mountain in the late 1980s, lost her entire 2003 vintage, about 7,400 cases, in the warehouse fire. Viader's wine was not even supposed to be at Wines Central. She had to move it there because she ran out of room at her winery when the expansion of her caves was not completed on time. Viader's insurance company declined to reimburse the $4.5 million she lost, forcing Viader to sell the vineyard in Italy she had hoped to retire to. *(Photo courtesy of the author)*

Ted Hall, who started Long Meadow Ranch with his wife, Laddie, and son, Chris, established his winery's brand by making more than 5,000 visits to restaurants and stores around the country. The fire destroyed Long Meadow's 2002 vintage and part of its 2001 vintage, meaning there was no wine to send to all those outlets. Hall made an impassioned speech at Anderson's sentencing about the lingering damage of the fire, and it appeared to persuade the judge to hand down a long sentence.

Only a few bottles of Isaias Hellman's 1875 Port and Angelica remain after 175 bottles were destroyed in the warehouse fire. *(Photo courtesy of the author)*

CHAPTER THIRTEEN

THE ERA OF THE GREAT SAN FRANCISCO WINE HOUSES

The two-story B. Dreyfus & Co. wine house on Brannan Street in an industrial section of San Francisco was not an impressive sight. The only adornment on the stark brick building was a stone statue of an eagle with outstretched wings over the front entrance. The eagle was the company's trademark; the building was called Eagle Wine Vaults.

A visitor stepping inside, however, could not fail to be impressed. In the center of the main hall stood a 12,500-gallon oak wine cask decorated with carved grape leaves and clusters of fruit. The massive cask, which held only a minute portion of the wine the company distributed each year, was surrounded by dozens of 2,500-gallon carved oak casks that rose ten feet high.

By the 1890s, San Francisco had become the most important wine region in the state, even though there was not a single commercial vineyard in the city's boundaries. Its economic dominance was the result of the shift of winemaking to northern California, as well as a peculiar system that made wine houses involved in every single aspect of wine making in California, from the grape to the store shelf.

The hills and valleys of California were filled with grape growers, yet few small-scale winemakers sold their own products. Instead, they made wine and sold it in bulk to wine houses, which then blended it, stored it in huge barrels and vats, and shipped it around the world. The wine houses also had their own vineyards and cellars throughout the state. B. Dreyfus & Co., for example, brought wine to its Eagle Wine Vaults in San Francisco from the Cucamonga Vineyard, which it then managed, among others.

The number of wine houses in the city had grown rapidly in the latter years of the century. The San Francisco city directory listed only twenty businesses that sold, bought, and shipped wine in 1860. By 1885, there were more than forty-eight wine houses. Six years later in 1891, the number had doubled to 100 wine houses in San Francisco.[127]

Many of these wine houses were clustered south of Market Street, just a few blocks from the harbor. The port of San Francisco, where train lines, freighters, and clipper ships converged, was the center of wine exports in the state. It was not uncommon to see steamers, their decks heaped with barrels, pull up to the docks after a trip down the Napa River. Workmen would unload the wooden casks into open-air wagons, and horses would pull them to the wine houses, sometimes leaving a trail of dripping wine behind on the cobblestones. Rail lines crisscrossed the south of Market section of San Francisco as well, and locomotives often hauled carloads of barrels through the streets.

The wine houses had tremendous power as a result of this concentration, which at times they used for good. In 1893, for instance, as the country geared up for the Chicago Columbian Exposition that celebrated Columbus's arrival in America, four of San Francisco's leading wine houses came up with an arresting way to promote California wine, which still wasn't as popular as French wine on the East Coast. C. Carpy & Co., J. Gundlach & Co., Arpad Haraszthy & Co., and the Napa Valley Wine Company commissioned a forty-foot-high replica of a sequoia redwood tree, covered with natural bark, as an exhibit.

From the start, the towering fake tree garnered attention. A curious reporter from the *San Francisco Call* newspaper noticed it under construction on a vacant lot on Octavia Street. He went by and asked the carpenter, M. Schuman, if he was building another Tower of Babel. He then printed up the exchange. "Mr. Shuman is a master carpenter and when he gets through with the trunk, no one will be able to tell the difference between it and a real tree," the reporter concluded in a March 21, 1893, article.

The replica tree, once assembled inside one of the 400 buildings that made up the fair, was hollow. It held a tasting room that featured the wines of the four wine merchants, a painting of San Francisco Bay, and signs reading "Welcome Stranger to the Realm of the Golden State," and "Ye Who Enter Leave Your Cares Behind."

A statue of "Viticulture," draped in robes and crowned with grape clusters entwined in her hair, stood by the entrance. She held a long staff topped by a pineapple, which was the classical accessory of those who worshipped the wine god Bacchus. To her right was a statue of an Indian maiden holding a basket of grapes and to her left was a statue of a Franciscan missionary planting the state's first vines.

L. L. Palmer, the Chicago correspondent for the *Pacific Wine and Spirits Review*, an industry trade paper based in San Francisco, called the Big Tree exhibit "the most striking feature of the whole wine exhibit, be it foreign or domestic."[128]

More often, however, the wine houses used their power to control sales and prices and maximize their own profits. Small winemakers and grape growers couldn't shop around for the best deals because wine house managers often colluded on how much they were willing to pay. The San Francisco merchants "want to monopolize the whole market and try to crush all others by their price-cutting methods," one grower complained.[129]

The problem became particularly acute in the final decade of the nineteenth century. The Panic of 1893, the worst financial crisis the country had suffered in twenty years, prompted the closure of banks and railroads throughout the United States. Hardly anyone was making a profit on anything, including wine. There was a bumper crop that year as all the vineyards that had been planted in the 1880s to take advantage of France's phylloxera misfortunes produced millions of tons of grapes. The huge harvest drove down prices. Grape growers had trouble finding buyers. When they did, the prices were calamitous. Grapes that sold for twenty-five dollars a ton in 1884 only fetched from six to eight dollars a ton in 1893.

Winemakers received just seven cents a gallon for the wine they sold to the wine houses, making wine cheaper than milk. That was less than a one-cent profit per gallon of wine. The wine merchants, though, would then resell the same product for about fifty-three cents a gallon, pocketing the difference. The farmers resented the wine houses' strong-arm tactics and price collusion.

Wine houses claimed they weren't making much money, either. They constantly undercut one another's prices until wine in New Orleans was going for less than it cost to make.

"Competition is said to be the life of trade, but as a fact it is largely the death of the wine business," read an article in an industry paper in May.

Drastic action was needed.

CHAPTER FOURTEEN

THE WINE WAR

From the outside, Percy Morgan seemed like an unlikely candidate to rescue the California wine business. An Englishman by birth, an accountant by training, and a mining executive by choice, Morgan didn't know much about wine. Yet in 1894, he accomplished the seemingly impossible task of bringing together seven of the leading wine houses in San Francisco—all of whom competed fiercely against one another—to form the California Wine Association, or CWA. Its name suggested it was a trade association, but it was in fact a company that at its height controlled 80 percent of the wine production in the state.[130] The CWA wielded tremendous power—and yielded tremendous profits—and would elevate the reputation of California's wine to new heights until Prohibition decimated the industry.

But Morgan and the six other men sitting around a table in a law office on Pine Street in San Francisco on August 10, 1894, couldn't have foretold the future.[131] All they knew was the wine business was in terrible straits. The market was glutted with grapes. Prices had plummeted. And no one was making any money.

Sacrifice and a tolerance for risk were needed to save the industry. The men knew they had to take a bold step, one that subsumed their individual companies and fortunes into a bigger entity. They weren't alone in their vision. Trade papers and other influential business leaders had been crying out for months for someone, something, to seize control and regulate a business that was draining money from people's pockets.

Just a day earlier the seven men had filed papers to incorporate as the California Wine Association. The seven wine houses—Kohler & Frohling, B. Dreyfus & Co., Charles Carpy & Co., Arpad Haraszthy & Co., Kohler & Van Bergen, and the Napa Valley Wine Company—had pooled all their assets into the new concern in return for shares of stock for the new company.

By banding together, the new company instantly dominated the California wine business. Its assets included dozens of vineyards around the state, from Napa and Sonoma counties in the north, to Alameda and Santa Clara counties on the south end of San Francisco Bay, to vineyards in Orange and San Bernardino counties, including the Cucamonga Vineyard. There were thirteen wineries to crush, press, and store wine, including Greystone Wine Cellar in St. Helena, a spectacular three-story stone cellar that used gravity to process its wines, Tokay Vineyards and Winery in Glen Ellen, and the Scandinavian Colony Winery in Fresno, among others. There were cooper shops and bottling departments. The company also had relationships with merchants from New York to New Orleans, and shipping contracts to Europe, Mexico, and Central America. The CWA's assets were valued at $2.75 million.[132]

With his aquiline nose, receding hairline, and large bushy brown mustache, Percy Morgan was definitely the odd man out at the table. Unlike his new CWA colleagues, he had never planted a grape or fermented a batch of wine in his life. But Morgan was a number cruncher, a man who brought a clear eye to the profit and loss statements of the various wine houses. He could see that consolidation was the only answer to the problem. Perhaps his distance from the wine business gave him an advantage over those mired in its details.

There was no doubt of Morgan's brilliance. He had passed Oxford University's junior candidate scholarship examination at the age of thirteen. In 1881, at just nineteen, he was sent to America to work as a book-keeper at the Kingston Mine in Austin, Nevada. The change from crowded cosmopolitan London to a silver boom town on the high desert must have been jarring. But Morgan embraced the opportunities available in the developing West. He would spend the next few years as an accountant for various mining firms in some of the most isolated and mountainous territory around.

A photo taken of Morgan in 1885 shows a fresh-faced young man with a mild countenance and a calm demeanor. Morgan, who was then twenty-three, is standing in a snowy field on a snowy day, wrapped in a huge overcoat that reaches down almost to his ankles and envelops his slim frame. His face is open, unconcerned, and he stares off into the horizon. He looks like an innocent abroad.

Behind the boyish exterior, however, was a man who refused to be intimidated. That same year, after two "miscreants"[133] known as Red River Dick and "Dunk" McGregor terrorized Cooke City, Montana, by shooting their way through town, Morgan organized a vigilante committee to send a posse after the bandits.[134] Morgan also possessed the presence of mind to once find his way home through a raging blizzard by following a telegraph line.[135]

Morgan moved to California in 1886, an experienced accountant who intended to branch out into advising businesses. After working for a time in "steam boating" on the Sacramento and San Joaquin rivers, he joined companies that were developing electrical devices, telephones,[136] and a water system in Berkeley.[137]

Morgan would be best remembered for his key role in the birth of the California Wine Association. Although he initially focused on the company's accounts, he soon became general manager.

The CWA set up its headquarters in the Kohler & Frohling wine house in San Francisco. It was a building designed to wow. Built in 1890 by the sons of Charles Kohler, the musician and wine merchant who started the Anaheim wine colony and who was the first to market California wine in New York, the brick building on the corner of Second and Folsom streets stood three stories tall and was capped by a tower with a cupola. One newspaper called the structure "the finest in San Francisco"[138] and another complimented it for its "harmonious proportions."[139] Inside, hundreds of oak casks were lined up on the main floor. Four 18,000-gallon redwood casks stood in the basement for blending, as did a cooper shop where workmen made casks and barrels. Hydraulic elevators lifted grapes and wine to every floor. The large building radiated strength, confidence, and, perhaps, the ability to crush smaller rivals.

It's no surprise that not every one was pleased by the formation of the CWA, which trade papers began to refer to as "The Syndicate." If growers had difficulty getting a decent price for their grapes in the past when the wine houses competed with one another, what would happen now that seven had merged into one? There were still some independent wine houses remaining, but growers were worried.

So the growers formed their own large entity that November, the California Wine-Makers' Corporation. The grape growers intended to use their collective might to insist on higher grape prices. Within a few months, more than 160 grape growers had signed up to join the Corporation, as they referred to it.[140]

One of the driving forces behind the Corporation—and a man who would soon face off against Morgan—was Pietro C. Rossi, a thirty-nine-year-old university-trained chemist and pharmacist who immigrated to San Francisco in 1875. Within six years he found himself overseeing the wine operations of an agricultural cooperative called the Italian Swiss Colony located in Asti in northern Sonoma County. Rossi, like Morgan, had no previous experience making wine. But he understood chemistry. Using his laboratory skills as a guide, Rossi soon insisted on clean vats, controlled fermentations, and temperature control, efforts that propelled Italian Swiss Colony into the forefront of winemakers in California. Under Rossi's leadership, the company expanded its vineyards, established its own storage cellars in San Francisco, and set up wholesale accounts with merchants across the country. No wonder, then, that he bristled at the threat posed by the humungous CWA to his and other growers' financial independence.

While the Italian Swiss Colony and a few other vineyardists, like Isaac de Turk of Santa Rosa, were large and powerful, most members of the

Corporation were small farmers with modest vineyards, men who had struggled to survive the ravages of phylloxera and prices that dropped to six dollars a ton for grapes. When they had negotiated over the years with the powerful wine merchants in San Francisco, they found they had no leverage. Many wine men were frustrated that they saw little profit for their work. That led them to join forces with the Corporation.

At first the two sides seemed well matched. After an intense negotiation, the CWA agreed in 1895 to pay a decent price: twelve and a half cents a gallon for the 1894 vintage. The CWA even proposed a long-term contract guaranteeing to purchase 5 million gallons of wine a year in the next three years at a price to be mutually agreed upon. The CWA also announced it would stop making wine and focus instead on sales and marketing. An ecstatic Corporation agreed, in exchange, to lease the CWA's vineyards and wineries. The deal meant that the CWA would get the wine it needed to sell, and the grape growers would get the prices they needed to thrive.

"It pays to organize," an exultant Rossi told the newspapers. Rossi, with his brown hair and mustache and soulful brown eyes, had worked harder than anyone else to bring the grape growers together. "We know our power and so did the wholesale men. We can understand and respect each other and as a result we can do business on an equitable basis. It is no longer a fight, each trying to get the better of one another."

Soon prices for both wine and grapes increased substantially. Winemakers who had only gotten seven cents a gallon for their *vin ordinaire* in 1893 realized twenty cents a gallon in 1896. Those selling Cabernet saw their wine sell for twenty-five cents a gallon, up from twelve cents. Grape prices went from $6 to $20 a ton, and up to $25 or $26 for the best grapes.[141] "After a long period of depression, of overproduction, of pest-infected vineyards, mortgages and of low prices, better times have come,"[142] read one editorial.

But cooperation soon faltered. Three months after signing a contract, the CWA and the Corporation started fighting again. The two sides couldn't agree on a price for the next vintage. When the Corporation demanded fifteen cents a gallon, the CWA turned it down. The

Corporation retaliated by cancelling its contracts to rent the CWA's vineyards and wineries.

By early 1897, the CWA and the Corporation were battling in court and on the shelves of markets and streets of cities around the country. Each side looked for every opportunity to squash the other. "The war has begun and will be carried out to the bitter end," said Morgan. "There will be no compromise."[143]

One of the most heated battles took place in New Orleans. The Louisiana city had always been cosmopolitan. Founded by the French in 1718, settled by many Jews and Germans in the 1840s, the city had a polyglot population that loved wine. New Orleans's love for the beverage had deepened in 1878 when yellow fever ravaged the area, killing more than 180 people and as many as 20,000 in the lower Mississippi Valley. Panicked inhabitants blamed the disease on the city's inadequate sewer system, which allowed mosquitos carrying the disease to breed. People turned from drinking water to drinking California wine. By the late 1890s, New Orleans was the second largest export market for California, consuming almost as much as New York. Wholesale grocers and San Francisco wine houses with branches in New Orleans sold 90,000 to 110,000 gallons each year. That was around one barrel for every three inhabitants.[144]

The New Orleans market was lucrative, and the CWA had no intention of losing its dominance there. Morgan, in his most aggressive tactic to date, wanted to make sure the Corporation couldn't afford to sell its wine there. He reduced the price of the wine the CWA sold in New Orleans by five cents, to twenty-two cents a gallon. That price would be disastrous for members of the Corporation.

The Corporation refused to be bowed. If it couldn't sell its wine to the CWA, it would find other buyers, merchants who weren't embroiled in the war. Rossi and other leaders struck a deal with the A. Marschall Company of New York. The company agreed to purchase 2 million gallons of wine for eighteen cents a gallon—more than the Corporation had wanted from the CWA. A. Marschall also took out an option to purchase 1.5 million gallons more.

The CWA retaliated. It started to sell wine on the East Coast for less than the eighteen cents A. Marschall had paid. That meant the New York firm had no incentive to exercise its option and get even more wine from the Corporation.

What followed was a race to the bottom with the CWA and Corporation rushing to offer the lowest prices in a dangerous gambit to capture the largest market share. With millions of gallons of wine stored in its warehouses, and the financial backing of the powerful wine houses, the CWA could afford a price war. The Corporation, in contrast, still had to pay its growers for the wine they produced, which became increasingly difficult as prices declined. Prices dropped to seventeen cents a gallon. Then fifteen cents. Then thirteen and a half cents. Then ten cents a gallon.

"There seems no longer any doubt whatever but that the present wine fight will be one to the death," read one editorial.[145]

Throughout the war, Morgan denied that the CWA was attempting to crush its rivals, although, that, in fact, was exactly what it was doing. "We haven't done any cutting, are not doing any cutting, and don't propose to cut. We do make cuts but we meet those of our competitors."[146]

The Corporation decided the only way it would survive was to become more like the CWA. Rossi conceived a plan to allow the Corporation to store more of its members' wine in bulk, which would give it time to find new markets in which to sell. It took out a lease at the Pioneer Warehouse on Eighth and Bryant streets in San Francisco and converted it into a storage facility that could hold 1.5 million gallons.[147] In August of 1897, Rossi announced that the Italian Swiss Colony would build the largest wine storage tank in the world at its property at Asti: a 500,000-gallon concrete storage tank, which could hold an equivalent of 2.5 million bottles of wine. The tank was twenty-four feet high, eighty feet long, and thirty-four feet wide, with a glazed surface to prevent the wine from contamination.[148] That fall it was filled with a bumper crop of wine.

The next spring, after the red wine in the vat had been shipped to stores, restaurants, and grocers, Rossi threw an elegant party inside the vat to advertise the Italian Swiss Colony's recent successes. He chartered a train to carry 100 guests from San Francisco north to Asti. The party-goers, who included some State Supreme Court justices, members of the San Francisco Board of Supervisors, and foreign officials, boarded the train at 7:30 a.m. for the two-hour ride. When they disembarked, they were led through a grape arbor that stretched a quarter mile to eat lunch among the vines, sitting at tables decorated with white linen and crystal.

Then they went to the aboveground storage vat, which one news-paper said resembled "one of the Pyramids of Egypt with the top sliced off." Four sets of concrete staircases led to a roof garden with meander-ing gravel paths, a stone fountain, and flowerbeds. Guests descended into the vault via a spiral staircase to a dark and cool interior with walls stained a dark red from the wine once stored inside. One paper described the atmosphere as "lurid." A band played Strauss waltzes and the celebrants danced away deep underground.[149]

Elegant luncheons among the vineyards may be commonplace in the twenty-first century, but they were unusual when Rossi wined and dined many of the city's opinion makers. He may have earned their gratitude, but the party did nothing to lessen Morgan's and CWA's determination to smash the Corporation and seize control of the California wine in-dustry.

It took the courts to settle the bitter and protracted fight. In October 1898, Judge George Bahars of the San Francisco Superior Court ruled on competing lawsuits that the California Wine Association and the Wine-Makers' Corporation had filed against each other in early 1897. The judge split his ruling, declaring that the CWA and the Corporation had both violated their contracts with each other. Although the judge levied a heftier fine on the Corporation, his ruling gave each side a win, so they both saved face. It was enough to prod them to settle their dif-ferences.

On December 15, 1898, after the two sides reached a private agreement, order was restored. The CWA agreed to buy 5 million gallons for 12.5 to 15 cents a gallon—a price the growers could live with.

"After a two years' contest, marked by the use of every weapon known in commercial warfare, and by bitterly fought litigation, the end has come," remarked the *Pacific Wine and Spirit Review.*

The wine war was over.

The Corporation went out of business a short time later. The CWA had won.

CHAPTER FIFTEEN

EARTHQUAKE AND FIRE

The jolt on April 18, 1906, came at 5:13 a.m. Deep under the ocean, miles off the coast of San Francisco, two massive tectonic plates slipped past each other, letting loose shock waves that traveled 7,000 miles an hour through rock and dirt, swamps and hills. Seconds later, the tremor reached San Franciscans as they slumbered. The first shock lasted forty seconds and threw people out of their beds. Then came a ten-second pause. The second spasm lasted twenty-five seconds and it sent pictures, chimneys, and brick facades crashing to the ground. After a series of shudders, the earth went still again.

In the south of Market area, the earthquake shook loose tens of thousands of oak wine casks stored in the wine houses that crowded the area. Some casks had been stacked as high as the ceilings, yet they tumbled down like a house of cards, spilling their vinous contents. Large tanks holding thousands of gallons of wine cracked open as well, sending red rivers of wine into the streets.

Percy Morgan, like most everyone living in San Francisco, was shaken by the temblor and must have rushed from his home on Buchanan Street to survey the damage.[150] When he reached Third and Bryant streets, Morgan would have seen that the facade of the California Wine Association headquarters, with its proud tower, was damaged. Bricks lay in a heap on the sidewalk below. Dust from falling debris obscured the rising sun. But while many barrels had busted open, the majority of the wine stored in the Association's storage cellars was unharmed.

But what the earthquake had left untouched, the fires would destroy.

By early afternoon on Wednesday, April 18, 1906, San Francisco was an inferno. For the next three days, as shocked city dwellers wandered, dazed, through the parks, dragging their meager possessions, or rushed to the ferry building to get on a boat out of town, the city burned. There was no water to fight the fires, since the underground pipes of the Spring Valley Water Company had broken in soft ground. No amount of dynamiting by troops seemed to stop the fire's progress. The industrial area south of Market went first, followed by downtown with its massive banks, office towers, and hotels. Flames obliterated the Nob Hill mansions of the men who had built the railroads, as well as the ornate homes of the lesser merchants lining tony Van Ness Avenue.

There was little water, but there was wine. Up on Telegraph Hill and in North Beach, some determined Italian immigrants used the barrels of their homemade wine to stave off the flames.

The Italian Swiss Colony was able to save its three-year-old brick cellar at Battery and Greenwich streets through ingenuity and muscle. There was a spring on the property and the company's founder, Andrea Sbarboro, an Italian from Genoa, rushed down from Asti after the earthquake. When he arrived, he ordered his workers to jury-rig a hose to pump water from the spring-fed well. They sprayed the cellar's walls and laid down a puddle on the roof.

"We fought unceasingly for three days and three nights," Sbarboro later recalled. They managed to save the two million gallons of wine in the cellar.[151]

Most other wine houses were not as lucky. By Saturday, when the flames were finally extinguished, twenty-eight of San Francisco's thirty-one wine houses were smoldering wrecks of twisted metal and blackened bricks. The remains of the huge tanks that had held the 1905 vintage lay underneath feet of debris. About 12 to 15 million gallons of wine had been ruined. Sbarboro told the newspapers that the lost wine was worth about $3.5 million,[152] equal to about $93 million in 2013 dollars. It was the largest natural disaster ever to hit the wine industry.

The California Wine Association bore the brunt of the loss. The company had expanded considerably since the wine war of the late 1890s. In 1900, it acquired a half interest in three of the state's largest wine concerns: Lachman & Jacobi,[153] C. Schilling wine company, and Italian Swiss Colony, whose leaders eventually concluded it was easier to join the CWA than fight it. Then in 1901, three prominent bankers, Isaias Hellman, whose Cucamonga Vineyard was already under the CWA's management, Daniel Meyer, and Antoine Borel invested $1 million in the CWA, allowing them to assume a controlling interest in the organization. Henry Huntington, the nephew of one of the Big Four builders of the transcontinental railroad and a tycoon in his own right, would also soon invest. The capital infusion allowed Morgan to go on a buying spree unseen in the history of the business. The CWA would eventually control fifty-two wineries and vineyards spreading out over 100,000 acres—half of the vineyards in the state. By 1902, it produced 30 million gallons, or 68 percent of the wine made in California.[154] Its storage facilities were vast.

CWA's size had allowed it to improve the overall quality of wine in California by blending it to a standard level in its central cellars in San Francisco. Once it had made sure of its product, CWA started to aggressively market its Calwa brand, whose trademark seal featured a young Bacchus, the Roman god of wine, and a California bear standing on the prow of a ship.

The losses from the fire were staggering. Morgan estimated that 10 million gallons of the company's wine had spilled or burned. The fire was so intense that it obliterated casks and melted glass.

"To give an idea of the heat to which these bottles were subjected, it can be stated that they were packed in rows in racks, and that of the first five rows, all were melted into a solid mass of glass," a reporter wrote in the "Calamity Edition" of the *Pacific Wine and Spirits Review.* "Only one of five retained corks; the rest blew with the sudden expansion of the liquid."[155]

Morgan soon heard that some of the company's other properties had been seriously damaged. The huge brick I. Turk Winery in Santa Rosa was a total loss, like most of the brick buildings in that city. The Brun & Chaix winery in Oakville was also seriously damaged.[156]

One of Percy Morgan's biggest regrets was the destruction of thousands of bottles of wine the company had been storing for ten or more years. The notion of aging California wine was new, and Morgan had intended to show those on the East Coast that California wines, like French wines, could develop with time. That dream now had to be deferred.

But as in most disasters, new opportunities emerged. The wine in the basement of CWA's headquarters on Third and Bryant had spilled out of its casks. But a plugged sewer line had prevented the wine from flowing into the street and the concrete cellar inadvertently turned into a 2-million-gallon wine vat. After the flames had passed and the twisted timbers had cooled, one of CWA's men came up with a way to save that wine. Louis Wetmore, who was in charge of the company's George West & Son winery in Stockton, rented barges from around the bay and had them towed by steamer to San Francisco. Workmen cut a hole into the side of the wine house, and Wetmore somehow convinced members of the busy fire department to pump the wine through 2,000 feet of pipe laid down on Bryant Street toward barges on the bay. The barges were then towed to the El Pinal winery in Stockton and other river cities, where the scorched wine was turned into brandy. CWA rescued about 1.5 to 2 million gallons of wine this way.[157]

The CWA was also able to save 35,000 bottles from one of its cellars. Despite the fact the wine was exposed to high heat, the company decided that the wine was still sound. The CWA offered it as a souvenir of the conflagration. "These wines by reason of tremendous superheating and slow cooling have developed marvelous qualities," claimed Morgan in an advertisement that was reprinted in the newspapers. "In richness of bouquet and body and color, they are probably the finest wines ever produced in California. Of course this is a very expensive way to produce fine wines, and the Association will certainly not endeavor to repeat their success in this way. However the wines will be cased and specially labeled and sold throughout the United States as souvenirs of the great conflagration."

The earthquake forced the wine houses to rethink their operations. For the previous twenty-five years, ever since the grape-planting boom of the 1880s, the center of the wine business had been in San Francisco. Wine was made in outlying areas and shipped to the city to be blended and stored. San Francisco's temperate weather, with its cool summer fogs, made it an ideal place to age wine, particularly since temperatures in Napa and Sonoma counties often hit 90 or 100 degrees in the summer. The country wine cellars also had to be emptied regularly to make room for the next vintage.[158] The earthquake revealed the downside to that centralization.

Morgan had been frustrated for years by the way the California Wine Association was physically organized. Since the company had started when seven wine houses merged, it had had numerous buildings scattered around San Francisco. Each of them had been allotted a specific function: one held sweet wines, one was used for aging, one for blending, one for storage, and so on. Morgan had long talked about consolidating those facilities as a way to cut costs and increase efficiency. The earthquake gave him that chance.

Morgan wanted to build a showcase, a facility that would demonstrate that the California Wine Association was the most successful wine company in the world. Morgan never used the word monopoly to describe the corporation he had built, even though others did. He preferred "community of interests," a phrase coined by the banker J. P. Morgan (no relation). Congress had passed the Sherman Anti-Trust Act in 1890 to break up trusts that dominated certain industries. Even though the

California Wine Association was "vertically integrated," meaning it controlled winemaking from the field to the grape to the making of wine to distribution, no regulator ever sought its dismantling. Morgan may have gobbled up as many wine concerns as he could buy, but he was strategic. He didn't push wine prices so high that consumers or merchants became outraged.

The CWA also had allowed its various divisions to operate under their own names, giving the illusion that there were many separate wine businesses in the state. That also may have deflected federal scrutiny.

Morgan decided to consolidate all the CWA's operations in one facility. In late 1906, CWA began construction of Winehaven, which would become the world's largest wine depot and would strip away any pretense that the CWA wasn't the mighty muscle of wine. Winehaven crushed more grapes, blended more wine, and shipped more casks than any entity before it. Its dominance lasted until Prohibition. One historian called Winehaven a "city-state," because hundreds of workers lived on the grounds, either in the Winehaven Hotel or in small bungalows scattered around the property. The manager had his own two-story house on a hill with a magnificent view of San Francisco Bay. There was a school for workers' children, a social hall, and a fire station.

Morgan built Winehaven on forty-seven acres on a promontory called Point Molate, which sat at the eastern edge of the bay about four miles from the city of Richmond in Contra Costa County. It was ideally located for sea and rail travel, being next to deep water and numerous rail lines. The company noted this attribute in its slogan, "Where rail and water meet for the worldwide distribution of California wines."

Having just gone through the catastrophe, the directors of the CWA wanted to build a structure that could withstand another major earthquake. The company constructed a brick building that resembled a medieval castle with crenellated parapets and corner towers. Its wine cellar was lined with concrete and could hold 10 million gallons of wine. There were bottling shops, cooperages, a sherry house, and laboratory. A pier that stretched 1,800 feet into the bay allowed casks to be loaded directly onto waiting ships. The rail lines that ran though the property connected directly with the transcontinental railroads.[159]

Construction on Winehaven began just months after the earthquake, but the plant wasn't fully operational until 1908. That year, the company produced 675,000 gallons of wine on site. So much fruit was brought in from the San Joaquin Valley that the railroads had to add two additional freight trains a week.[160] Immigrants started to arrive directly from Italy to work at Winehaven.

When it was completed, Winehaven not only became a critical part of the state's economy, but a popular tourist attraction as well. The CWA had a steamer and it would invite dignitaries on board for a cruise along the bay. They would pull up to the long dock at Winehaven and disembark for a tour and a gourmet lunch overlooking the facilities.

The California Wine Association operated Winehaven for eleven years before the threat of Prohibition prompted the company to shutter the facility in 1919. The company managed to sell about 50 million gallons of wine (the equivalent of seventy-five Olympic size swimming pools) before the sale of wine became illegal, but was left with millions of unsold gallons when the Volstead Act became law on January 16, 1920.

Winehaven remained vacant for more than twenty years. In June 1942, seven months after the U.S.'s entry into World War II, the U.S. Navy seized the property and evicted the Santa Cruz Oil Company, which had purchased the property a few months earlier. The Navy mostly left the Winehaven buildings alone, but installed massive 2.2-million-gallon concrete fuel tanks on the hill to hold aviation and bunker fuel for the Pacific Fleet.[161]

As I was driving the narrow and winding road to Winehaven in the winter of 2010, it occurred to me that its hidden setting was an apt reflection of its hidden history. Even though I had driven past the freeway exit leading to Winehaven hundreds of times on my way to the Richmond–San Rafael Bridge crossing San Francisco Bay, and had even spotted the cluster of brick buildings on my return trips, I never knew what the complex was. I am not alone in this. Winehaven has been off limits to most visitors since 1942 when the Navy seized the property for the war effort. Even after the city of Richmond acquired the land in 2003, access was limited.

But when a developer made plans to transform the old wine complex into an Indian gambling casino, people started to pay attention. That, in fact, is why I was navigating my car over the rutted and narrow road that bright winter day. I was writing about the controversy over the casino.

The road led up and around a ridge, and then dropped to parallel the shoreline. A cyclone fence, rusted and bent in parts, separated most of the road from the property. Off in the distance the bright blue of the bay sparkled in the sun.

I pulled my car into the parking area outside Building 123, a Navy Quonset hut then being used as a security checkpoint. Up ahead, I could see a redbrick building with crenellated towers and a group of other warehouse structures. I was to meet Don Gosney, a former steamfitter and union leader turned photographer, who knew more about Winehaven than anyone else in Richmond. He had been appointed to a Navy board established to examine possible reuses for the old fuel depot. By Gosney's estimates, he had read from 70,000 to 80,000 pages on Winehaven. He not only knew details about the California Wine Association, but about contamination left by the Navy.

Gosney had agreed to lead me on a tour of the shuttered property. As he led me around various buildings and detailed how they had been used over the past century, his love of history was apparent. So was his concern about the fate of the buildings. Richmond was divided over the casino. Some thought the proposed gambling palace and 500-room Marriot Hotel was a travesty. Richmond is largely poor and African American and Latino, and casino opponents expressed concern that poor people would be lured into needlessly spending their money. Others, including Gosney, believed that the casino would create jobs and revenue for the city; in fact the developer promised to pay Richmond $12 million in annual fees. As we walked, he convincingly explained that it would take Las Vegas–style money to restore the buildings at Winehaven.

They had a dilapidated air. One brick building had been condemned. Peeking through the windows I could see that part of the roof had fallen in. The doors and windows of the twenty-nine bungalows built for married workers were covered with plywood. Squatters had slept in the wine-master's house, perched on a hill with a commanding view of the bay. There was a sleeping bag laid out in one tiny closet, with magazines and old drug paraphernalia heaped nearby.

There were times when I felt I was walking through a time warp. The old nuclear fallout shelter set up by the Navy still stood, tucked away in a main building. Rusting cans of tinned drinking water dated 1953 were stacked along one wall, along with folding cots that doubled as stretchers. Five-gallon cardboard sanitation kits stuffed with toilet paper, tampons, deodorant—and a portable toilet seat that could be placed on top to make a commode—sat in another area.

But there was beauty, too, in the old buildings. The brick wine warehouse's rounded towers and crenellated parapets seemed to be straight out of the medieval era. I kept wondering when knights in chain-link armor would pour boiling oil on us below. Huge, red iron beams supported the brick walls and ceiling of the building, and they looked like they would withstand the strongest of earthquakes. The bottom floor, the place where wine was stored, had walls of concrete, including the stairs leading down into the cellar.

I was struck by the size of the place. In the twenty-first century, wineries often market their wine through the story of their founders. It usually involves tales of a couple taking a risk by buying a winery and making it a success through hard work and determination. The key is that these wineries are presented as small, family-owned operations. And in fact, individuals own most of the wineries in Sonoma and Napa County. Of course the corporate wineries, with their millions of gallons of production, overshadow the small places. But in the first decade of the twentieth century, bigness was a virtue. Size conveyed strength and prosperity and hope for a bright future. The California Wine Association had been all about size and dominance.

Now Winehaven, once the world's largest winery, was decaying on the edge of the bay. It was a discard, a place that held relevance long ago, now relegated to the proverbial dustbin of history.

What a blow Prohibition must have been to the California Wine Association. Here it was, the biggest wine concern in the world, a company that had tamed and transformed the California wine industry. Suddenly it was out of business.

Prohibition must have been a shock to Percy Morgan, too. Building Winehaven had exhausted him and in 1911, partly on his doctor's orders, he had resigned from the presidency of the CWA. After his departure, he built a home in Los Altos on the San Francisco Peninsula that resembled a baronial manor. He joined the boards of Wells Fargo Nevada National Bank and Stanford University. He took his family on an extended trip to Europe.

But on the morning of April 16, 1920, Morgan walked down the grand wood staircase of his mansion and into a sitting room right off the front door. He picked up a hunting rifle, sat down on the couch, and blasted a hole through his chest. His young son and wife rushed into the room, but there was nothing they could do. Morgan was dead. He was fifty-eight years old.

The newspapers attributed Morgan's suicide to his despondency over his health. He had been in a car accident two months earlier, and was worried he would never recover completely. Perhaps the accident had shaken Morgan's confidence and willingness to face the new, prohibitionist era, then just three months old. It must have been terrible to know that you had created the world's most successful wine company, a monopoly that restored order to the chaotic and self-destructive California wine industry, and that it had to be dissolved. A change in social attitudes had branded the CWA and other winemaking operations criminal enterprises. For a man who had spent seventeen years promoting California wine and the CWA, that shift must have been difficult to accept.

By 2010, the year I toured Winehaven, Morgan's most lasting legacy, he had been almost completely forgotten. There was not even a Wikipedia page for him or the California Wine Association. Maybe that was appropriate since Morgan and the CWA dealt in wine, a product that was meant to be ephemeral, to be drunk and savored, not kept forever.

I am a history buff, the kind of person who walks down a street and doesn't see the twenty-first-century sign for Starbucks, but thinks back about what store had been in that spot in the nineteenth and early twentieth centuries. So I was grateful to get the chance to walk through Winehaven and contemplate the scale of the wine business up until Prohibition. I could imagine the 400 workers toiling with the huge storage casks, loading barrels onto seagoing ships or rail cars that were traveling cross country. The industrial nature of the enterprise, even though it was long dead, was impressive. I knew then that I wanted to write about the CWA some day, even though only five words about it ever made it into my *New York Times* story about the casino.

By July 1916, the vineyard at Cucamonga looked tired. Many of the Mission vines that spread out over hundreds of acres had been planted almost sixty years earlier when John Rains had expanded his vineyard. The vines were woody and gnarled, leafy in the summer months, but bearing little fruit. As the vineyard had grown less productive, the vines had been allowed to grow whichever way they pleased. They were so tall and overgrown that a horse-drawn cultivator couldn't even traverse the rows.[162]

The vineyard looked "worn out," Jackson Graves, the vice president of the Farmers and Merchants Bank in Los Angeles, wrote to Isaias Hellman.[163] He took care of Hellman's business affairs. For that reason, the CWA had cancelled the lease it had held for ten years on the vineyard, which meant Hellman once again resumed control of the 580-acre property. "It looked like a place with a mortgage on it, weeds rank, and a general air of dilapidation," wrote Graves.[164]

Graves cast around for a future for the depleted vineyard. A number of wine men in the region came calling, men like Secondo Guasti, whose nearby Italian Vineyard Company would one day span 5,000 acres, making it the largest contiguous vineyard in the world. Guasti offered to rent the land for $1,500 for one year. Graves turned him down. Then Guasti offered to buy 1,100 acres for $100 an acre.[165] Graves turned him down a second time. He thought the land was worth about $350 an acre.[166]

"I suppose it will be necessary to take out these vines," Graves wrote to Hellman. "There are between three and four hundred acres of them. To do it by hand will cost a little fortune."

It would also be extremely difficult. The roots of the Mission grapes extended deep into the ground, perhaps as far as ten feet, little voyagers in search of water. For more than a half century they had anchored themselves in the sandy dirt of Rancho Cucamonga, and they would not be easy to extract.

Graves had heard that the trustees of Stanford University had a similar problem with the vines at Vina Ranch. The trustees needed to uproot 2,500 acres, and they purchased a special machine for the job, a tractor that pulled a "snaking apparatus," that dug out the vines below the surface.

"The machine works something like a road-scraper, has a knife that sinks two feet underground and cuts the vines off there," wrote Graves. "Mr. Stowe told me that he removed 25 acres a day with it, at a slight expense, whereas to grub them up by hand would cost $25.00 an acre. I don't think the Stanford estate will ask us very much for the old machine."[167]

The machine from Stanford's old vineyard arrived by train to Rancho Cucamonga in early January 1917. It had rained heavily that month and the ground was so saturated that work couldn't start immediately. The man in charge of uprooting the vineyard, Mr. Stowe, only got going on the job a few weeks later. He drove the machine through the old vines, ripping and tugging them from the ground. In the first three days, he took out forty acres. "Our vines are so big, much bigger, I guess, than this machine ever tackled, that there is some difficulty in getting rid of the vines after they are dug up," Graves wrote Hellman. "So we had to put two Mexicans on the job to grab a vine as quick as it is cut off and pull it out of the way. This allows the machine to go ahead without stopping."[168]

It took the foreman three months to remove all the grapevines from the vineyard.

I was sitting in the reading room of the Huntington Library in San Marino, California, when I read Graves's letters about the old machine rented from Stanford University. It was astonishing to learn specific details about the demise of the vineyard, one that had been planted during the rancho era of the *Californios* and ended seventy-eight years later in the middle of World War I. Just a few years later, Prohibition would put a different kind of end to the California wine industry.

When I read Graves's description of the vines' tenacity, I gave a silent cheer. Good for them to protest their destruction, I thought, and to cling with their roots to life as long as possible. I liked the idea that the grapevines that had been planted before California was part of the United States had resisted their death. I doodled on my notebook: "RIP: 1839–1917."

PART FIVE

DECEPTION

CHAPTER SIXTEEN

THEFT AND DECEPTION

In December 2003, Samuel Maslak's tortuous court case over the bankruptcy of his South San Francisco restaurant was nearing resolution. It was time to sell his wine and distribute the funds. Maslak had hired the London-based Christie's to auction off the restaurant's collection. Christie's had a good reputation in the wine world, and selling a wine collection through the company signaled its excellence. Maslak hired a trucking company to pick his wine up from Sausalito Cellars so the Christie's wine experts could catalogue it.

But the driver who pulled his big truck up to the loading dock of Sausalito Cellars faced a surprise. Maslak had told him he would be picking up around 756 cases of wine. But when the driver arrived, Anderson said there was much less wine—a total of just 144 cases. Baffled, and not sure what to do, the driver left Sausalito. As soon as he arrived at the office he alerted his supervisor to the discrepancy.

When Maslak heard the news he was furious. How could Anderson claim he had not left 756 cases worth around $650,000 at Sausalito Cellars, especially since he had been spending $600 a month for the privilege? How could some of them "disappear"?

Maslak immediately called Anderson to demand an explanation. But the answers he received made him even angrier. Anderson spun wild tales about the missing cases, one so complicated and convoluted it was hard to follow. In Maslak's mind, the transaction was simple: he had dropped off 756 cases of French Bordeaux, Burgundy, and many California varietals in May 2001. Now he wanted them back.

That would not be possible, Anderson insisted. When they had first communicated, he had gone to the restaurant to look at the wine cellar to estimate the scope of the contract. When he arrived, the wine cellar was in disarray with bottles out of boxes stacked on shelves, Anderson claimed. Anderson offered to box the wine, but Maslak decided to do it himself—meaning that the bottles were all jumbled together when they arrived at Sausalito Cellars.[169] Moreover, Sausalito Cellars stored fewer boxes than Maslak contended, according to Anderson. The first driver dropping off cases in 2001 only left 200 cases of wine, not the 756 cases that Maslak remembered, said Anderson. There was no way the old location of Sausalito Cellars could have held so much wine, said Anderson. It was a tiny facility.

And didn't Maslak remember that he had sent someone in December 2002 to pick up about forty cases for a party that he was throwing? He had nothing to do with the missing wine, Anderson insisted.

"I called Mark and said, 'There should be roughly 7,000 bottles of wine,'" Maslak said. "Mark's answer was, 'I was wondering when you were going to deliver (the rest of) those wines for storage.'"[170]

The explanation Anderson provided was lengthy and complicated, full of long-ago actions that didn't quite make sense. Even though he and Maslak had a signed contract stating how much wine Sausalito Cellars would store, Anderson just dismissed what was written on it. This would be his modus operandi during the next few years—offering convoluted explanations for why a client's wine was missing. The wine was there, just not available. Or there had been a flood in the storage cellar and many saturated boxes fell apart, so wine got mixed up. Or it was a case of bad record keeping. Or one of Sausalito Cellars's employees might have taken the wine. It was always someone else's fault, never Anderson's.

Maslak didn't believe a word Anderson said. In the two and a half years Maslak's wine had been at Sausalito Cellars, Anderson had never once mentioned that some of it had not been delivered. And Maslak, a successful businessman who lived in a spacious home in Woodside, a tony suburb south of San Francisco, was not the kind of guy who let himself get hoodwinked.

So one cool gray December day in 2003, Maslak drove to the headquarters of the Sausalito Police Department, then operating out of a trailer near the waterfront. It was a small police operation with fewer than twenty-five officers, a department that spent most of its time dealing with tourist theft, burglaries, and parking issues. When Maslak walked in and started talking to Sgt. William Fraass, a second-generation Sausalito police officer, he kicked off one of the biggest investigations ever launched by the department. Solving it would demand many years of Fraass's attention.

Two months later, Fraass had enough information to file criminal embezzlement charges against Anderson. On February 25, 2004, the Marin County district attorney's office filed one felony count of embezzlement against Anderson. No warrant was issued for his arrest; instead the court sent Anderson a letter informing him of the charges and ordering him to appear in court.

On March 17, 2004, Anderson drove north from his Sausalito apartment to the Marin County Civic Center, a landmark building with distinctive blue roof that had been Frank Lloyd Wright's last commission. Anderson's back was bothering him so he slowly made his way up to the "C" floor, where courtrooms lined the hallway. His attorney, Douglas Horngrad, was there to represent him. Dorothy Proudfoot was the deputy district attorney for the prosecution. Anderson entered a "not guilty" plea.

Three months later, Jack Rubyn, president of the Marin chapter of the International Food and Wine Society, went to Sausalito Cellars to pick up some bottles of Château Cheval Blanc for a vertical tasting of the prized Bordeaux varietal. The group had been started in 1996 and its 600 members met numerous times a year to drink and feast and revel in the sense of community that wine appreciation could bring. The members always gathered at top restaurants. In 1997, for example, the society had hosted two meals at Alice Waters's Chez Panisse in Berkeley, the restaurant credited with launching the nation's push for fresh and local ingredients, as well as a luncheon at the French Laundry, Thomas Keller's Michelin three-star restaurant in Yountville. The Society also hosted a party to celebrate Julia Child's birthday at Roland Passant's Left Bank in Larkspur.

Anderson was a longtime member of the club. There was nothing he liked better than sitting around a table, eating delicious food, drinking excellent wine, and talking with friends. Over the years he and Rubyn had become close—so close that Rubyn agreed to move the society's wines into Sausalito Cellars. Anderson had fenced off a section of the storage facility and told Rubyn that he would be the only one with a key.

Because Anderson was a trusted, longtime member of the group, the International Food and Wine Society had placed a number of its best wines in Styrofoam packaging on shelves in the rear portion of Sausalito Cellars. But when Rubyn entered the area that June day, he noticed that the containers, each marked with a unique identification number, were out of order.[171] He opened a case that was supposed to contain a magnum of 1929 Cheval Blanc. It was empty. He then reached for the container that should have held a magnum of 1959 Cheval Blanc. It, too, was missing. An increasingly worried Rubyn also discovered that a 1961 Cheval Blanc was not in its container. Pale with shock—after all, he considered Anderson a close friend—Rubyn found wine in boxes that it should not have been in, and more wine missing from where it should be.

Rubyn returned to Sausalito Cellars the next day and discovered that a box that should have contained a jeroboam (equivalent to six bottles) of 1995 Musigny-Vogue worth about $2,600 "looked odd." Instead of the fine French wine, Rubyn found a jeroboam of Estancia Chardonnay nestled inside. It was worth about $50. That wine did not belong to the Society. Other large-format bottles, including a 1959 jeroboam of Château Lafite Rothschild valued at $29,000, were also missing. All told, 482 bottles, worth $282,289, were not where they were supposed to be.

The next day Rubyn went down to the Sausalito police station and filed a report.

News of the embezzlement charges reached across San Francisco Bay in mid-June. John Fox, the owner of Premier Cru, a retail wine store and auction business in Emeryville, was disturbed. His company had been buying wine from Anderson for more than two years, and Fox had to consider the possibility that some of it might have been stolen. Fox was concerned his company's reputation would be tainted if customers learned they had purchased stolen wine. Fox contacted Anderson and told him his business was no longer welcome. The last transaction between Premier Cru and Anderson was on June 7, 2004.

The news was a blow to Anderson. He was increasingly dependent on his illegal wine sales. While he had relied on his father's largesse for decades, his father's bank account had finally dried up. He couldn't lend his son any more money. Sausalito Cellars wasn't bringing in much cash, either. Anderson's clients had started cancelling their contracts when they heard about the embezzlement charges. Anderson was now behind in his rent for the large space at 30 Libertyship Way.

But Anderson thought he might be able to get around Premier Cru's banishment. It was simple, really. All he had to do was use a different name.

Anderson had long associated the word "Kansai" with wine. After all, he had learned so much about wine when he hung out with the group of Japanese businessmen in the 1980s. They had dubbed themselves the Kansai Wine Club, named after a region in the southern-central section of the main island of Japan. So Anderson created a new entity, "Kansai Partners," with which to sell wine. Anderson sent off an email to Premier Cru offering the store twenty-four bottles of high-end French wine.

On June 14—just a week after telling Anderson his business was no longer welcome—Premier Cru purchased those twenty-four bottles from Kansai Partners for $34,800.[172]

Anderson needed another place to sell the purloined wine, some place well out of town that had never heard about his embezzlement charges. Anderson settled on the Chicago Wine Company, a well-regarded auction house. But to be sure, he approached the auction house not as Mark Anderson, but as Kansai Partners. On September 29, 2004, the Chicago Wine Company purchased forty-five cases of wine from Kansai.

Despite all these sales, Anderson found himself $5,000 behind in rent at Sausalito Cellars. His relationship with the building's owner and manager had let him postpone his debt, but he needed to find a less expensive alternative to storing his clients' wine than in a Class A office building in Sausalito.

Another business acquaintance of Anderson's, Jack Krystal, a commercial property developer born in Argentina, had opened a large wine storage warehouse on the old Navy base on Mare Island in Vallejo, about thirty-seven miles northwest of Sausalito. Anderson had known Krystal for more than a decade, mostly through Chamber of Commerce events and other business gatherings, and they were friendly. Anderson had been with Krystal the day he and his business partners took over the lease for the former Navy warehouse they planned to turn into a fine wine storage facility.

Mare Island was the first naval station on the West Coast, opening in 1851. It had once been a bustling naval hub teeming with service men and those who repaired Navy ships and submarines. But the Navy moved out in 1996 after a 143-year occupation, leaving behind a collection of concrete bunkers, huts, and miles of cracked pavement. Lennar Corporation had won the right to redevelop the land for the city of Vallejo.

Krystal and his three partners had been looking to start a boat storage company when they toured Building 627 on Mare Island. They were impressed with what they saw. The warehouse was huge, around 600 feet long and 300 feet wide, with large rolling doors and numerous loading docks. Rumor had it that the parts for Little Boy, the atomic bomb dropped on Hiroshima in 1945, had been stored in that warehouse, but that may have only been an urban myth. What was provable was that the USS *Indianapolis* had stopped by Mare Island during World War II and had picked up a top-secret payload it then carted to Tinian in the Northern Marian Islands where the A-bomb was assembled. Four days after delivering the atomic bomb, a Japanese submarine torpedoed the USS *Indianapolis*, killing 200 and tossing 880 men into the ocean. The men had to tread water and fight off vicious shark attacks for five days before they were rescued. Only 317 sailors survived.

When Krystal and his partners saw the space, they jettisoned their plans for a boat storage business and decided to start a wine storage business instead. Vallejo was ideally situated: it sat at the intersection of a number of highways connected to San Francisco, Sacramento, Napa, and Sonoma. It was also close to the railroad. There was also an increasing demand for wine storage services. Land was so expensive in Napa and zoning restrictions so tight that there weren't many storage facilities near the bulk of the wineries; instead they were clustered at the southern end of the valley and places like Vallejo.

The men's vision was big: they not only wanted to offer storage of wine cases, but of barrels of wine. They wanted to purchase a wine trucking company so they could pick up and drop off deliveries. They wanted to offer wine tastings to lure in retail customers. They wanted Wines Central to cater to small and large wineries, from one-person operations to corporate giants that produced 100,000 cases a year. And since the warehouse's walls were three feet thick, they marketed the building as particularly safe from earthquakes, little realizing how the concrete walls would later bake the wine.

Wines Central was successful from the start. Krystal and his partners attracted a number of large corporate clients, including Sterling Vineyards and Beaulieu Vineyards. There were small clients as well, such as Sinskey Vineyards, an organic and biodynamic vineyard on the Silverado Trail, and Saddleback Cellars, whose owner, Nils Venge, had earned the nickname "King of Cab."

Sean Thackrey was attracted to Wines Central because he thought the three-foot-thick walls of the former naval bunker would be indestructible in an earthquake. Amazon Ranch liked the place because its rents were reasonable. None of the winemakers thought to inquire if Wines Central had fire sprinklers. It didn't.

Since Anderson needed to leave his Sausalito cellar, he rented Bay 14, a 2,500-square-foot space on the second-floor mezzanine in an area reserved for individual collectors and special collections. Anderson got permission to erect a chain-link fence to segregate Sausalito Cellars' wine from the rest of the wine on the mezzanine, allowing him complete control over his space. No one else had that privilege. Anderson's storage space was directly above the space used by Long Meadow Ranch.

Anderson started to transfer his clients' wine from the Libertyship Way facility in Sausalito to Wines Central in the summer of 2004. He was in no hurry to inform his clients about the move; in fact he retained a small office space in his old building so he could keep the same address. By fall, Sausalito Cellars had relocated about 100 pallets of wine, which works out to 5,600 cases or 67,200 bottles.

Pressure on Anderson continued to build. Maslak filed a civil lawsuit against Sausalito Cellars and Anderson on July 23, 2004. Susan Guerguey, the secretary for the Society of Medical Friends of Wine, a group started in 1939 by doctors, nurses, and other medical professionals to explore the medicinal benefits of wine, heard about the embezzlement charges around then. Troubled, she called Anderson and demanded to see the group's wine. To her astonishment, Anderson told her the wine was no longer in Sausalito, but at a warehouse in Vallejo. So Guerguey and the group's president drove to Wines Central. When they arrived, Anderson pointed them to a collection of boxes. Guerguey checked each box off against her inventory and found that a lot of wine was missing. She told Anderson that the society was terminating its contract with Sausalito Cellars immediately. She marched down to the office of Wines Central and arranged to rent some space in the mezzanine—space to which Anderson had no access.

On December 17, 2004, the Marin County district attorney filed four additional embezzlement charges against Anderson, alleging he had stolen 6,600 bottles of wine worth more than $870,000 from his Sausalito Cellars clients. The new charges sparked the local newspaper, the *Marin Independent Journal*, to splash a story about Anderson on the front of its local section. Soon, other clients of Sausalito Cellars started to call wanting to know the whereabouts of their wine.

The year 2005 was *annus horribilis* for Anderson. Ron Lussier, who had been renting space from Anderson for almost four years, heard about the embezzlement charges in January. Lussier called Anderson, who downplayed the situation. Everything was a mix-up, Anderson said. The guy (Maslak) who was complaining hadn't delivered the amount of wine he was now claiming. Lussier didn't care. At that point he wanted out. He and his boyfriend were building a wine cellar in their Sausalito home that could accommodate their wine.

Anderson told Lussier that he could get his wine, but he would have to wait a week. It was only then that Anderson revealed that Lussier's wine was in Vallejo, not Sausalito. Anderson gave a meandering explanation that he was forced to move the wine because of unexpected, and unresolvable, cooling problems in the Sausalito facility.

A week later, Lussier drove in a rented truck to Wines Central. He expected to spend a few hours with Anderson clearing out his collection, and was surprised when Anderson departed, leaving an employee to move Lussier's thirty cases of wine.

Lussier had poured his heart and soul into that collection. In addition to tracking down Sine Qua Non bottle by bottle, Lussier had purchased great California Cabernet Sauvignon from top wineries like Silver Oak, in the Oakville portion of Napa, and Stag's Leap. Every time he made a wine purchase, Lussier thought about the parties he would host for his friends, creating memorable evenings with good food, good wine, and good cheer.

When Lussier returned to his hillside home in Sausalito, he took inventory. It looked like Anderson had returned all his cases. He selected a wooden box that held wines made by Stag's Leap Vineyards from 1992 to 1998. He tried to take off the top. It wouldn't budge. It was glued shut. That was odd, Lussier thought to himself. Lussier got a lever and pried open the top. He was shocked by what lay inside. Instead of six beautiful bottles of Cabernet Sauvignon, made from some of Napa's finest vineyards, worth about $650 each, there were six bottles of Two-Buck Chuck from Trader Joe's. The price for each bottle? Less than two dollars.

"It was painful," said Lussier. "When we bought it we thought we would have a fantastic party one day. We were going to taste it to see how it changed every year."

Lussier called Anderson on the phone and demanded an explanation. Anderson delivered his usual litany of excuses and suggested the wine must have been misplaced when Sausalito Cellars moved to Wines Central in Vallejo.

"The rest of the wine never showed up," said Lussier. Mark "would always mumble excuses. Kind of like street people, he would mumble. He would just go on and on and on." He seemed to put on an endless stream of ever changing excuses.

Lussier went to the police.

On Monday April 25, 2005, Anderson and his girlfriend, Cynthia Witten, were in their apartment along Sausalito's waterfront when there was a loud knock on the door. When Anderson answered, he saw Sausalito Police Department Sergeant Fraass, an agent from the Internal Revenue Service, and a number of Sausalito police officers dressed in SWAT outfits. They had a search warrant for his apartment, his Audi and Cadillac, and his computer.

The officers rushed into the apartment and started opening drawers, filing cabinets, and closets. They looked under the bed, scoured the bookshelves, asked for the car keys to search the cars, and carted off the computer. Some of the material the police carried off shed a suspicious light on Anderson and suggested he was thinking of leaving town. Police found a stack of books on how to disappear, including some with titles like *The Modern Identity Changer* by Sheldon Charrelt; *Bullet Proof Privacy: How to Live Hidden, Happy & Free* by Boston T. Party; *Swiss Bank Accounts and Investment Management* by David Falkayn; and *Hide Your Assets and Disappear: A Step by Step Guide to Vanishing Without a Trace* by Edmund Pankan.[173]

The police also seized check registers, receipts, a printout of an email with the phrase "Missing Wine" at the top, a shipping box labeled Sausalito Cellars, various VHS tapes, including two in an envelope marked "Attorney-Client privilege," and Anderson's and Witten's passports.

The raid indicated the seriousness of the police investigation, but the ratcheted-up pressure did not seem to faze Anderson. About two weeks later, he sent off four pallets of wine worth about $50,000 to Chicago Wine Company.

By this time, the managers at Wines Central were regularly receiving calls about Anderson. Clients who couldn't reach him would call and ask Debbie Polverino to pass on a message or to try to find out when he would be there. Some of the winemakers who stored their wine in the warehouse also started to complain about Anderson to Polverino. They reported that some cases of their wine were missing. They suspected Anderson was the thief.

Anderson was becoming a distraction; his storage bay occupied only a tiny fraction of the 240,000-square-foot business, but he needed a lot of attention. Also, despite repeated requests, Wines Central had still not gotten a detailed inventory of Anderson's collection. As a business practice, Wines Central needed to know what wines were in its possession, regardless of who owned them. The company had more than ninety-five winery clients at that point and forty private collectors. But Anderson gave excuse after excuse about why he hadn't prepared an inventory.[174] And he was also overdue on his $750 a month rent.

On June 5, Anderson met with Jack Krystal, the owner of Wines Central, and Linda Childs Hothem and Scott Hothem, the two owners of Pac-Am, a company that had taken over day-to-day management of

Wines Central in February. They told Anderson he had to move out, and that he had ninety days to do so. However, to put a pretty face on the eviction, they wrote Anderson a letter referring to a "change in business model" at Wines Central, which would affect Sausalito Cellars.

"This letter will serve as official notice to you that no later than September 3 at 5:00 p.m., all products owned or controlled by Sausalito Cellars and/or Mark Anderson must be removed . . ."

Anderson behaved calmly in the meeting, but inwardly seethed. He was furious. He felt snubbed, cast out of a club he had helped create. Not only had Anderson been with Krystal in the warehouse before it became Wines Central, he had looked for people to invest with Krystal, who needed an infusion of cash after he became embroiled in costly litigation with his original partners. Anderson had gotten Orlando Lobo, the owner of the Marinship building where Sausalito Cellars used to be, to take a look at the investment. Lobo passed on the deal. Anderson had then introduced the Hothems to Krystal. They had struck a deal.

Anderson later told Linda Hothem that "he would make things difficult" if the eviction proceeded. He could sue, he told her, for financial hardship. He could claim he hurt his back at Wines Central. Anderson tried to make her feel guilty for his troubles. Then he announced he would never pay Wines Central another cent.[175]

It must have felt as if the world was spinning out of control. Anderson faced trouble on many fronts: he was fighting criminal charges in Marin (two more clients had stepped forward to talk to police), a number of his former clients were suing him, and he needed money to pay his lawyers.

Still, Anderson kept on selling his clients' wine. The day he got a formal letter asking him to leave Wines Central, he sent off another pallet worth $22,700 to the Chicago Wine Company. By now, Bill Mazer, the owner of the auction house Golden West, which had been buying Anderson's wine for a few years, was demanding proof that Anderson had the right to sell wine. While Premier Cru believed it had severed its relationship with Anderson in the middle of 2004, Golden

West had continued to purchase his wine. Anderson wrote Mazer and told him that he had formed a relationship with a new entity not connected to Sausalito Cellars: Kansai Partners. Anderson then offered more wine to Mazer, who cut two checks for Kansai Partners on July 13, 2005—one for $5,000 and another for $6,385.

On September 26, 2005, Anderson sat down before his computer. The world looked bleak. He was now facing numerous embezzlement counts for stealing 8,000 bottles of wine worth $1.1 million. If convicted, he faced a lengthy prison sentence. His business had fallen apart. His friends were avoiding him. The mayor of Sausalito had suggested he resign from his commissions. His father, long a financial spigot, was running out of money. And his younger brother, Steven, declined to even talk to him.

Anderson had always been a good teller of yarns, a man who could smooth away awkwardness with a joke or funny story. But there was no humor in his current situation, no dexterous phrase that could make the trouble go away. Ten days earlier, the Marin County district attorney had filed more embezzlement charges against him. Anderson now faced eleven counts for stealing from his Sausalito Cellars clients. Anderson had been juggling the charges since February 2004, but the law was closing in.

As his mind raced, Anderson began to type. He was looking for a way out, for an end to all his troubles. He needed something that would take care of all his problems at once. A fire would do that. A fire at Wines Central would make it impossible for authorities to prove that the missing wine hadn't burned up.

Anderson began surfing the Internet. He Googled cell phone triggers. Thousands of articles popped up. He scanned some and when he found one that seemed helpful, he saved it to a shortcut on his computer. It joined other articles on how to build time bombs and destruction by fire.[176]

Anderson had been thinking about burning down Wines Central for months. In May, right around the time the owners of Wines Central had told him he would have to vacate his storage bay, he told Jason Greer, one of his employees, that "It would suck for Jack (Krystal) if the whole place went up in flames." The comment was so chilling that it lodged in Greer's memory.[177] Then, a short time later, Anderson said: "Wines Central is old; the wood is brittle, and it would go up in flames easily."

After the fire, when Anderson's name emerged as a suspect, a man— most likely his brother Steven—speculated on his motive. "After being charged with 10 counts of embezzlement, Anderson set the warehouse ablaze in an attempt to destroy the evidence," "Steven" wrote on the website of Moonstone Cellars. "This is how Mark works . . . if he doesn't get his way, he will wreck everything for everybody. Out of Spite. He lit that fire possibly to hide evidence, but knowing him (I am as close as you can get), he was getting back at Wines Central for not rolling over for him like the Sausalito crowd. Yeah, he is that mean. Not Crazy . . . Criminal Mean. And he has not a Scrap of Remorse."

It's remarkable how little it takes to ruin 4.5 million bottles of wine. In the end, it didn't involve cell phone triggers or fancy incendiary devices. All it took was a bucket of gasoline-soaked rags, a plumber's propane torch, and fuel—in this case the Styrofoam, cardboard, and wooden boxes used to protect wine bottles.

No one knows where Anderson bought that plumber's torch, a standard propane torch available in almost any hardware store in the United States. ATF Agent Brian Parker became obsessed with that torch. He spent hours combing every hardware and automotive store near Sausalito he could think of, but didn't turn up a receipt with Mark Anderson's name on it. There was no evidence of the purchase on Anderson's credit card receipts, either.

By October 12, the pressure on Anderson was unrelenting. He had been enduring the scorn of the outside world for close to two years by then. His vaunted position as a member of two city commissions had evaporated. His invitations to feasts that featured wine by the world's great chefs and wine made in the world's great vineyards had dwindled. Even his closest friends, like Yoshi Tome, owner of Sushi Ran, didn't know what to think when they looked at Anderson. Was he a scoundrel, a thief, a con artist? Or was he a man falsely accused?

Something finally snapped. Anderson felt compelled to act, to lash out at all of those who wronged him.

Anderson backed his car out of his driveway on Bridgeway Avenue in Sausalito in the early afternoon and headed north on Highway 101. Hidden in his truck was a bucket inside a duffle bag. The gas-soaked rags were stuffed inside, along with the propane torch. The drive took him past the Marin County towns of Mill Valley, Corte Madera, and San Rafael. When he reached Highway 37, he headed east toward Vallejo, getting off on the Mare Island exit. The trip took less than an hour.

Anderson had been cleaning out his storage locker for a few weeks by then. He had rented more space in a warehouse in American Canyon, just a few miles north. A large truck had hauled away most of the wine Anderson still had from clients, but about seven pallets and a lot of garbage remained.

Wines Central had a peculiar physical layout. To reach the mezzanine, where Anderson's wines and various library wines were stored, visitors had to walk through the office. Anderson arrived in the early afternoon of October 12, although Debbie Polverino, the warehouse manager, did not see him going up the stairs to the mezzanine. But a worker saw Anderson later, cleaning out his storage bay.

It was afternoon in the middle of the harvest, and no one else was on the mezzanine. From his second-floor vantage point, Anderson could have looked down onto the main floor of Wines Central and seen cases of wine stacked up into the distance. The wine that lay in bottles inside cardboard cases reflected hundreds of thousands of hours of work, maybe even millions of hours. Laborers had prepared the ground, planted and tended the vines, and carefully picked the grapes. Winemakers had sorted, crushed, and fermented the fruit, the first steps in the long process to turn the grape juice into an alcoholic liquid that could please, delight, and inebriate. The winemakers tasted and blended wine from different parts of different vineyards to create a signature product, one that expressed their taste and vision.

But Anderson probably didn't give that a moment's reflection.

When he was sure he was alone, Anderson reached into his bag and took out the bucket and gasoline-soaked rags. He pulled the ignition switch on the propane torch and touched the blue flame to cloth. The fire took hold.

The last time Polverino saw Anderson was around 3:15 in the afternoon. Anderson came rushing through the office, sweating profusely, almost galloping through while using his cane as a third leg. She had never seen him move so fast.

The warehouse exploded into flames about twenty minutes later.

CHAPTER SEVENTEEN

DISMAY

The days after the fire were gloomy ones for Delia Viader. She tried to maintain a bright outlook, but the uncertainty was crushing. She had about 7,400 cases in the warehouse with a retail value of about $4.5 million. Viader had been counting on sales from that vintage to pay the bills that were piling up. But now no money was coming in.

Viader phoned her insurance company regularly, pushing for the time they would mail her a check for her loss. The insurance broker kept saying "soon," but the mailbox remained empty.

Viader tried to focus on other business. The fire happened smack in the middle of the 2005 harvest, and there were still grapes hanging on her vines. She had three quarters of an acre of Petit Verdot grapes on her hillside vineyard and they were always slow to ripen. While Cabernet Sauvignon grapes might be ready to pick in September or early October, Petit Verdot weren't fully ripe before the end of October or early November. So even though Viader felt distracted by the fire, as a winemaker she had to be engaged in the harvest.

Viader also needed to do damage control. She called all the restaurants that carried her wine and all the distributors who sold it. The loss of the 2003 vintage meant that there wouldn't be Viader products on store shelves or on restaurant wine lists for at least a year, an eternity in the wine world. The business was extremely competitive. Placement was everything. Convincing a restaurant to carry your wine could take years. Once a wine was off a wine list, it might be off forever. There were always other winemakers, other wineries, waiting in line to talk to that sommelier, to pour him or her a glass and discuss the soils in which the grapes grew. Viader wanted to maintain the relationships she had built up over fifteen years. She needed to personally explain to her clients that although the 2003 vintage was a total loss, she hoped to release her 2004 vintage, now aging in oak barrels in her caves, early. Could they hold a spot for her?

As she waited for word from her insurance company, Viader got the idea that she could learn something from the fire. Heat had always been an issue with wine. It didn't take much to cook a bottle and change a wine's flavor. Viader had an extensive chemistry background and had always been fascinated by the chemical transformation that happened with wine. She decided to send samples of wine that she and her crew had pulled from different parts of the warehouse to a laboratory in St. Helena that specialized in wine analysis. Viader would ask them to test it and see how different levels of heat exposure had affected the bottles differently.[178] It was a variation on the "if you've got lemons, make lemonade" theory.

As the days rolled by, Viader's financial troubles began to mount. She owed money everywhere—to the people who had purchased wine futures, to members of the wine club, to restaurants that had made down payments—and she had negative cash flow. She had a lot of bills to pay and nothing to pay them with. "In this business, you live from one harvest to the next."[179]

Viader had to take out an emergency loan from the bank.

A communication from the insurance company finally arrived. It was not what Viader had been expecting. The insurance company denied most of her claim. It would pay her $500,000 but not the $4.5 million she had lost when her wine was destroyed in the fire.

It all came down to fine print. The policy insured Viader's wines at her winery on Howell Mountain and at the warehouse she had long used on Tower Road in southern Napa County. But the destroyed wine wasn't in either place. It was at Wines Central. It was "in transit," according to her insurer.

Viader was devastated. She sat in her office in the winery, a large room crowded with desks, computers, and various size bottles, and fumed. And cried. And cried some more. Then she vowed to contest the ruling.

Seven years earlier, Viader had invested in a dream: to make wine in Italy. She loved that country, with its emphasis on food, wine, and gentle living. While land was expensive, it wasn't as costly as Napa Valley, where prime vineyard land could be $300,000 an acre. Viader got the idea to develop a small vineyard and eventually retire there.

Viader knew where she wanted to plant grapes: in the increasingly respected area around Bolgheri, about seventy-five miles south of Florence in Tuscany. Italians had been making wine there for generations, wine that was well regarded, but had no special designation. It was table wine, or *vino de tavola*. But forty years ago, an ambitious group of winemakers started to blend Sangiovese grapes, the backbone of Chianti, with Cabernet Sauvignon, Merlot, and other varietals. Old-time Italian winemakers thought they were crazy. They denounced the invention. Most of the world ignored the controversy.

But in 1974, two years before California wines gained recognition and respect at the famous Judgment of Paris tasting, a similar thing happened in Bolgheri. *Decanter* magazine, a well-regarded British wine magazine, sponsored a competition between French Bordeaux wines and those from Bolgheri. Guess who won?

In the next twenty years the region became one of the most respected wine areas in the world. A few producers made rich, complex wines dubbed "Super Tuscans." They began to be almost as esteemed as French Burgundy and Bordeaux.

The popularity of the Super Tuscan wines meant that property was at a premium and difficult to find. Viader, who had an Italian business partner, scoured the countryside for years. They finally found a twenty-acre parcel near Bolgheri.

Viader called the vineyard "Preselle," which means small parcel in Italian. She later bought a farmhouse nearby. Viader traveled each month to Italy to oversee the vineyard and home, frequently taking her then seven-year-old son. He was soon speaking Italian fluently.

But the Italian vineyard and its upkeep were expensive. Now that her income had been slashed—and now that the insurance company was denying her claim—Viader wondered how long she would be able to hold on to her retirement dream. The thought of losing it, though, tormented her.

A few weeks after the fire, Cathy Corison ran into Ted Hall at the farmers' market in a park in St. Helena. The normally gregarious man looked shell-shocked, his round face a grim reminder of all that he had lost. Hall usually had a greeting for everyone, and was quick to offer his opinion on anything from the quality of the produce his ranch's stand had for sale to the state of the American political system. But as Corison and Hall stood there among the eggs and end-of-the-year tomatoes, her former boss was uncharacteristically quiet.

Corison could relate to Hall's feelings of loss. She had been Long Meadow Ranch's consulting winemaker for ten years while simultaneously starting her Corison label. She had been in charge of the 2002 vintage, the one that the fire had completely destroyed. Corison could remember the details of that harvest: it had been a cool ripening season, but an extended heat spell in the second half of September condensed the harvest, ripening all the grapes at once. Now none of it was left.

Nor were the other vintages on which Corison had worked. The thought made her stomach turn. When the library area in the cave at Long Meadow Farm had filled up with bottles of previous vintages, Hall had sent them to Wines Central. It included large-format bottles, magnums and jeroboams of wine beginning with the 1994 vintage. The loss of all that history made Corison sad. Corison considered herself a steward of Mother Nature's gifts. Each of the vintages she made was a snapshot of time, a reflection of that year's weather and soils. The wines had also been made to age, to improve and develop over the years. The fire wiped out the chance to see that evolution.

Corison greeted Hall. There wasn't much to say. The pain in Corison's eyes reflected the pain in Hall's.[180] As they looked at each other, Ted Hall began to cry.

In the weeks after the fire, Hall worried most about the fate of Long Meadow Ranch's nineteen employees. The destruction of the 2002 vintage and some remaining cases of the 2001 vintage meant the winery had nothing to sell. With no income, how could he keep so many people on the payroll? The question kept him up at night.

Hall knew he had to take drastic action to bring in money—and to keep Long Meadow Ranch's name in front of the public. Before the fire, he had been pleased by how the winery's reputation had grown. Hall had personally made 5,000 visits to wine stores and restaurants around the country to convince them to carry his wine. Those hard-won placements would now vanish since there were no new vintages to send them.

Hall tried some unusual things to create cash flow. He decided to make grappa, a strong, clear Italian liqueur, from pomace, the leftovers from the pressing of the juice out of the fermented grape skins. It is usually thrown out or composted. Hall hired some flatbed trucks to cart away about three and a half tons of pomace. Hall sent it about sixty-five miles southeast to St. George's Spirit, a spirit manufacturer in Alameda, an island near Oakland.

Long Meadow Ranch had always been the type of winery that aged its wine longer than most and released it later than other wineries. These were all red wines, Cabernets that took time to reach their peak. But after the fire, Hall decided to upend his business model. White wine doesn't need to be aged as long as red. Hall bought Sauvignon Blanc grapes and turned out 500 cases of white wine to sell.

Dick Ward found that people were gifting him bottles of his own wine. When word got out that Saintsbury had lost its 3,000-bottle wine library on the eve of its twenty-fifth anniversary, customers and clients started shipping back the older bottles they had ferreted away in their own cellars. The outpouring of support was remarkable, and moved Ward deeply.

Saintsbury wasn't the only winery that had lost its library. So many places had that the Napa Valley Vintners' Association created a bulletin board on its website listing the wineries that had lost their histories. Soon, people from around the country had sent back old wines from those wineries.

In late 2006, Sainstbury held the long-awaited party for its twenty-fifth anniversary. Dick Ward and David Graves rented a room at Per Se, Thomas Keller's four-star restaurant in New York City's Time Warner Center. Both men had been frequent visitors to Keller's French Laundry and Bouchon in Yountville, and chose Per Se for that geographical connection. It was a theme that Keller also played up: the bright blue door leading into the modern Per Se in New York was the same color as the door leading into the rustic French Laundry in California.

The guest list was a who's who of East Coast publications. There were writers from *Forbes*, *Food and Wine*, *Gourmet*, the *New York Times*, and *Decanter*.

Ward and Graves had laid out more than twenty vintages on tables around the room. They had managed to find examples of wine from almost every year of Saintsbury, thanks in part to the generosity of customers. They started with samples from the 1986 vintage. One critic later wrote, "Beautifully mature but still lively and appetizing, the wines from the 1980s and 1990s seem to prove the pair's early beliefs were well founded." The evening helped Ward put the fire behind him

For months the broken bottles of wine sat in the Wines Central warehouse as winemakers and insurance companies negotiated payments and coverage. Mold soon took over. It was a fertile environment. There was damp from the wine pooled on the floor, a foot deep in some spots. There was "food"—the wine. Slimy mold soon started to grow over the tops of everything: the sodden cardboard boxes holding the bottles, the heaps of broken glass, the charred wood. It was black, white, pink—and disgusting.

Mold even grew inside the bottles. Debbie Polverino, the manager of the warehouse, said the corks and the bottoms of Ted Hall's wine blew off because of the heat of the fire. His empty bottles were soon filled with white mold. I. W. Hellman's Port was stored next to the wine from Hall's Long Meadow Ranch. Those bottles were invaded by mold as well.

The smell was rank—a combination of sour wine, smoke, and decay. The mice and rats were so bad that Wines Central kept an extermination company on contract. They came regularly to set traps every few feet both inside and outside the warehouse. The Vallejo fire department hosed down the interior of the building a few times to clean it up and dissipate the mold and mildew.

It wasn't until a few months after the fire that disposal of the damaged bottles began. While most of the wine was ruined, winemakers could not destroy it before they settled with their insurance carriers and informed the Alcohol and Tobacco Tax Trade Bureau, the federal agency that regulated alcohol taxes, that it would be trashed.

It took almost two and a half years to clean out the warehouse. Disposing of four and a half to six million bottles of wine, as well as numerous barrels, was no simple exercise. One winery, Sterling Vineyards, had to destroy 40,000 cases of scorched wine.

Wines Central hired Upper Valley Disposal to come in with huge front-loaders to pick up pallets of wine. As soon as a vintner had the okay from his or her insurance company to dispose of the wine, UVD would search out the wine in the warehouse, pick it up, and carry it outside to a huge sorting machine. The boxes of wine would be dumped into a funnel-like mechanism. The machine would crush everything. The wine would go through a strainer into a 20,000-gallon tanker where it was carted off to be converted into ethanol. The wood, cardboard, and glass was sorted onto conveyer belts, removed, and stacked in the parking lot until it was dumped. The piles of wood, glass, and cardboard grew to be thirty to forty feet long and taller than a human.

Delia Viader was one of the winemakers who came to watch the destruction of her wine. She needed to witness its demise, both for the insurance company and for her own sense of closure. On the day her bottles were set to be crushed, Viader left her winery on Howell Mountain, with its spectacular view of rolling vineyards and distant peaks, and drove south to Vallejo to a completely different vision of winemaking. The parking lot at Wines Central had become an industrial disposal center: loud, dirty, smelly, and distasteful. But Viader did not flinch from the mess. She wanted to see the end of the wine she had nurtured, the wine she had turned from grapes into something magical. She had helped create it, so it was only appropriate that she attend its funeral.

CHAPTER EIGHTEEN

THE TRAP IS SET

The five pallets of wine came into the Chicago Wine Company by truck, arriving at the Wood Dale, Illinois, warehouse on October 11, 2005. After a forklift operator unloaded the 2,600 bottles, the shipment was given a quick visual inspection. Something was off. It looked like someone had blacked out initials written on some of the boxes and had pasted strips of paper over other identifying marks.

The correspondence from the shipper was odd, too. The sender, Kansai Partners, wrote that they hoped to make $100,000 when the Chicago Wine Company auctioned off the wine. Yet the wine was worth more than $150,000. Why would a company purposely undervalue what it was selling? A staff member made a mental note to look further into the situation.

The next evening, the wine company was abuzz with news of the fire in the Wines Central warehouse near Napa. There had been other wine warehouse fires in the past, but none were as large or as costly as this. As television stations around the country showed video clips of the plume of black smoke rising from the building, reporters mentioned that as many as 6 million bottles of wine worth $100 million were feared destroyed.

To the woman who coordinated shipping for the Chicago Wine

Company, there was something disturbingly familiar about the address of the burning warehouse. After pondering for a bit, she realized that Kansai Partners, the company that had sent the problematic shipment of wine, used the same address as the warehouse that went up in flames.

Like other retail and auction houses, the Chicago Wine Company often did business without knowing much about its clients. In the case of Kansai Partners, the two men who said they owned the company, Peter Martin and Joseph Throckmorton, had communicated with the Chicago Wine Company by email. But when a staff member put the telephone number for Kansai Partners into Google, it came back as a number for Sausalito Cellars and a man named Mark Anderson. Another couple of computer clicks showed that the police were investigating Anderson in connection with the warehouse fire.

The Chicago Wine Company got in touch with the Federal Bureau of Investigation.

Brian Parker, the lead ATF investigator, had been working on the assumption that he had a straightforward arson case. Of course there is never anything simple about arson. Most of the time there are no witnesses. Searching for the ignition point is laborious. ATF agents often have to build a circumstantial case one small piece at a time.

The evidence collected from Anderson's storage bay at Wines Central was damning. But the call from the Chicago Wine Company to the FBI, which referred it to the ATF, proved a propellant of its own. All of a sudden, Parker no longer had just an arson investigation. If Anderson had shipped wine from California to Illinois using a fake name, the criminal charges would include mail fraud. If that wine had been stolen, the charges would include interstate transfer of stolen property. To determine that would prove time-consuming. Parker had to figure out who actually owned the wine that had been sent to Chicago.

Parker used the BlackBerry that police had seized during a search of Anderson's apartment to compile a list of Sausalito Cellars clients. He then tracked as many of the 100 clients he could reach and found out what wine they had stored at Sausalito Cellars. He then compared that list to the wines sent to Chicago. It took Parker eighteen months to prove that at least 80 percent of that wine belonged to the clients of Sausalito Cellars, not to Kansai Partners, or Anderson.[181]

In the months after the fire, Anderson didn't hide. Friends often saw him walking around Sausalito, near the small shopping district on Caledonia Street with its movie theater and hardwood store or along trails that ran by the bay. He didn't seem worried or overly concerned about the pending embezzlement charges or the fact that various police agencies had twice stormed his apartment looking for evidence connecting him to wine theft and arson. Anderson still joked and told his stories. At meetings of the Rotary Club at the Sausalito Yacht Club, Anderson just brushed off the mess as an administrative mix-up, one that was sure to be sorted out eventually.[182] When "I saw him . . . in the parking lot of the Sausalito Yacht Harbor, Mark was absolutely confident this would go away," recalled Paul Anderson, the publisher of the *Marin Scope* (and no relation to Anderson). "Everything was absolutely fine; he was innocent."

There were signs of tension, though. Yoshi Tome threw a twentieth anniversary party for Sushi Ran in August 2006. He invited Anderson, his longtime friend and former member of the Sushi Lovers' Club, for old times' sake. Tome no longer regarded Anderson with affection. In a strange way, Tome felt responsible for introducing Anderson to many of his customers, people whose wine had been stolen or burned. Anderson had used his close association with Sushi Ran as a calling card to meet wealthy people who might become his clients, Tome thought. He couldn't get the image out of his head of Anderson at Sushi Ran, holding a cup of sake, deep in conversation with a future victim.

When Anderson showed up to the party, Tome was shocked by how much weight he had gained. He had ballooned to 300 pounds. His skin was a pasty white. He looked stressed. Yet Anderson acted as if nothing was the matter. He mingled, drank, and ate sushi as if he had not a care in the world.

Shortly after that party, process servers bearing legal papers started to stalk Anderson to compel him to appear in court for the numerous civil cases his former clients had filed. Anderson laid low. He holed up in his apartment and didn't answer his phone. He pasted cardboard over the small window in his front door, leaving a peephole three inches square. Even then he didn't open the door to strangers.

Caffe Trieste, the Italian espresso bar and café at the edge of the Sausalito Yacht Harbor, was a favorite local hangout, a place to spend hours nursing a cappuccino or munching on a plate of antipasto. Mothers with toddlers were lunch regulars. Bicyclers returning from a ride on Mount Tam clustered around the entrance on weekends.

The crowds let the undercover detectives mingle without detection as they scoped out Anderson's apartment in mid-March 2007. Agents from the ATF and detectives from the Sausalito and Vallejo police departments set up an around-the-clock surveillance to determine Anderson's habits. For three days straight they hunched over cups of coffee at the café that sat kitty-corner from the apartment or hunkered down in cars in a lot across from the duplex.

Around ten a.m. on Friday March 16, 2007, Anderson and his girlfriend shut the door of their apartment and descended the steep flight of stairs toward the garage. Anderson leaned on his cane for support. When they got to the sidewalk, Anderson opened the garage door and eased his large frame into his Cadillac. Witten got in the passenger side. Before Anderson could pull out of the garage, a police car rolled up and blocked the way. An ATF agent got out, walked to the driver's side, and asked Anderson to get out of the car. He was handcuffed and placed under arrest.

"Mark, what's going on?" Witten screamed. "What's going on? Talk to me, Mark. Talk to me."[183]

Anderson didn't say much as he was taken to the Sausalito police station, nor did he talk as ATF Agent Brian Parker sat down with him in a locked holding room. This was only the second time Parker had come face-to-face with Anderson; he had met him once before when he served a search warrant in late 2005. They had exchanged a few glib generalities then. But Parker had studied every aspect of Anderson's life in the intervening months and felt he knew the man and his secrets.

Parker pulled out a card to read Anderson his Miranda rights. "You have the right to remain silent. Anything you say and do can be used against you in a court of law. You have the right to an attorney . . ." and so on.

When Parker had finished, Anderson looked up at him. "I don't think you've got that quite right," he said. Parker was stunned by that response. Anderson didn't look sad, he didn't look shocked or mad that he was under arrest. He acted like he could have been anywhere, not in handcuffs in the trailer that was the Sausalito police headquarters. But he was still the kind of know-it-all who corrected a federal agent reading out his Miranda rights. Parker handed Anderson the card with the Miranda warning printed on it. "You read it then," he said.[184]

Three days later at a press conference in Sacramento, the U.S. attorney for the Eastern District of California, McGregor Scott, stood at the front of the room flanked by agents and investigators from the ATF, IRS, and U.S. Postal Service. He announced that a grand jury that had been meeting for more than a year had handed down a nineteen-count indictment. Anderson was charged with arson, interstate transportation of fraudulently obtained property, mail fraud, use of a fictitious name in connection with a scheme to defraud, and tax evasion. He faced 240 years in prison. "Mark Anderson put lives at risk to cover his tracks," Scott explained.

Anderson had been hauled to jail first in San Francisco, then in Sacramento. He spent the next five days in a small cell with a narrow bed, sink, and metal toilet. He was released from federal custody on $500,000 bail. (Witten's father may have put up the funds.) When Anderson returned to his apartment he must have been happy to see his harbor view—and desperate not to go back to that claustrophobic jail cell.

Anderson looked for ways to cast suspicion on others. On April 4 he logged onto Wine Expressions, a website for wine lovers, using the screen name "carlmwood." Anderson wrote two comments saying that he had heard Wines Central was a "leaky" warehouse and its manager had been involved in the disappearance of some wine years earlier. "Hasn't anyone ever looked into the other people at Wines Central? It wasn't a wine warehouse, it was a front for all kinds of other business scams. Anderson had moved out long before."[185] In another comment he wrote: "Jack Krystal (owner of Wines Central) . . . was bankrupt and needed the insurance to get out of town."

Two days later, a federal court judge determined Anderson was a flight risk and cancelled his bail. Anderson had no known family ties in the area, no steady employment, no substantial financial resources, used aliases, and traveled overseas frequently, the court determined. He also owned books on how to flee and hide. He was thrown back in jail.

The court appointed Mark Reichel to represent Anderson. He was the tenth attorney in the previous few years to represent Anderson in various civil and criminal proceedings, and the second federal defender. (The original federal defender excused himself because of a conflict of interest.) Reichel was a Sacramento attorney who had spent thirteen years as a federal public defender handling both white-collar crimes and major felonies, including arson. He had argued one case all the way to the U.S. Supreme Court, and would soon appear in the pages of *People* magazine for defending a twelve-year-old boy accused of fatally stabbing his eight-year-old sister. Reichel, whom journalists could always rely on for a pithy quote, had set himself up in private practice in 2006 and took on government cases to augment his work. Both defense attorneys and prosecutors regarded him highly, although they acknowledged he was a bit disorganized—until he got in court. Then he was a bulldog.

Reichel would be facing off against R. Steven Lapham, who had been intimately involved in the pursuit of Anderson since he was identified as a suspect in late 2005. Reichel and Lapham were old adversaries who had argued against each other numerous times. But the legal community that spent its time in the wood-paneled courtrooms of the glossy Robert T. Matsui United States Courthouse in Sacramento was small and congenial. Reichel and Lapham had a good personal working relationship that transcended individual cases.

At the start, Reichel crafted a strategy that would limit the amount of time Anderson spent in jail. Reichel didn't think he could get his client off completely—there was too much evidence against him for that—but he believed he could minimize his jail time. The key was to split off the fraud charges from the arson charges.[186]

Reichel thought it would be easy for Lapham to prove that Anderson had sent stolen wine to the Chicago Wine Company. The paper trail was clear: clients had entrusted their wine to Sausalito Cellars. Anderson or Kansai Partners had sold similar wine, and money from that sale was deposited into bank accounts controlled by Anderson. The scheme was amateurish and greedy, and Reichel thought jurors would be insulted by Anderson's conduct.[187]

But if Anderson pleaded guilty to the four counts of interstate transportation of fraudulently obtained property, Reichel could try to block details of that fraud in the trial about arson. The jail sentence for the fraud would not be severe, and Anderson might get time served.

Then Reichel would be able to focus on the arson charges during the trial.

The arson evidence was mostly circumstantial. Reichel thought he could also poke holes in what the government said was the motive for the fire: that Anderson set the fire to the warehouse to "cover his tracks," to make it harder to prove he had illegally sold his clients' wine. Anderson had moved most of his clients' wine out of Wines Central to another warehouse before the fire. There were no computers or paper records. Reichel planned to argue that there was nothing left to cover up, no evidence to destroy, so there was no motive for Anderson to light the fire.

But when Reichel told Anderson about his strategy, he found an uncooperative client. Anderson insisted he had not stolen the wine and he wanted Reichel to present his convoluted explanations for why it went missing.

Sitting alone in a jail cell with a bad back and constant pain is one way to focus the mind. Anderson never got a license to practice law in California. He graduated from law school, but failed the bar exam twice. Maybe that partial knowledge led him to try to outsmart the judicial system from the isolation of his jail cell. He showered the court with letters and claims. And to a large extent, his manipulations worked.

Letters in his large block print handwriting poured into the court. Anderson complained constantly about his health. He wasn't getting his pain medicine. The sheriff's deputies had taken his egg carton mattress topper, which meant he couldn't sleep. They had broken his CPAP machine when they searched his cell. They had stolen dozens of boxes of important defense documents. Because of his complaints, he had been tossed into solitary confinement for twenty-eight days, he told the judge.

That's not all Anderson complained about. He was dissatisfied with Reichel. In January 2008, he wrote to the judge in the case, Judge Lawrence Karlton, and said he hadn't seen or heard from Reichel for months, even though he had written and called the attorney four dozen times. Anderson accused Reichel of not interviewing key witnesses, not hiring a computer expert to examine his hard drive, and being disorganized. "Where is my court appointed attorney?" Anderson wrote on June 18, 2008—his five hundredth day of incarceration. "Why has virtually nothing been done on my case, in my defense, since my arrest?"

Inmates have a lot of time on their hands, and they often use it to reach out to whomever they think can help—reporters, women sympathetic to the incarcerated, prison rights organizations. But Anderson's tendency to cry wolf at any opportunity would come back to haunt him.

He sat in the Sacramento jail and stewed. A date was set for his trial, and then postponed. A new date was proposed, and put aside. Finally, two years and nine months after he had been arrested, the courts set November 17, 2009, as the date for the start of Anderson's trial.

Lapham was ready. He had been working on the case for four years and had spent weeks preparing, interviewing witnesses, poring over wine inventories, examining the forensic arson evidence. He likened trial prep to planning a military campaign where moves and contingencies are plotted out in advance. Lapham intended to put fifty-six witnesses on the stand—people whose wine Anderson had embezzled, former employees, winemakers, detectives, and Wines Central employees. One of them would be flying in from Japan. Others were coming from out of state. He had interviewed every one of them at least once, and intended to talk to them a second time before they walked up to the witness stand.

As Lapham sat in his office on the eleventh floor of the federal building, reminders of other arson cases surrounded him. There was a photo of a nine-year-old Vietnamese girl pinned above the bookcase. She had died in 1997 when her father threw a Molotov cocktail into the house where his estranged wife was living with her child and new boyfriend. There was a drawing made during a trial of a Sacramento developer who torched a warehouse to collect insurance. A plaque with grape leaves was a reminder of his successful prosecution of Fred Franzia, who had substituted cheap grapes for expensive Zinfandel ones.

In the days before Anderson's trial was set to begin, Lapham's attention was focused on an easel at the center of his office. He had diagrammed the case day-by-day, with notations of which witnesses and which evidence would be presented. Lapham thought the prosecution part of the trial would last at least three weeks since it was a complex case with many moving parts. The stakes were high: Anderson faced up to 240 years in prison.

Lapham is always open to resolving a case before trial. He has had a lot of experience, having argued around sixty cases before juries, so his reputation is secure. He is not one of those young Turk attorneys who are afraid to show weakness. He doesn't feel that settling a case is a capitulation.

The U.S. attorney in the Eastern District of California has a policy that if there is going to be a plea bargain, it must be negotiated two weeks before a trial is set to start. That ensures that the attorneys get to focus on trial preparation in the days leading up to court, rather than hammering out a plea bargain. But Lapham knew he would have to make an exception for Reichel, whom he considered a good attorney but one who took things down to the wire. Reichel always juggled up until the last moment.

A few days before the trial was set to begin, way past the office's official deadline, Reichel called Lapham. He wanted to deal. Reichel had talked to his client and Anderson, the man who had shouted his innocence to anyone who would listen, had agreed to plead guilty to all nineteen counts. Laphman listened. He said that in exchange for a guilty plea he would ask that Anderson be sentenced to fifteen years, eight months in prison. The suggested sentence meant Anderson, then sixty-one, might not die in jail.

Anderson's day of reckoning came on Monday, November 16. He was rousted early from his hard jail bed, which he had tried to make more comfortable by piling on two mattresses and three mattress pads. He dressed in his orange jail jumpsuit and then joined the line of prisoners who had court dates that day. But Anderson couldn't walk next door to the courtroom. His back, with its ruptured discs, hurt too much. A sheriff's deputy had to push Anderson into the hearing in a wheelchair.

Anderson managed to hobble from the defense table to a spot in front of Judge Karlton. His attorney stood by his side. Lapham was just a few feet away. When the judge asked Anderson if he wanted to plead guilty, if he understood what he was doing, Anderson replied, "Yes." He said he agreed to give up his constitutional rights, his right to remain silent, and his right to appeal the sentence. Anderson said "yes" more than twenty times to the judge's questions. When asked how he would plead, he said, "Guilty." He later signed a document admitting that "he used gasoline soaked rags to intentionally start a fire in Bay 14 of Wines Central warehouse," and that he "embezzled his clients' wine through the use of Kansai Partners."

The judge set the date for sentencing six weeks in the future.

If only it had ended there.

I was sitting at my desk in mid-November 2009 when the phone rang. I picked up the receiver. There was a recorded message on the line, asking if I would accept a collect call from the Sacramento County jail by an inmate named Mark Anderson. Would I accept the charges?

Would I? Of course I would. I pressed the phone key that would patch through the call. Nothing. I pushed it again. At that point the line died.

I was puzzled. I had started to report on Anderson and the fire, but had not reached out to him directly. How had he heard I was interested in talking to him? Was it because the story about wine was for the *New York Times*? I hurriedly wrote him a letter asking if we could talk, and received one back just a few days later. "Yes! I heard through the grapevine you were making inquiries and yes, I would very much like to speak with you or even meet with you," Anderson wrote. I would soon come to know his big, blocky print handwriting well. The letters came regularly, six, seven, sometimes ten pages on white-lined binder paper. He usually wrote front to back, in pencil. In the first year, Mark wrote me more than twenty times.

In his letters, Mark was charming and expansive, writing chatty tomes with references to wine, history, and countries he had visited around the world. I would send him a list of questions. He would answer them in detail. He always asked me to make a copy of our correspondence and send it back to him. Every letter contained a jab against the jail system.

He said it was too bad we weren't communicating face-to-face. "A personal conversation . . . like at Yosemite's Ahwahnee Hotel, with a bottle of old Cabernet in front of a snowy landscape, recounting this entire story would be much more interesting."[188]

In later letters Mark played the aggrieved victim. There was no truth to anything the prosecution said, he insisted, even though he had pleaded guilty to the federal charges of arson, mail fraud, and tax evasion. He never embezzled any wine; missing bottles were due to flooding in the cellars or an errant employee who helped himself. The prosecutors had blown up what should merely have been a civil case into something criminal. He had nothing to do with the Wines Central fire—and by the way, most of the burned wine was plonk, not Napa Valley's best as claimed by the U.S. attorney's office. "I'm just as much of a victim," he wrote, "if not more—I'm being charged for something I didn't do."[189]

The letters evolved into occasional calls. Mark would telephone collect from the Sacramento County jail. We would have a few frantic minutes to talk before a robo-voice announced that the time was up.

Two things marked my communications with Mark: incredible detail and an amazing lack of specificity. He could write for pages about his childhood in Berkeley or the wine adventures he took with his friends around the world. He went into depth about the time he drank wine in a thatched hut in Bora-Bora and the time by the pyramids in Egypt. Mark created such vivid portraits that his stories would leap off the page.

But when I pushed Mark for verification of his history, people I could interview who could confirm those events actually happened, he suddenly became unable—or unwilling—to provide me with names. All his old friends from the Kansai Wine Club in Japan were dead, he insisted, so I couldn't verify the tales of his amazing international travels. As for other friends, etiquette required he contact them first. But unfortunately, he had fallen out of touch with most of them.

Mark's inability to connect me with anyone who could corroborate his stories increased my suspicions. It's one of the first things you learn as a reporter: when a story is complicated, it is frequently false. All the warning signs were there: Mark was evasive. He constructed elaborate explanations about what happened to him and where the wine had gone. He usually cast the blame on someone else.

At first I didn't understand why Mark wouldn't be frank and admit he had set the fire. After all, he had pleaded guilty to arson and assorted other crimes. Why wouldn't he try to grab a different kind of glory? The brass ring of crime? He could be known as the man who destroyed the largest collection of wine in history, a caper so outrageous that it ruined a quarter of a billion dollars of property. I imagined there would be a kind of relief in admitting what he had done, of coming clean. I was wrong.

"Involving yourself in the life of a great liar, once you understand that he's a liar but go on seeking the truth from him, is a swan dive through a mirror into a whirlpool," Walter Kirn wrote in his memoir about dealing with a man who claimed to be a Rockefeller descendant. I dove into that whirlpool with Mark Anderson. I learned there was no coming up for air.

It didn't take long for Anderson to decide he made a terrible mistake. In April 2010, five months after pleading guilty and before he had been sentenced, Anderson wrote Judge Karlton and said he wanted to vacate his guilty plea. He insisted he had been tricked into accepting a deal because his attorney told him it meant he would only spend eighteen more months in jail. Anderson said he didn't realize his guilty plea would be final. He figured it was just his attorney's maneuver to get more time for a trial for which he was not prepared. Plus, Anderson said, Reichel rushed the process, only giving Anderson a few hours to decide. "I can't remember a time I was under more pressure," Anderson wrote.

It's hard to believe that Anderson didn't know the stakes when he accepted the plea bargain. This was a law school graduate who had worked as a legal researcher for the twenty-six judges at San Francisco Superior Court. He had "negotiated hundreds of civil agreements, in several languages." Yet he felt "like a deer in the headlight with Mr. Reichel urging him to take the plea."[190]

The Ninth Circuit Court of Appeals, which oversees the federal court in California, has ruled that defendants can withdraw their guilty pleas before sentencing under certain circumstances. And one of those is a defendant's belief that their attorney's deficient performance and bad legal advice motivated their decision to plead guilty. In fact, one ruling seemed to speak to Anderson's case. In *United States vs. Davis*, the Ninth Circuit ruled in 2005 that the defendant has the right to withdraw his guilty plea if "the defense counsel's gross mischaracterization of the likely sentencing range could have motivated defendant to plead guilty." That was precisely Anderson's claim.

It's impossible to know if Anderson had concocted a strategy early on to delay his sentence based on inadequate counsel. But he laid the groundwork for that claim with his first complaint to Karlton in 2008. Many other letters chastising Reichel's representation had followed. On August 16, 2010, Judge Karlton felt compelled to appoint an independent attorney to assess whether Anderson's claims of inadequate representation were true. Anderson's sentencing was postponed once again.

It became Reichel's word against Anderson's. The complaint meant that Reichel was no longer bound by attorney-client privilege. Out poured a torrent of stories showing how working with Anderson was extremely strange.

"It was a bizarre experience," wrote Reichel in his declaration to the court. "It was not an easy task. From the beginning of that representation he was not candid with me, changed his story often, and did not ever want to admit hard truths. He is extremely difficult to work with, and that is an understatement."

Reichel said talking to Anderson was like going into the carnival fun house where everything is distorted. He had "bizarre defense theories." He constantly lied and changed his story. Reichel would ask Anderson a simple question, like "Who is Joe Throckmorton," and Anderson would repeat the question back verbatim. He would tell Reichel about "important" defense witnesses who did not exist. When one of Reichel's investigators interviewed Anderson, he was castigated for not knowing enough about certain types of French red wine. Anderson seemed to prefer "to discuss anything other than his case; he desired that my time . . . be spent listening to him spin yarns with stories of all the great things he had done in his life."

Reichel eventually had a psychiatrist examine Anderson. The report "confirmed all my concerns about his characteristics of narcissism and a complete unwillingness to deal with difficult matters and preferring to simply lie about things."

Despite the difficulty, Reichel denied he pushed any plea bargain on Anderson. He had been prepared to go to trial. Anderson even admitted to Reichel he had set the fire, Reichel wrote in his court statement.

When Anderson saw the government's overwhelming evidence against him and the jail sentence it could bring, Anderson had willingly taken the fifteen years, eight months, said Reichel.[191]

Anderson submitted a point-by-point rebuttal to Reichel's affidavit. His version was diametrically different. He claimed Reichel rarely showed up to talk to him, had no handle on the case, and had done the barest of preparation. "If one were going to ask someone to attempt to castigate, humiliate, and pontificate, about something he does not understand or comprehend, with all the pomposity and subtlety of a Victorian coster-monger, Mr. Reichel would certainly win a penny at the circus," Anderson wrote. "There are no metes or bounds to his lack of vacuous creativity."

In August 2011, almost two years after Anderson pleaded guilty, Judge Karlton removed Reichel as Anderson's counsel. There was evidence, he said, that Reichel had performed poorly. Then he gave time to Anderson's new attorney, Jan Karowsky, to prepare to argue why Anderson should be able to withdraw his guilty pleas.

That meant more delays for Anderson's victims.

I had been following Anderson's case closely for almost two years at that point, driving from Berkeley to Sacramento whenever there was a hearing. Mark and I were communicating by letter and telephone, but I did not visit him in jail after my initial visit in 2010. Instead, I only saw him in the courtroom. It got to be a cozy crowd at the courthouse. The group included Steven Lapham, the prosecutor, Brian Parker, the lead ATF agent, and Jan Karowsky, Anderson's newest attorney. Anderson's girlfriend, Cynthia Witten, was frequently in attendance, although she never talked to the press. She was always dressed demurely in a long-sleeved dress, skirt, or powder blue suit. One time when I was sitting in an aisle seat and she needed to get by, I smiled and said hello. "No comment," she murmured.

Of course, the central actor in this drama was Mark. Even his entrance into court resembled theater. Accompanied by a sheriff's deputy, he would enter by a side door into the wood-paneled courtroom and make his way to the defendant's table. He had gained even more weight in jail—his attorney said he weighed 330 pounds—and his stomach bulged against his bright orange uniform. Sometimes he arrived in a wheelchair. Sometimes he walked in leaning on the wheelchair for support. One time he even asked the judge's permission to lie down on a wooden bench while the proceedings continued because his back hurt too much to stay seated. Apparently, Anderson had to lie down when he met his attorney in jail, too. Karowsky told the court how strange it was to hear "this disembodied voice" coming from the floor during their strategy sessions.

There were numerous hearings on Anderson's case. As Judge Karlton said from the bench, how could this man take up so much of the court's time? Anderson seemed disconnected from reality. Despite the evidence, he kept arguing that he was innocent—even after he pleaded guilty. He even started to insist he was not at Wines Central the day of the fire. "He almost seems like he likes the attention," Lapham, the prosecutor, said outside the courtroom. "As soon as he gets packed off to federal detention he becomes a number. At least here he gets attention."

While Anderson dallied, Ted Hall stewed. He thought it was unconscionable that so much time had lapsed from crime to judgment to justice. While Lapham didn't seem to mind the delay—Anderson was sitting in a jail cell, after all—Hall and others wanted closure. They wanted justice. They felt jerked around. There had been eleven hearings set for Anderson's sentencing, eleven delays. Six years had passed since the fire and four since Anderson's arrest. To Hall, the delays were "not in the public interest."

DELAY

On February 7, 2012, six years and four months after the fire at Wines Central, Mark Anderson was rolled into federal court to finally be sentenced for the crime. Anderson's new attorney could not convince Judge Karlton to let Anderson withdraw his guilty plea. Karowsky, a white-haired former district attorney turned criminal defense attorney, had fought hard for his client, however. He had hired his own wine appraiser to look at the value of the four and a half million to six million bottles destroyed that day. The appraiser, who had been recommended by the well-regarded Sotheby's auction house, put the loss at $54 million—significantly lower than the government's estimate of $250 million for the wine alone. (Lapham thought the loss was actually more than $400 million but had agreed to the lower number for sentencing purposes.) Karowsky had hoped the lower figure would reduce the severity of the crime and Anderson's time in jail.

"The day has actually arrived," Judge Karlton said as he settled in the chair behind the high desk on the dais.

The judge then began to think aloud, casting around scenarios for Anderson. The plea bargain worked out in November 2009 that would have sentenced Anderson to fifteen years, eight months—and given him a chance to spend his later years out of jail—was no longer in effect, the judge noted. Anderson had breeched it when he made a motion to withdraw his guilty plea.

Karowsky asked for a sentence of ten years. "Here we have a gentleman who never had a traffic ticket, a respected member of his community, finding himself in a financially precarious position, who took an extreme action."

Lapham asked for thirty years. He pointed out that the losses were huge. Insurance companies had paid out about $65 million in claims. And he revealed for the first time that Sterling Vineyards, a unit of the gigantic British beverage firm Diageo, suffered the largest uninsured loss—$37 million.

Judge Karlton couldn't seem to decide what to do. He started throwing around different scenarios. If Anderson had been twenty or thirty years old, a sentence of thirty years would be a deterrent, he said, but now that he was sixty-three, that jail term would almost certainly mean he would die in jail. Thirty years was "an outrageously heavy sentence."

"Ultimately the question in the court's mind is what is sufficient? I'm not certain thirty years, given Mr. Anderson's age, is appropriate . . . Mr. Karowsky, you suggest ten years. I'm going to tell you, that's not going to happen. Everything else is a life sentence, probably." Judge Karlton looked to be hovering at a sentence of about fifteen years.

Then Ted Hall stood up. Lapham had invited some of Anderson's victims to talk about what impact the fire had on them. It was a strategy that Lapham often used to show a judge the human side of a tragedy. Hall, dressed in a gray suit and looking more like the management consultant he used to be than the winery owner he was currently, slowly made his way from the audience gallery to a podium before the judge. He held a white piece of paper with his statement typed on it. Almost as soon as Hall started to speak, he began to cry. Tears rolled down his cheeks. He choked up, and was barely able to get out his words for a minute. The fire may have happened years earlier, but it still carried an emotional impact.

The fire had ruined many people's lives, Hall told the court. Wineries lost millions. Some went out of business. Hundreds of people lost their jobs. But while the court focused on the financial implications of the crime, Hall asked the judge to think about the personal implications.

"This was a crime against families: those that owned the businesses and many everyday working men and women who helped us produce these irreplaceable wines," said Hall. "Our farm workers, our winemaker, and our entire team dedicated themselves to producing these wines for which there is no replacement. We can't simply call up a factory and ask them to make us another vintage of 2001 Cabernet Sauvignon. It is gone forever. The fruit of our hands and of our hearts is irretrievably gone, like a piece of fine art trashed by a barbarian sacking a city . . . May his sentence reflect the havoc he wreaked and may it be long to reflect the lasting damage to our lives."

Delia Viader was not in the courtroom. She had planned on giving a statement, but so many of Anderson's hearings had been postponed or changed that she hadn't been sure if it was worth the effort to drive the hour from Napa. Dick Ward also decided to skip the hearing. The only other person who testified was Catherine Williams, the daughter of Julie Johnson, who had lost thousands of cases of her Tres Sabores wine. My mother "has not taken a day off since that fire," said Williams. "She cannot stop working because the devastation that it caused brought her to the brink of financial insolvency. It not only ruined her business, it ruined her spirit. He stole her wine and he stole her spirit."

The testimony of the two victims changed the atmosphere in the courtroom. Judge Karlton reacted visibly to Hall's statement, lifting his eyebrows as if he suddenly understood the stakes of Anderson's crime.[192] While before there had been banter about Anderson's sentence, with a few jabs made by the judge about how wine lovers think every bottle of wine is worth $10,000, there seemed to be a new awareness of the devastation and pain Anderson had wrought.

The judge asked Anderson if he had anything to say. Anderson did not.

"This was a grievous crime," said Judge Karlton. "It's important the court recognize that. Whatever I do is a life sentence anyway."

He then sentenced Anderson to twenty-seven years in prison and ordered him to pay $70.3 million in restitution, even though Anderson was broke. That meant Anderson would be jailed until 2034, when he was eighty-six years old.

As Anderson heard the sentence, all he did was shake his head in disbelief.

Anderson has never publicly expressed remorse for setting the fire. He never apologized in court for his actions, something his victims have long wanted. Apparently, he told a probation officer in 2009 that "he was very sorry for his conduct and remorseful for the impact of his actions on others," but that document has never been made public and its contents have only turned up in court filings. "My position regarding the event was that it was indeed a catastrophe and obviously a devastating loss to the owners of the contents and the owner of the business," Anderson wrote me after he was sentenced. "Notwithstanding the event, I had nothing to do with it; was not a party or directed the theft of any wines and certainly did not have any part in anything of which I was accused."[193]

Over time, I stopped expecting a confession from Mark, or even any acknowledgment that he had hurt people. If his own brother felt compelled to create a website attacking him as a way to get his attention, as a way to say he thought his brother was guilty, how could anyone else expect to penetrate the web of self-denial he had spun around himself?

Our last conversation was in the spring of 2012, right before he was about to be sent to Terminal Island, a low-security federal penitentiary in San Pedro, right near the entrance to the Los Angeles Harbor. Al Capone, Charles Manson, and Timothy Leary were all once inmates there. Anderson had hoped to be sentenced to Lompoc, probably because it was closer to where Witten lived, but he didn't get his wish. She eventually moved back to her home state of Oregon. But Terminal Island, with 975 inmates, is one of the better federal prisons. It sits on the edge of the Pacific Ocean and most of the year the weather is sunny. Anderson had appealed his case, he told me, arguing to the Court of Appeals that he had had insufficient representation, which led him to accept the guilty plea. He wrote me one more letter. Then our correspondence stopped.

PART SIX

REDEMPTION

CHAPTER TWENTY

LEGACY

The bottle of Port had been lying on its side in a storage room beneath my home's staircase for almost fifteen years. A present from my stepmother, I had taken it from its cool, dark resting place only twice: once, after my cousin told me that 175 bottles of Hellman's wine had been destroyed in the Vallejo warehouse fire and again, after I visited Mark Anderson in the Sacramento County jail in 2010. On both of these occasions I held the green bottle in my hands and wondered about the discolored label and sediment stuck to the sides. I also pondered: what would it taste like? It seemed too precious to open for even a special birthday or anniversary. But what kind of occasion would justify drinking a wine made in 1875?

I had begun researching the Port's provenance in 2010, and by the summer of 2014 I had scoured history books, assessors' records, court cases, archives, and museum exhibits. I knew when the grapes were first planted in Cucamonga Vineyard (1839) and when the last grapes were pulled out (1917). I knew that the vineyard had passed through the hands of at least five men and a smattering of companies. I knew five people with a connection to the vineyard had been killed. But all those facts didn't tell me a crucial thing: how good was Hellman's Port? What exactly was lost in the fire?

My mother and stepfather had also been curious about the value and quality of the wine, and in the 1970s had sent a bottle of Hellman's Port to Julio Gallo, the proprietor of E. & J. Gallo, now the biggest wine company in the world. At that time Gallo was mostly focused on making bulk wine from grapes in the Central Valley; it would only be later that the firm also moved into high-end wine.

The Port impressed Gallo. He recounted his reactions in a typed letter to my mother. For two paragraphs he talked about the amber color of the wine, its viscosity, and its strong, but pleasant, perfume. It was only in the last paragraph that he admitted that he had dropped the bottle on the floor, where it shattered and spilled. He had to crouch down on his knees, sniff the juice, and dip a finger into the puddle to evaluate the Port.

Long Meadow Farms proprietor Ted Hall and Fritz Hatton, a wine appraiser and a regular auctioneer at Auction Napa Valley, also turned their expert attention to Hellman's Port. They tasted samples from the bottles my cousin Miranda Heller had sent Hall in 2003 for evaluation. "We were dazzled by it," Hall told me. There was "a surprising amount of fruitiness, and it was more sophisticated than Fritz or I expected given the state of the wine industry at the time."

Through the years, Hellman's wine has occasionally been put up for sale at auction, and buyers have posted their tasting notes on the Internet. Eric Ifune, a surgeon, bought some of Hellman's Port and Angelica, the slightly fizzy fortified white wine, in 2102 at an auction at Zachy's Wine House in New York. He paid $800 for two bottles. He drank the Port with his family in Las Vegas on Christmas Day. He had the Angelica a few months later with friends in Seattle. He considered both bottles extraordinary and posted his tasting notes on Wineberserkers.com. He wrote that the Port's aroma was rich with hints of sweet, dark fruit, maple syrup, and tangerines. The taste was nutty and sweet, almost like pecans and pralines.

I decided I needed someone with an expert palate to help me determine the quality of Hellman's wine. So I contacted Fred Dame, who is a Master Sommelier, a title held by only 147 people in North America.

Getting the title is famously difficult, as it requires memorizing thousands of facts about different wines and regions around the world, as well as being able to recite unimaginable minutiae about hospitality. The test on wine involves blind tasting six wines and accurately identifying the grape, where the wine comes from, and the year it was made. Most people don't pass the first time, despite thousands of hours of study. Many people don't pass the second or third times, either.

Dame took the exam in 1984 and became the first American to pass all three parts on the first try. Only thirteen other people in the world have accomplished that. For their achievement, they were awarded the "Krug Cup," an honor bestowed by the historic Champagne company.

Dame was recently featured in the documentary *Somm*, which traces four men as they study to take the Master Sommelier test. He was busy enough before the film, traveling around the world to consult with companies about wine, but the movie's release has put even more demands on his time. Food festivals from El Paso to Boca Raton routinely ask Dame to make an appearance.

Dame lives in San Francisco. I was introduced to him in the fall of 2012 at a party after the screening of *Somm* in Napa. I mentioned Hellman's Port to him then and asked if he might assess it. Over eighteen months, I emailed him about a dozen times and sent photos of the Port. I was hoping to tempt him into meeting me, but he resisted my efforts. When I finally got him on the phone, Dame was polite but initially explained he was too busy. When he wasn't working, his priority was to spend time with his young children.

But Dame is fundamentally a teacher, a man who explains wine and spirits to those who know less than him. His instinct is to help. And even though his schedule was tight, he has a hard time saying no when he knows his knowledge is needed. He finally relented and invited me over to his house.

The empty bottle of Mumm's Champagne propping up Dame's front door was the first clue I had of Dame's stature in the wine world. It was the largest I had ever seen. Green, with a white and red label, it stood three feet high and three feet around, the height but not the width of a fire hydrant. The formal name for that size bottle is nebuchadnezzar, named after an ancient king of Babylon, and it holds fifteen liters, or about twenty bottles of wine. The Champagne house had hand-blown the bottle as a gift for Dame's 1996 wedding.

I brought Dame, a tall, imposing man in his sixties, an empty bottle of Hellman's Port. At the time, it hadn't occurred to me to ask him to taste the wine; that idea came later. I had long wondered about the size and shape of the bottles. They were larger and fatter than an average wine bottle.

I handed Dame the bottle. Sediment still clung to one side, but the label was pristine. It took him about thirty seconds to pronounce judgment. He twirled the bottle. He walked over to a window to get more light. "It's hand-blown. This was nicely done," he said.

There weren't many bottle factories in the early 1920s as Prohibition gripped the country, explained Dame. Up until 1920, most California wine was sold in bulk, in barrels. So whoever had wanted the Port in bottles had hired a craftsman.

Dame pointed out that the bottle did not have a seam, which meant it was not made in a mold. Instead, its entire surface was smooth and unlined. An air bubble was lodged in the bottle's neck, another clue that it was hand-blown. The deep indentation on the bottle, known as the punt, is a classic sign of a hand-blown bottle, he said.

Dame has taught himself about old glass bottles. He grew up on the Monterey Peninsula, a descendant of merchants who arrived in California in 1842, before the Gold Rush. Another branch of the family was in the raisin business, growing grapes in Madera in California's Central Valley. Dame, who first got interested in wine when he was eighteen and traveling through Europe, went to work after college for the Sardine Factory, a restaurant on Cannery Row in Monterey known for having one of the world's greatest wine cellars. Dame said it carries 3,200 different types of wine, about 105,000 bottles in total.

Dame began consulting about the age and provenance of wine after British inheritance laws changed in the 1980s, allowing the English to sell wine without prohibitive taxes. A flood of old wine came into the United States and people hired Dame to authenticate it. Dame remembers seeing a bottle of 1870 Château Lafite Rothschild, its bottom still encrusted with dirt from sitting on the cellar floor. Dame had to learn a lot about bottle manufacturing in a hurry, and he talked to glass blowers and artisan glassmakers and scrutinized thousands of bottles from the nineteenth century.

So Hellman's bottles were hand-blown. That explained their strange shape. But who had made them? Who had filled them with Port and Angelica?

I thought I understood the timing. The Port had been placed in barrels in 1875, where it sat for forty-six years. Isaias Hellman died in April 1920 and his only son died a month later. His other children, Clara Hellman Heller and Florence Hellman Ehrman, and their husbands must have decided to bottle and distribute the wine. The year 1921 was the second year of Prohibition and many alcohol-related companies were casting about for ways to survive. While the law prohibited the commercial sale of alcohol, there were a number of loopholes. Wineries could sell sacramental wine to churches or synagogues. The law also allowed households to make 200 gallons of wine each year for personal use. The Hellmans probably used this loophole to legally bottle the wine.

I couldn't find any mention of the bottling in any of the 40,000 documents that make up the Hellman papers at the California Historical Society. The only family member who had any recollection of the bottles was my uncle, Bill Green, who told me, before his death in 2014 at age ninety, that he thought Grace Brothers had something to do with it. Grace Brothers Brewery was a Santa Rosa beer-making company, and one of its partners, Joseph T. Grace, was a close family friend. That must be it, I thought. Grace had to close its beer-making operations because of Prohibition and Joseph Grace bottled the wine as a favor to the Hellman family.

It was only months later that I discovered the true connection, and it came while I was browsing through a book on the California Wine Association. I read that in 1920, after Prohibition went into effect, the California Wine Association split its operations in two. One company kept the property and another kept the wine. Joseph Grace then purchased the CWA name and its wine.

That was a Eureka moment. I realized that Grace probably took an inventory of his new assets. And during that process, he probably discovered the two neglected barrels of 1875 Port and Angelica sitting in a warehouse somewhere. That's the way Grace came to bottle the wine as a favor to his friends.

It was only as I was leaving Dame's house that I realized I should have asked him to taste some of Hellman's Port. After all, he was a man who knew wine better than almost anyone else on earth. He had an encyclopedic memory of wines he had tasted over the decades. That included Port, too. Dame had showed me an empty bottle of an 1868 Port sitting on his kitchen table. He and his friends had just finished the bottle the week before. The oldest Port he had ever drunk had been made in 1780 or 1790. And I had thought I would be giving him something special with a taste of an 1875 Port!

Getting a second appointment with Dame was just as hard as the first. I emailed him. No answer. I emailed him again. Silence. I finally caught him on his cell phone while he was driving to Sacramento. When I asked if he would taste the Port, he was reluctant. He was about to go on a long trip to Australia. But once again Dame couldn't bring himself to turn me down. I promised the visit would be brief.

It rained the night before my appointment, the first wet weather the drought-stricken Bay Area had seen in months. The traffic across the Bay Bridge was bumper to bumper and never went faster than twenty miles an hour. Even though I had allotted an hour for the drive, I had been delayed leaving my house in Berkeley and didn't think I would arrive in time. As the car inched along, I worried that if I was late, Dame would shut the door in my face.

I did sense some impatience on Dame's part as he led me through the garage to his kitchen. He didn't greet me warmly, or offer up chitchat.

He was all business. I handed him a full bottle of Hellman's Port. It was one that I had been saving for around fifteen years. Forest green wax covered the top. Dame tipped the bottle over a garbage can and began gently hitting the wax with a knife to break it apart.

Dame then eased a corkscrew into the cork. It crumbled into a few pieces as he extracted it, but he finally managed to pull it out. "The seal is still good," he said, as he showed me a piece of the moist cork. That was a good sign, since the flavor of wine deteriorates if a cork dries out, permitting oxygen to enter the bottle.

Almost immediately a sweet aphrodisiacal scent filled the air. I was standing about four feet away from the bottle yet I could smell the Port's fumes. The aroma, cooped up inside a bottle for ninety-three years, rushed out. "It smells fantastic," said Dame.

Dame brought the bottle into his dining room. We sat down and Dame poured the Port into two glasses. It was dark amber, almost the color of the redwood it was once stored in. The liquid was translucent. I had thought it would be opaque. It's comparable to an "old, beautiful tawny Port," said Dame.

I lifted my glass and let the Port swirl over my tongue. I wasn't prepared for the intensity of the flavor. Sweetness exploded over my taste buds, followed by a pleasant sharpness. I have never been good at thinking of adjectives to describe wine, but Dame, with decades of practice behind him, didn't have that problem.

"It has a wonderful old clay smell that I love," he said as he lifted the glass to examine it more closely. "It's delicious. It has almost a sour cherry quality to it, like cherries soaked in brandy. There is a sweetness of fruit here."

He paused and thought. His brown eyes softened. "It's phenomenal," he said.

The longer we sat there, the mellower the Port became. The exposure to oxygen softened the alcoholic sharpness I had tasted when the bottle was first opened. Time seemed to mellow and slow down, too. The anxiety I had been feeling about imposing on Dame's time melted away. He also appeared to forget he was busy. We talked. I told him a little about the history of the bottle, how my great-great-grandfather had purchased the land in the 1870s and how excited I had been when I discovered Jean Louis Sainsevain was the winemaker.

Dame had drunk many old wines during his career and always enjoyed them for their history, but Hellman's Port actually tasted good, he said. Many of the old wines he had tried had lost their fruitiness, and tasted flat, but this Port was bursting with fruit flavor. There was no way this Port had been forgotten in the back of the winery, Dame said. It must have been deliberately set aside because it was so special. Dame said he wished he could have tasted the Port with the friends he was with the previous day—the other thirteen Krug Cup winners, the people who had passed the Master Sommelier exams in the first try.

"Wines like this must be shared," said Dame. "It is history. It is an honor to drink it with you as a descendant."

Suddenly Dame jumped up and went into his bedroom. When he came back he was holding a solid gold cravat pin. At the top was a tiny gold nugget. One of his ancestors had found a large nugget during the Gold Rush and had made it into five gold cravat pins for his five sons. Dame has a nineteenth-century photo of his relatives wearing the pin. Apparently, only three of the pins remain in the family.

That gesture gave me the answer I had been seeking for the last few years: Why is wine so special? What drives people to become fascinated by it?

The answer, of course, is that it brings people together. Here I was with a man I barely knew, a man who was pressed for time, yet who decided to help me better understand my ancestor's Port. We had sipped a bit together and thought about the past, about the era the grapes were pressed, about the men who brought the wine to fruition. Drinking the Port at ten a.m. had left me a little lightheaded—and also very happy. I had shared a piece of my family history with Dame, which prompted him to share his family history with me. We were doing what people had done for millennia, and would continue doing as long as there were grapes in the ground and wine to share. We were connecting. And wine was what brought us together.

"This Port has plenty of time left," said Dame, as he leaned back in his chair and twirled his glass. "It's going to outlive us."

EPILOGUE

R. Steven Lapham retired from the U.S. attorney's office in 2013. He is now a Superior Court judge for the Juvenile Division of Sacramento County Superior Court. He said he likes intervening in the lives of young people and helping them to stay out of the court system. The walls of Lapham's office still hold mementos of his days as a prosecutor, including court drawings of the Unabomber case. Lapham had to write about his top ten cases when he applied for the judgeship; one of those was the Mark Anderson prosecution.

Brian Parker is still a field agent for the ATF, based in Sacramento. He continues to investigate arson cases. When he started investigating Mark Anderson he did not have any children. Now he has three.

Ted Hall's Long Meadow Ranch continues to make highly regarded wine. The Halls have expanded the farming operation of the ranch as well. In February 2010, they opened Farmstead, a farm-to-table restaurant, in a former nursery barn on two and a half acres at the south end of St. Helena. The place has become a destination. In addition to a well-regarded restaurant, the property holds a tasting room, a fruit and vegetable garden, a seasonal farm stand where people can buy olive oil produced by the ranch, and a store. It wasn't until the Halls opened Farmstead that the fire subsided as a central influence on their business.

Delia Viader's Viader Vineyards is flourishing, although recovering economically from the fire was delayed even further by the 2008 recession. The operation is now a family affair: Alan Viader is the head winemaker and his sister Janet oversees sales and marketing and the wine club. Marciela Viader, Alan's wife, is the director of the culinary program. A professionally trained chef, she prepares banquets and meals for visiting VIPs. Viader also leads wine-related trips to places like Argentina, her ancestral home. Viader oversees the winery's operations and she assists Alan when he is blending the wine.

Dick Ward of Saintsbury keeps a few cases of wine that survived the Wines Central fire in a back area of his barrel room. Some of the white cardboard boxes are still covered with soot. The bottles were a custom blend for Premiere Napa Valley, the winter auction that mostly draws retailers looking for unique vintages they can sell to their customers. Saintsbury suffered a fair amount of damage when an earthquake hit Napa on August 24, 2014. Hundreds of bottles of the winery's remaining library wine fell to the floor and broke. Saintsbury estimated the damage as $50,000. The bottles were not insured.

Mark's brother Steven Anderson died, destitute, in 2013 of prostate cancer that had spread to his bones. He died one day before he would have turned fifty-nine. He is buried in a pauper's grave in Sonoma County.

Doña Maria Merced Williams Rains Carrillo moved out of her home on Rancho Cucamonga in 1876. She lived in poverty, but one of her and Rains's daughters married Henry Gage, who became the governor of California. She died in 1907 at the age of sixty-eight. One of Doña Merced's great-granddaughters, Lita Grey, married the actor Charlie Chaplin.

The 1875 Port and Angelica—A bottle of this Port is displayed at the historic Vintners' Hall of Fame at the Culinary Institute of America at Greystone in St. Helena. It is part of an exhibit of the history of California wine. There are probably a few dozen bottles left of this wine in private hands scattered around the country, most with Hellman's descendants. Bottles occasionally come up for auction.

Rancho Cucamonga—There are only about 500 acres of grapevines left in San Bernardino County, down from around 23,000 acres in the early 1960s. Just a few remnants remain of what was once the country's largest winegrowing region. The Hofer family, who once owned 1,000 acres of grapes, still has a five-acre parcel near the Ontario airport, with a small amount planted in vines. The Galleano family owns the largest vineyard in the county, the 300-acre Lopez Ranch, which sits between two freeways and a Staples and a Target store right near the San Gabriel Mountains. The Filippi family, which started to grow grapes in the 1920s and purchased the site of the Cucamonga Vineyard wine cellar, still makes wine in the area, although they now buy grapes from others. Despite this decline, the Cucamonga Valley was officially named an American Viticultural Area (AVA) in 1995.

The Cucamonga Vineyard—Wine is still being made at the site of the original vineyard, although not from grapes grown nearby. Bryan Farr is the owner of The Wine Tailor at 8916 Foothill Boulevard in the building that sits on the site of the old cellar. The Wine Tailor describes itself as a boutique winery. Customers come in, select a grape must (the juice from crushed grapes), and then sprinkle it with yeast. They return five to seven weeks later to get their wine. Customers also design their own labels and bottle their own wine. The fact that the facility has ties to Tiburcio Tapia from 1839 is a selling point.

The California Wine Association—Right before Prohibition the CWA operated fifty-two wineries and controlled more than 80 percent of the state's wine. The organization recognized that temperance was coming and stopped making wine around 1917. It was able to sell 4 million gallons right before selling wine became illegal, but it was stuck with 6.75 million gallons at Winehaven when the Volstead Act became law in 1920.[194] The company started to produce around 1,000 barrels of fresh grape juice in early 1920.[195] The CWA was officially dissolved in 1935. It has mostly been forgotten. An antique dealer named Dean Walters has become one of the world's biggest collectors of CWA memorabilia and has started a website that showcases the company's beautiful labels. He hopes to build a wine museum one day. Another wine entrepreneur, Norman Hersch, recently acquired the trademark rights for the label of the California Wine Association, and is intending to revive it.

Mark Anderson is serving out his twenty-seven-year prison term in Terminal Island, a federal penitentiary near Los Angeles. He filed an appeal in 2012. Since then he has gone through three different appellate attorneys. The appeal was denied in July 2015.

APPENDIX: HISTORY OF THE OWNERSHIP OF CUCAMONGA VINEYARD[196]

1839

Juan B. Alvarado, the governor of California, then owned by Mexico, granted the 13,000-acre Rancho Cucamonga to Tiburcio Tapia.

1845

Upon Tapia's death, his daughter Maria Merced Tapia Prudhomme and her husband Victor Prudhomme inherit the land.

1858

The Prudhommes sell the Rancho to John Rains, who does not put his wife's name on the deed.

1863

The courts rule that Maria Merced Rains is the owner of the rancho. She deeds half the land to her five children.

1870

When Maria Merced Rains cannot pay the mortgage taken out by her husband, the rancho is auctioned at a sheriff's sale. Isaias Hellman, a banker, buys the property and immediately sells off chunks for development.

1871

Hellman sells the 580-acre vineyard to Joseph Garcia, a Portuguese sea captain, for $25,000. Garcia then sells it to Pierre Sainsevain, the younger brother of Jean Louis Sainsevain, who has been managing the vineyard since 1867.

1873

Hellman buys back the vineyard for $35,000. He brings in investors to expand the planting and build a new winery. They include John G. Downey, a former California governor, and Hellman's business partner in the Farmers and Merchants Bank, Isaiah M. Hellman, his cousin and a dry goods merchant, and wine man Benjamin Dreyfus.

1878

Dreyfus takes over management of the Cucamonga Vineyard, although the partnership still owns the land. When he dies in 1886, his firm, B. Dreyfus & Co., continues to manage most of the vineyard. Hellman, however, had started taking a portion of the annual vintage to sell in 1881.

1894

B. Dreyfus & Co. becomes part of the California Wine Association, which continues to manage the Cucamonga Vineyard.

1895

After all the original partners of the vineyard, except Hellman, had died, the partnership incorporated as The Cucamonga Vineyard Company, with a capital stock of $100,000. The directors were Isaias W. Hellman, his brother Herman Hellman, L. P. Weil, J. M. Harvey (the nephew of John Downey), John Milner, P. D. Martin, and Max Meyberg (a cousin of Hellman's).

1910

Hellman rents the Cucamonga Vineyard to the California Wine Association for six years.

1917

The vines are dug up and the Cucamonga Vineyard is sold to the Cucamonga Investment Company for $91,011. Hellman also sells the land the Rains house sits on to the same group for $76,532.[197]

1920

Hugh and Ida Thomas buy the vineyard and winery and plant new grapes.

1967

The descendants of the Thomases sell the winery to Joseph Filippi, whose family has made wine in the region for decades.

1980

A developer acquires the property and builds a strip mall called Thomas Winery Plaza at 8916 Foothill Boulevard. The remnants of the old winery still stand, along with huge redwood barrels that supposedly were brought around the horn by John Rains.

2004

Ken and Angela Lineberger open The Wine Tailor, which brings winemaking back to the site of the original winery. Bryan and Joey Farr now own the business.

ACKNOWLEDGMENTS

When I would tell people I was working on a book about wine they would roll their eyes and say something like "Tough life." It's true that I got to spend a lot of time in the Napa Valley, one of the most beautiful places in California, and drink my share of fantastic wine. But the most satisfying part of writing any book is the people encountered on the way.

The winemakers who were intimately affected by the Vallejo warehouse fire didn't have to open up to me, but did. Thank you, Delia Viader, Dick Ward, Ted Hall, and many others. It was the Wines Central warehouse manager Debbie Polverino who tipped me off to Steven Anderson's websites about his brother. Thank you for leading me to that invaluable information and sharing your story. A shout-out as well to Fred Dame, whose mastery of hand-blown bottles and historic vintages gave me important insights into what makes an old wine shine.

There were two men who didn't seem to mind my dozens of emails, phone calls, and requests for interviews. This book would not exist without the help of ATF Agent Brian O. Parker and former assistant U.S. attorney Steven Lapham. Thank you for your time and all your careful explanations. The ATF also generously allowed me access to files on Mark Anderson.

Many people who knew Mark Anderson in Sausalito also agreed to meet with me. A big thank you to Yoshi Tome, who had not talked to the press before; Ron Lussier, who shared a bottle of Sine Qua Non, an experience I will never forget; and Martin Brown, Mervyn Regan, Eric Johnson, Tom Johnson, and others.

I also have to thank Mark Anderson for being as open with me as he was, however much his credibility was in doubt.

This book happened because Felicity Barringer, then the editor of the short-lived, but much admired, *New York Times* San Francisco section, assigned me to write about Anderson's upcoming trial. It turned out to be one of the best assignments of my life and I thank her for letting me pursue what became a six-year long story.

Demian Bulwa of the *San Francisco Chronicle* was also particularly helpful. In addition to writing great stories on Anderson, he shared with me some of the material he had gathered during his reporting. I also want to thank James Conaway, a southern gentleman if I ever met one, for his advice and guidance.

There has been a small but dedicated group of people researching and writing about the history of California wine. Without their scholarship, I could never have written about the Cucamonga Vineyard, the California Wine Association, or other aspects of the nineteenth-century wine industry. I relied heavily on Thomas Pinney's two-volume opus on the history of wine in America, Charles Sullivan's many books, and the work done by Gail Unzelman and the late Ernest Peninou on the CWA. When I was growing up in San Francisco, I used to regularly walk by Peninou's French Laundry on Sacramento Street (which has been in the same location since 1903) little realizing that Ernest's second job was amassing data on California wine. Esther Boulton Black's exhaustive book on Rancho Cucamonga and Doña Merced was also invaluable.

Thank you to Dean Walters for preserving (and showing me) labels and bottles and pamphlets of the CWA. Bernadette Glenn, Doug Murray, and Dora Calott Wang graciously hosted me while I pored over documents at the Huntington Library.

When I first got the idea to write a book, I didn't know much about wine except that I liked to drink it. Thankfully, the Symposium for Professional Wine Writers at Meadowood Napa Valley was there to fill in the gaps—and please my palate. Thank you, Jim Gordon, the director of the symposium; Bill Harlan, who hosted us at Meadowood; and Linda Reiff and the Napa Valley Vintners, who donate such delicious wine. Hess Winery also generously provided support for a fellowship.

For the last ten years or so I have been blessed by the wisdom and support of an extraordinary group of women. Every question I asked North 24th Writers, every doubt I expressed, every hope I dreamed, was met with sensitivity and acceptance. Thank you, Allison Bartlett, Leslie Berlin, Leslie Crawford, Kathy Ellison, Sharon Epel, Susan Freinkel, Katherine Neilan, Lisa Okuhn, and Jill Story. I want to make an extra shout-out to Julia Flynn Siler for reading and editing so many versions of the manuscript and always being willing to do so.

I want to thank my agent, Michael Carlisle, and his team of assistants at Inkwell Management, Ethan Bassof, Lauren Smythe, and Hannah Schwartz for their advice and hard work on my proposal and manuscript. Michael, your faith in me has been so important. Michel Flamini, my editor at St. Martin's Press, has also been a terrific cheerleader. I appreciate the delicate care he took with my manuscript. Vicki Lame saved me from many a mistake.

And last but not least, my friends. I have to thank my Berkeleyside colleagues who always told me to take the time I needed to write this book, even though the press of news in Berkeley means we can all be working 24/7: Tracey Taylor, Lance Knobel, Emilie Raguso, and Wendy Cohen.

Finally, my family. My mother, Georganne Conley, died before I completed this work. She was such a staunch cheerleader for my first book, *Towers of Gold*. I know she would have been at my readings and talks, sitting in the front row, encouraging me on. Mom, I miss you every day.

My brothers Lloyd and Steven—if only there was a family tree in this book. I would not leave you off. Thank you for your love and support. Steven, an extra thank you for making sure I didn't repeat the same word in a paragraph. My cousin Miranda Heller was gracious in repeatedly talking to me about a difficult experience.

That leaves my husband, Gary Wayne, and my two lovely daughters, Charlotte Wayne and Juliet Wayne. Once again, with love, this book is for you.

NOTES

INTRODUCTION

1. The retail value of the wine sold in the United States in 2014 was $37.6 billion, with $24.6 billion coming from the sale of 269 million cases of California wine.

1. THE MYSTERY OF WINE

2. Mark Anderson, letter to author, January 11, 2010.
3. A 2011 report prepared by Stonebridge Research Group for the Napa Valley Vintners Association determined that the economic impact of the 789 licensed wineries in Napa County was $13.3 billion a year in Napa, $25.9 billion in California, and $50.3 billion in the U.S. Napa produced 20 percent of all wines made in California in 2011 and 17 percent of all the wine made in the U.S.
4. Patricia Leigh Brown, "Growing in Napa: Club, and Camp, for Wine Lovers," *New York Times*, October 21, 2005.
5. Ibid.

2. ALL IS LOST

6. An appellation is a legal definition for a specific geographical area. The Alcohol Tobacco Tax and Trade Bureau is the federal entity that awards the designation. While the entire Napa Valley is an appellation, small areas within it with specific subclimates are also appellations, including Los Carneros, Coombsville, Oakville, Yountville, Rutherford, Stags Leap, Spring Mountain, Howell Mountain, and Mount Veeder, among others.

3. THE WRECKED REMAINS

7. Martin Kasindorf and Jonathan T. Lovitt, "Harsh Details amid Unabomber Pleas," *USA Today*, January 23, 1988.

4. A SOGGY, CHARRED MESS

8. David Ryan, "Complex Legal Mess May Await Wineries That Lost Vintages," *Napa Valley Register*, October 20, 2005.

9. *United States of America v. Mark C. Anderson*, statement of R. Steven Lapham,

10. Ben Conniff, reprint of "A Winemaker Turns Disaster into a Delicious Barbecue Sauce," from *Tasting Table Everywhere*, May 22, 2009.

5. JOE SAUSALITO

11. Undated, unmarked newspaper clippings. Steven Anderson presented them to *San Francisco Chronicle* reporter Demian Bulwa in 2007. Bulwa gave them to the author.

12. Jeff Greenwald, "Livin' on the Dock of the Bay," Smithsonian.com, April 3, 2012.

13. The schools Anderson attended included Santa Rosa Junior College, the University of San Francisco, San Francisco Law School, Golden Gate University, the University of California at Berkeley, and the Sorbonne in Paris, among others.

14. Mark Anderson, letter to the author, March 12, 2010.

6. THE BEGINNING OF RANCHO CUCAMONGA

15. Thomas Pinney, *A History of Wine in America: From Prohibition to the Present* (Berkeley, Los Angeles, London: University of California Press, 2005), 209.

16. Esther Boulton Black, *Rancho Cucamonga and Doña Merced* (Redlands, CA: San Bernardino County Museum Association, 1973), 197.

17. Roy Brady, "The Swallow That Came from Capistrano," *New West*, September 24, 1979.

18. Ibid.

19. Thomas Pinney, *A History of Wine in America: From the Beginnings to Prohibition* (Berkeley, Los Angeles, London: University of California Press, 2005), 239.

20. Irving McKee, "The Beginnings of Los Angeles Winemaking," *The Historical Quarterly of Southern California,* v. 29, no 1., 59–71.

21. Richard Steven Street, *Beasts in the Field: A Narrative History of the California Farmworkers, 1769–1913* (Stanford, CA: Stanford University Press, 2004), 40.

22. Street, 39.

23. Charles Franklin Carter, "Duhaut-Cilly's Account of California in the Years 1827–28," *California Historical Society Quarterly,* 8 (September 1929), 246.

24. Letter by Father Bachelot as quoted by Léonce Jore and L. Jay Oliva, "Jean Louis Vignes of Bordeaux, Pioneer of California Viticulture," *Southern California Quarterly*, 45 (December 1963), 289–303.

25. Edwin Bryant, "What I Saw In California," as quoted by Blake Gumprecht in *The Los Angeles River: Its Life, Death and Possible Rebirth*, (Baltimore, MD: Johns Hopkins University Press, 1999), 48

26. Pedro Sainsevain to Agoston Haraszthy, June 22, 1886, in The Haraszthy Family MSS C-D 418, Bancroft Library.

27. W. H. Emory as quoted in Pinney, "Notes of a Military Reconnaissance from Fort Leavenworth, in Missouri, to San Diego, in California," 249.

28. Sainsevain to Haraszthy.

29. Ginoffvine, "Thomas Vineyards, California's Oldest Winery," www.ginoffvine .wordpress.com, May 8, 2010.

7. WINE FEVER

30. John Walton Caughey, "The Jacob Y. Stover Narrative," *Pacific Historical Review* 6, no. 2 (June 1, 1937): 165–181.

31. Undated news clipping, Hayes Scraps on Emigrant Notes II, V 14, Bancroft Library.

32. A legal document in Hayes Scraps, v. 14, the section of Cucamonga, says that Merced and her sister had about $91,000 worth of cattle and sheep. Rancho del Chino was divided with Merced getting $25,000, bringing her net worth to at least $70,000. The same legal document described how much stock Rains owned.

33. Undated news clipping, Hayes Scraps on California Agriculture.

34. *Los Angeles Star*, Volume VII, Number 24, October 24, 1857.

35. Joseph Warren Revere, *A Tour of Duty in California* (New York: C. S. Francis & Co.), 282.

36. Pinney, *From the Beginnings to Prohibition*, 252.

37. *California Farmer and Journal of Useful Sciences,* Volume 6, Number 7, September 5, 1856.

38. Daniel J. Thomas, "On Agricultural Statistics of the State" in *California State Agricultural Society*, Transactions 1859, Table XXV, 344.

39. Pinney, *From the Beginnings to Prohibition*, 253.

40. Charles Kohler, "Wine Production in California: Account Made Up from Material Provided by Charles Kohler," 1878, p. 7, Bancroft Library MSS C-D 111.

41. J. J. Warner, Benjamin Hayes, and Dr. J. P. Widney, *Historical Sketch of Los Angeles County, from the Spanish Occupancy, by the Founding of the Mission San Gabriel Archangel, September 8, 1771, to July 4, 1876* (Los Angeles: Lewis Lewin & Co. 1876), 62.

42. Pinney, *From the Beginnings to Prohibition,* 251.

43. W. W. Robinson, *The Indians of Los Angeles: Story of the Liquidation of a People* (Los Angeles: Glen Dawson 1952), 2.

44. Horace Bell, *Reminiscences of a Ranger: Early Times in Southern California* (Los Angeles: Yarnell, Caystile & Mathes, Printers, 1881), 35–36.

45. Harris Newmark, *Sixty Years in Southern California* (Boston and New York: Houghton Mifflin Co. 1930), 202–203.

8. BLOOD ON THE LAND

46. Benjamin Hayes to Col. Couts, November 26, 1862. Hayes Scraps, vol. 14, Bancroft Library.

47. It is difficult to determine exactly how much Rains owed. While he noted his debt as $14,600 on this piece of paper, the historian Esther Boulton Black put the debt at $16,000, or even more, based on testimony delivered in an 1863 trial, *Rains vs. Dunlap,* in Santa Clara County. Isaias Hellman testified that he was also a mortgage holder; he had lent Rains $5,352 shortly before his death. The author was unable to locate the court files as Santa Clara County had disposed of them.

48. Benjamin Hayes, *Pioneer Notes from the Diaries of Judge Benjamin Hayes*, edited and published by Marjorie Tisdale Wolcott, 147.

49. Black, 90.

50. *Los Angeles Star,* Feb. 28, 1853.

51. Richard Henry Dana, *Two Years Before the Mast* (Boston: James R. Osgood & Co., 1873), 179.

52. Benjamin Hayes letter to Col. Couts, December 3, 1862, LA Court Case 1017, Huntington Library.

53. Benjamin Hayes to Col. Couts, November 26, 1862.

54. *Los Angeles News,* December 2, 1863.

55. Ramón Carillo testimony in Hayes Scraps, vol. 14.

56. John W. Teal in *Arizona and the West: A Quarterly Journal of History*, diary edited by Henry Walker, University of Arizona, Tucson, spring 1971, pp. 70, 71, as cited by Black, p. 119, and footnote 11.

57. George William Beattie and Helen Pruitt Beattie, *Heritage of the Valley: San Bernardino's First Century* (Pasadena, CA: San Pasqual Press, 1939), 160.

58. Joe Blackstock, "Rains House Saved by a Hair," *Daily Bulletin*, March 27, 2011.

9. SAUSALITO CELLARS

59. Ron Lussier, interview with author, May 2014.

60. Anderson, letter to author, November 25, 2009.

61. Pinney, *From Prohibition to the Present*, 217.

62. Ibid., 225.

63. Ibid., 225–226.

10. FOR THE LOVE OF WINE

64. *Marin Scope,* August 28–September 4, 2000.

65. Bulwa, "Wine Scandal Leaves Sausalito with a Bad Taste," *San Francisco Chronicle,* May 29, 2007.

11. WINE FRAUD

66. Christopher Early, "The $2.7 Million Wine Heist," *Orange County Register*, November 27, 2013.

67. Sara Jean Green, "Men Plead Guilty in Massive Wine Theft," *Seattle Times*, July 14, 2014.

68. Jancis Robinson, ed., and Julia Harding, assistant ed., *The Oxford Companion to Wine* (Oxford, New York: Oxford University Press, 2006), 26–27.

69. Stanley Hock, *Harvesting the Dream: The Trinchero Family of Sutter Home: 50 Years in the Napa Valley* (St. Helena, CA: Sutter Home Winery, 1998), 37.

70. Hock, 44.

71. R. Steven Lapham, interview with author.

72. Richard Gahagan, ATF agent, interview with author, March 2014.

73. Donald Woutat, "The Other Players in the Scandal," *Los Angeles Times*, January 30, 1994.

74. Donald Woutat, "State Near Bottom of Barrel of Wine Grape Scandal," *Los Angeles Times*, January 30, 1994.

75. Michael Doyle, "Justice Department crushes Winemaker's Hopes of Pardon," *McClatchy Newspapers*, January, 8, 2009.

76. Maureen Downey, interviewed in "What Makes a Billionaire Cry? Bill Koch Duped by Wine Fakes," by *20/20*, June 13, 2014.

77. Lettie Teague, "The State of Fine-Wine Auction Houses: Less Flash, More Fire," *Wall Street Journal*, October 25, 2013.

78. Peter D. Meltzer, "Worldwide Wine Auction Revenues Fall in 2012," *Wine Spectator*, January 15, 2013.

79. Benjamin Wallace, "Château Sucker," *Vanity Fair*, July 2012.

80. Mike Steinberger, "Going, Going, Gone . . . for 11M," *Financial Times*, June 9, 2006.

81. Howard G. Goldberg, "Acker Starts Season with $10M Cellar," *Decanter*, January 18, 2006.

82. Peter Hellman, "The Crusade Against Counterfeits," *Wine Spectator*, December 15, 2009.

83. Jay McInerney, "His Magnum Is Bigger Than Yours," *The Juice* (New York: Alfred A. Knopf, 2012).

84. Mosi Secret, "A Koch Brother, on a Crusade Against Counterfeit Rare Wines, Takes the Stand," *New York Times*, December 13, 2003.

85. CBS Sunday Morning, "Counterfeit Wine: A Vintage Crime," interview with William I. Koch, December 22, 2013, http://www.cbsnews.com/news/counterfeit-wine-a-vintage-crime/.

86. *The Salt*, NPR, The Kitchen Sisters, "How Atomic Wine Particles Helped Solve a Wine Fraud Mystery," June 3, 2014, www.npr.org/blogs/thesalt/2014/06/03/318241738/how-atomic-particles-became-the-smoking-gun-in-wine-fraud-mystery.

87. Sausalito Cellars website, recovered from The Wayback Machine, http://web.archive.org/web/20001018174123/http://www.sausalitocellars.com/.

88. Brian O. Parker, interview with author. Parker showed author a copy of the time sheet.

12. THE STRUGGLE FOR RECOGNITION

89. Proceedings of the Farmers' Club from the Annual Report of the Institute of the City of New York, 1862, 86–87.

90. *Daily Alta California*, Vol. 12, No. 3900, October 17, 1860.

91. Proceedings, pp. 86–87.

92. Pinney, 257.

93. *Pacific Wine and Spirit Review,* February 6, 1893.

94. Carosso quoting Arpad Haraszthy, p. 132. S.B.V.C, Third Viticultural Convention, 1884, p. 140. *Proceedings of the California Pure Food Congress.*

95. *California Farmer and Journal of Useful Sciences,* December 2, 1859.

96. *California Farmer and Journal of Useful Sciences,* December 16, 1875.

97. *Sacramento Daily Union*, April 21, 1870.

98. Garcia deeded the vineyard to Pierre Sainsevain a few months later and Jean Louis Sainsevain's name soon appeared in the deed, according to Black. On June 27, 1873, Hellman bought back the vineyard from Garcia and J. L. Sainsevain, according to Black. Hellman brought in partners, including former governor John G. Downey, also a founder of the Farmers and Merchants Bank, his cousin, the dry goods merchant Isaiah M. Hellman, and Benjamin Dreyfus, the proprietor of B. Dreyfus & Co., a large wine concern.

99. *Daily Alta California*, July 20, 1870.

100. *Daily Alta California*, September 18, 1871.

101. Charles Sullivan, "Wine in California: The Early Years, Los Angeles, 1850–1870. Part I," *Wayward Tendrils*, vol. 21, 2011.

102. *Daily Alta California*, Vol. 9, July 11, 1857.

103. *Sacramento Daily Union*, Vol. 17, July 26, 1859.

104. *Daily Alta Californian*, February 16, 1858.

105. John Hittell, *Resources of California: Comprising Agriculture, Mining, Geography, Climate, &c., and the Past and Future Development of the State* (San Francisco, New York: A. Roman and Company, 1869), 204.

106. *Los Angeles Herald*, September 16, 1874.

107. Benjamin Truman, *Semi-Tropical California: Its Climate, Healthfulness, Productiveness, and Scenery* (San Francisco: A. L. Bancroft & Co., 1874), 198.

108. *Southern California Horticulturist*, vol. 1, no. 1, 1877.

109. Herbert B. Leggett, *Early History of Wine Production in California* (San Francisco: The Wine Institute, 1941), 61.

110. Frances Dinkelspiel, *Towers of Gold: How One Jewish Immigrant Named Isaias Hellman Created California* (New York: St. Martins Press, 2008), 88.

111. Hellman's purchase of the Cucamonga Vineyard was the start of a sideline business in winemaking. In the late 1870s he helped Matthew Keller, the proprietor of the 100-acre Rising Sun Vineyard in Los Angeles, restructure his debt and put his operation on a better financial footing. In 1882, Hellman was among the group that invested $500,000 in the San Gabriel Winery. After Shorb died in 1896, Hellman took over as president. His Farmers and Merchants Bank carried the mortgage, and after Shorb's widow tried to claim unsuccessfully in court that her husband had coerced her to co-sign the note, the bank foreclosed on the property in 1901. A short time later, Henry Huntington bought the land. It is now the home of The Huntington Library, Art Collections, and Botanical Gardens in San Marino, CA. Hellman was also part of the syndicate that bought a controlling interest in the California Wine Association in 1901.

112. Pinney, *From the Beginnings to Prohibition*, 290.

113. Dreyfus took over management of the Cucamonga Vineyard in 1878. One of the first things he did was fire Jean Louis Sainsevain and install his own vineyard manager. Dreyfus gave Sainsevain 30,000 gallons as severance, according to Norton B. Stern and William Kramer in "Benjamin Dreyfus: The Wine Tycoon of Anaheim," *Western State Jewish Historical Quarterly,* vol. XLIV: 3/4, Spring/Summer 2012, 15–31.

114. Ernest Peninou and Gail Unzelman, *The California Wine Association and Its Member Wineries, 1894–1920* (Santa Rosa, CA: Nomis Press, 2000), 50.

115. Pinney, *From the Beginnings to Prohibition*, 311.

116. Ibid., 313.

117. Ibid., 304.

118. Ibid., 322.

119. Ibid., 322.

120. Ibid., 322.

121. Ernest Peninou, *Leland Stanford's Great Vina Ranch, 1881–1919* (San Francisco: Yolo Hills Viticultural Society, 1991), 32–40.

122. Street, 242.

123. Peninou, *Leland Stanford's Great Vina Ranch,* 38.

124. Ibid., 45.

125. Ibid., 51.

126. Alberta Mary Snell, *Viticulture in California from 1870 to 1900: A Chapter in the Economic History of California,* thesis, UC Berkeley, 1926.

13. THE ERA OF THE GREAT SAN FRANCISCO WINE HOUSES

127. Peninou and Unzelman, 25.

128. *Pacific Wine and Spirit Review,* vol. 30, June 6, 1893.

129. *Pacific Wine and Spirit Review,* May 6, 1893.

14. THE WINE WAR

130. California Wine Association letter to stockholders, February 1903, MSS 300, Book 5, California Historical Society.

131. California Wine Association records, California Historical Society, Box 1.

132. Peninou and Unzelman, 38.

133. Christopher Carlsmith, "Percy Tredegar Morgan, 1862–1920, Portrait of a Stanford Trustee," *Sandstone & Tile, Stanford History Review,* vol. 28, no. 3, Fall 2004.

134. Peninou and Unzelman, 34.

135. Undated, unidentified newspaper clip in Percy T. Morgan scrapbook.

136. Peninou and Unzelman, 4.

137. Undated, unidentified newspaper clip in Percy T. Morgan scrapbook.

138. Thomas Pinney, *The Makers of American Wine: A Record of Two Hundred Years* (Berkeley: University of California Press, 2012), 73 (illustration).

139. *Pacific Wine and Spirit Review,* March 7, 1896.

140. Peninou and Unzelman, 74.

141. Ibid., 75.

142. *Pacific Wine and Spirit Review,* July 22, 1896.

143. Peninou and Unzelman, 76.

144. *Pacific Wine and Spirit Review,* September 30, 1898.

145. *Pacific Wine and Spirit Review,* June 24, 1897.

146. Peninou and Unzelman, 77.

147. Ibid.

148. Jack W. Florence, Sr., *Legacy of a Village: The Italian Swiss Colony and People of Asti, California* (Phoenix, AZ: Raymond Court Press), 64.

149. *San Francisco Chronicle,* May 14, 1898.

15. EARTHQUAKE AND FIRE

150. San Francisco Blue Book, 1905, p. 176, Internet archive.

151. Charles L. Sullivan, "The Great Wine Quake," *Wayward Tendrils Quarterly,* Vol. 16, No. 2, p. 3.

152. *San Francisco Call,* Vol. 99, No. 152, May 1, 1906.

153. Although no papers from Lachman & Jacobi remain, family influences may have played a small role in the firm's decision to join forces with the CWA, which was then controlled by Isaias Hellman and a syndicate of investors. Hellman's son, Marco Hellman, had married Frances Jacobi, the daughter of Frederick Jacobi, the co-owner of Lachman & Jacobi, in 1898. The author is their great-granddaughter.

154. Pinney, *From the Beginnings to Prohibition,* 236.

155. *Pacific Wine and Spirit Review,* April/May 1906 edition.

156. *San Francisco Call,* Vol. 99, No. 143, April 22, 1906.

157. *San Francisco Call,* Vol. 99, No. 155, May 4, 1906.

158. *Pacific Wine and Spirit Review*, Calamity Edition, April/May 1906.

159. Peninou and Unzelman, 103–104.

160. Ibid., 104.

161. "Everything you wanted to know about Point Molate in a 5 minute tour," by the Richmond Museum of History.

162. Jackson Graves to Isaias W. Hellman, January 8, 1915, Huntington Library.

163. Graves to Hellman, January 3, 1916,

164. Graves to Hellman, August 21, 1916.

165. This included the original 580-acre vineyard and an adjacent 534-acre parcel upon which the Rains house sat.

166. Graves to Hellman, January 19, 1916.

167. Graves to Hellman, October 25, 1916.

168. Graves to Hellman, January 22, 1917.

16. THEFT AND DECEPTION

169. Mark Anderson interview with author, April 5, 2010.

170. Bulwa, *San Francisco Chronicle,* May 29, 2007.

171. *International Food and Wine Society v. Mark Anderson*, Marin County Superior Court.

172. ATF telephone interview with John Fox on August 8, 2006.

173. *Marin County vs. Mark Anderson*, Marin County Superior Court.

174. October 13, 2005, interview by ATF Agent Parker with Jack Krystal.

175. October 13, 2005, interview by ATF Agent Parker with Linda Hothem.

176. *The United States of America v. Mark C. Anderson*, June 24, 2011.

177. ATF Agent Brian Parker interview with Jason Greer.

17. DISMAY

178. ETS Laboratories would determine that Cabernet Sauvignon and Petit Verdot were resilient to heat shock, while Syrah was not.

179. *Wine Spectator*, February 24, 2006.

180. Cathy Corison interview with the author, July 2014.

18. THE TRAP IS SET

181. *The United States of America v. Mark C. Anderson*, affidavit filed by Lapham June 24, 2011, 6.

182. Tom Johnson interview with author, December 2012.

183. Neither Sausalito police nor ATF officials have implicated Witten in Anderson's crimes. While it seems hard to believe she didn't have questions about the source of the million dollars suddenly at Anderson's disposal, there is no evidence to suggest she was any part of Anderson's operation.

184. Brian Parker interview with author.

185. *The United States of America v. Mark C. Anderson*, filed November 10, 2009.

186. *The United States of America v. Mark C. Anderson*, Declaration of Mark J. Reichel, June 24, 2011.

187. *The United States of America v. Mark C. Anderson*, Court document #163-1, 6. U.S. District Court, Eastern District of California.

188. Anderson letter to author, March 12, 2010.

189. Ibid.

190. *The United States of America v. Mark C. Anderson*, Anderson affidavit, March 29, 2011.

191. *The United States of America v. Mark C. Anderson*, Anderson affidavit, March 29, 2011, 3.

19. DELAY

192. Lapham interview with author, September 19, 2014. Lapham said he was watching Judge Karlton's face during Hall's testimony and saw him raise his eyebrows.

193. Anderson letter to author, January 18, 2013.

EPILOGUE

194. Ruth Teiser and Catherine Harroun, *Winemaking in California* (New York: McGraw-Hill, 1983), 160.

195. Peninou and Unzelman, 12.

APPENDIX

196. This is a simplified history meant to show the major owners and managers of the vineyard.

197. Black, 262.

SOURCES

ARCHIVAL COLLECTIONS

Benjamin Hayes scrapbooks, particularly volume 14, Bancroft Library.
Isaias W. Hellman papers, California Historical Society.
Jackson Graves papers, Huntington Library.
Vignes Family papers, Seaver Center for Western History Research.
California Wine Association Records, California Historical Society.
Los Angeles County court documents, Huntington Library.
San Bernardino County land records, San Bernardino Archives.
Percy Morgan scrapbook, private collection.
Wayback Machine, Internet Archive.

NEWSPAPER ACCOUNTS

The author consulted nineteenth- and twentieth-century accounts in the following newspapers and magazines.

Daily Alta California
Decanter
California Farmer and Journal of Useful Sciences
Los Angeles Star
Los Angeles Daily Times
Los Angeles Times
Marin Scope
Napa Valley Register
St. Helena Star

San Francisco Call
San Francisco Chronicle
Semi-Tropic California
Pacific Wine and Spirit Review
Wine Spectator

BIBLIOGRAPHY

Amerine, Maynard A. "An Introduction to the Pre-Repeal History of Grapes and Wines in California." *Agricultural History* 43, no. 2 (April 1, 1969): 259–68.

Apostol, Jane. "Don Mateo Keller: His Vines and His Wines." *Southern California Quarterly* 84, no. 2 (July 1, 2002): 93–114.

Asimov, Eric. "Rudy Kurniawan, Wine Dealer Accused of Fraud, Was Trusted by His Associates." *The New York Times*, March 12, 2012, sec. N.Y./Region. www.nytimes.com/2012/03/13/nyregion/rudy-kurniawan-wine-dealer -accused-of-fraud-was-trusted-by-his-associates.html.

Beattie, George William. "Development of Travel between Southern Arizona and Los Angeles as it Related to the San Bernardino Valley." *Annual Publication of the Historical Society of Southern California* 13, no. 2 (January 1, 1925): 228–57.

Black, Esther Boulton. *Rancho Cucamonga and Doña Merced*. Redlands, Calif: San Bernardino County Museum Association, 1975.

Brown, Patricia Leigh. "Growing in Napa: Club, and Camp, for Wine Lovers." *The New York Times*, October 21, 2005, sec. National. www.nytimes.com/2005 /10/21/national/21harvest.html.

Bryant, Edwin. *What I Saw in California*. Palo Alto: L. Osborne, 1967.

California and Los Angeles County (Calif.), eds. *Los Angeles Area Court Records*, 1850.

Carosso, Vincent P. "Anaheim, California: A Nineteenth Century Experiment in Commercial Viniculture." *Bulletin of the Business Historical Society* 23, no. 2 (June 1, 1949).

———. *The California Wine Industry, 1830–1895: A Study of the Formative Years*. Berkeley: University of California Press, 1951.

Caughey, John Walton. "The Jacob Y. Stover Narrative." *Pacific Historical Review* 6, no. 2 (June 1, 1937): 165–81.

Clucas, Donald L. *Light over the Mountain: A History of the Rancho Cucamonga Area.* Rev. ed. Upland, CA: California Family House, 1979.

Colburn, Frona Eunice Wait, and Dorothy Payne. *In Old Vintage Days.* John Henry Nash, 1937.

Collins, Dan. "In Vino Veritas? Inside the Bogus World of Wine." *Huffington Post,* August 7, 1920. www.huffingtonpost.com/2012/08/07/in-vino-veritas-inside -th_n_1751835.html.

Collins, Guy, and Scott Reyburn. "Wine Sales Drop for Second Year as Bordeaux Demand Wanes." *Bloomberg,* January 28, 2014. www.bloomberg.com/news /2014-01-29/wine-sales-drop-for-second-year-as-bordeaux-demand-wanes .html.

Conaway, James. *Napa: The Story of an American Eden.* Boston: Houghton Mifflin, 1990.

———. *The Far Side of Eden: New Money, Old Land, and the Battle for Napa Valley.* Boston: Houghton Mifflin, 2002.

Dinkelspiel, Frances. *Towers of Gold: How One Jewish Immigrant Named Isaias Hellman Created California.* 1st ed. New York: St. Martin's Press, 2008.

Duflot de Mofras, Eugène, and Marguerite Eyer Wilbur. *Duflot de Mofras' Travels on the Pacific Coast.* Calafia Series, no. 2. Santa Ana, CA: The Fine Arts Press, 1937.

"El Aliso: Ancient Sycamore Was Silent Witness to Four Centuries of L.A. History | LA as Subject | SoCal Focus." *KCET.* Accessed February 5, 2014. www.kcet .org/updaily/socal_focus/history/la-as-subject/el-aliso-silent-witness-to-four -centuries-of-la-history.html.

"Fine Wine and Fine Print." *The Underground Wine Letter.* Accessed February 19, 2014. www.undergroundwineletter.com/2012/02/fine-wine-and-fine-print/.

Florence, Sr., Jack W. *Legacy of a Village: The Italian Swiss Colony Winery and People of Asti, California.* Phoenix, AZ: Raymond Court Press, 2004.

Geraci, Victor W. "Fermenting a Twenty-First Century California Wine Industry." *Agricultural History* 78, no. 4 (October 1, 2004): 438–65.

Goldstein, Ben. "The Man Who Duped Millionaires into Paying Big Bucks for Fake Wine." *NPR.org.* Accessed March 11, 2014. www.npr.org/blogs/thesalt/2013 /12/18/255241685/the-man-who-duped-millionaires-into-paying-big-bucks -for-fake-wine.

Graves, J. A., and Isaias W. Hellman. *Papers of J. A. Graves,* 1878.

Green, Bertie. "List of Active Chapters of the: Sociedad Honoraria Hispánica." *Hispania* 85, no. 4 (December 1, 2002): 961–1002.

Greenwald, Jeff. "Livin' on the Dock of the Bay." *Smithsonian Magazine.* Accessed October 15, 2013. www.smithsonianmag.com/people-places/Everything

-Floats-Their-HouseBoats-What-Its-Like-to-Live-on-the-Dock-of-the-San
-Francisco-Bay.html.

Gumina, Deanna Paoli. "Andrea Sbarboro, Founder of the Italian Swiss Colony Wine Company: Reminiscences of an Italian-American Pioneer." *Italian Americana* 2, no. 1 (October 1, 1975): 1–17.

Gumprecht, Blake. *The Los Angeles River: Its Life, Death, and Possible Rebirth.* Creating the North American Landscape. Baltimore, MD: Johns Hopkins University Press, 1999.

Hermacinski, Ursula. *The Wine Lover's Guide to Auctions: The Art and Science of Buying and Selling Wines.* Square One Publishers, Inc., 2006.

Hittell, John S. *The Resources of California: Comprising Agriculture, Mining, Geography, Climate, &c., and the Past and Future Development of the State.* 5th ed., with an appendix on Oregon, Nevada, and Washington Territory. San Francisco, New York: A. Roman and Company, 1869.

Hock, Stanley. *Harvesting the Dream: The Trinchero Family of Sutter Home: 50 Years in the Napa Valley.* St. Helena, CA: Sutter Home Winery, 1998.

"Justice Department Crushes Winemaker's Hopes of Pardon | Justice Department | McClatchy DC." Accessed February 23, 2014. www.mcclatchydc.com/2009 /01/08/59310/justice-department-crushes-winemakers.html.

Lane, Elizabeth L. "Books and Articles Relating to Louisiana, 1966." *Louisiana History: The Journal of the Louisiana Historical Association* 8, no. 3 (July 1, 1967): 268–80.

Lehman, Anthony L. "Vines and Vintners in the Pomona Valley." *Southern California Quarterly* 54, no. 1 (April 1, 1972): 55–65. doi:10.2307/41170398.

"Lengthy Gang Trial Ends in Two Convictions." *Timesheraldonline.com.* Accessed September 15, 2013. www.timesheraldonline.com/ci_3688523.

Lukacs, Paul. *American Vintage: The Rise of American Wine.* Boston: Houghton Mifflin, 2000.

Monroy, Douglas. "The Creation and Re-Creation of Californio Society." *California History* 76, no. 2/3 (July 1, 1997): 173–95.

Newmark, Harris. *Sixty Years in Southern California, 1853–1913, Containing the Reminiscences of Harris Newmark.* New York: Knickerbocker Press, 1916.

Peninou, Ernest P. *A Directory of California Wine Growers and Wine Makers in 1860.* Berkeley, CA: Tamalpais Press, 1967.

———. *A History of the Los Angeles Viticultural District: Comprising the Counties of Imperial, Los Angeles, Orange, Riverside, San Bernardino, San Diego, San Luis Obispo, Santa Barbara, and Ventura: With Grape Acreage Statistics and Directories of Grape Growers.* A History of the Seven Viticultural Districts of California 4. Santa Rosa, CA: Nomis Press for Wine Librarians Association, 2004.

———. *Leland Stanford's Great Vina Ranch 1881–1919: A Research Paper: The History of Senator Leland Stanford's Vina Vineyard and the World's Largest Winery*

Formerly the Site of Peter Lassen's Bosquejo and Henry Gerke's Ranch. San Francisco, CA: Yolo Hills Viticultural Society, 1991.

———. *Winemaking in California.* San Francisco, CA: Peregrine Press, 1954.

Peninou, Ernest P., and Gail G. Unzelman, eds. *The California Wine Association and Its Member Wineries, 1894–1920.* Santa Rosa, CA: Nomis Press, 2000.

Pfanner, Eric. "Fraud Charges Threaten Burgundy's Vaunted Reputation." *The New York Times,* June 18, 2012, sec. Business Day/Global Business. www.nytimes.com/2012/06/19/business/global/fraud-charges-threaten-burgundys-vaunted-reputation.html.

Phillips, George Harwood. *Vineyards & Vaqueros: Indian Labor and the Economic Expansion of Southern California, 1771–1877.* Before Gold: California under Spain and Mexico, v. 1. Norman, OK: Arthur H. Clark, 2010.

Pinney, Thomas. *A History of Wine in America from the Beginnings to Prohibition.* Berkeley: University of California Press, 1989.

———. *A History of Wine in America: From Prohibition to the Present.* Berkeley: University of California Press, 2005.

———. *The Makers of American Wine: A Record of Two Hundred Years.* Berkeley: University of California Press, 2012.

Robinson, Jancis, ed. *The Oxford Companion to Wine.* 3rd ed. Oxford; New York: Oxford University Press, 2006.

Saloutos, Theodore. "The Immigrant Contribution to American Agriculture." *Agricultural History* 50, no. 1 (January 1, 1976): 45–67.

Siler, Julia Flynn. *The House of Mondavi: The Rise and Fall of an American Wine Dynasty.* New York: Gotham Books, 2007.

Street, Richard S. "Rural California: A Bibliographic Essay." *Southern California Quarterly* 70, no. 3 (October 1, 1988): 299–328.

Street, Richard Steven. *Beasts of the Field: A Narrative History of California Farmworkers, 1769–1913.* Stanford, CA: Stanford University Press, 2004.

Sullivan, Charles L. *A Companion to California Wine: An Encyclopedia of Wine and Winemaking from the Mission Period to the Present.* Berkeley: University of California Press, 1998.

———. *Napa Wine: A History from Mission Days to Present.* San Francisco: The Wine Appreciation Guild, 1994.

———. *Sonoma Wine and the Story of Buena Vista.* Board and Bench Publishing, 2013.

Taber, George M. *A Toast to Bargain Wines: How Innovators, Iconoclasts, and Winemaking Revolutionaries Are Changing the Way the World Drinks.* New York: Simon and Schuster, 2011.

Teiser, Ruth, and Harroun, Catherine. *Winemaking in California.* New York: McGraw-Hill, 1982.

Truman, Benjamin Cummings. *Semi-Tropical California: Its Climate, Healthfulness, Productiveness, and Scenery.* San Francisco: A. L. Bancroft & Company, 1874.

Wallace, Benjamin. Published May 2012. "Château Sucker." *NYMag.com*. Accessed February 22, 2014. http://nymag.com/news/features/rudy-kurniawan-wine -fraud-2012-5/.

Warner, J. J., Benjamin Hayes, J. P. Widney, and Los Angeles (Calif.), eds. *An His-torical Sketch of Los Angeles County, California: From the Spanish Occupancy, by the Founding of the Mission San Gabriel Archangel, September 8, 1771, to July 4, 1876*. Los Angeles: Louis Lewin & Co., 1876.

Wilson, Iris Ann. "Early Southern California Viniculture 1830–1865." *The Historical Society of Southern California Quarterly* 39, no. 3 (September 1, 1957): 242–50. doi:10.2307/41169133.

Winther, Oscar Osburn. "The Colony System of Southern California." *Agricul-tural History* 27, no. 3 (July 1, 1953): 94–103.

Woutat, Donald. "State Near Bottom of Barrel of Wine Grape Scandal : Fraud: Wineries That Unwittingly Bought Overpriced Grapes Simply Used Them to Make Overpriced Wine. New Safeguards Are Now in Place." *Los Angeles Times*, January 30, 1994. http://articles.latimes.com/1994-01-30/business/fi-18304_1 _wine-industry.

Writers, Susan Sward, Greg Lucas, Chronicle Staff. "S.F. Lawyer's Quest Contin-ues / On Case since '93, He'll Help Weigh Evidence against Kaczynski." *SF-Gate*, April 13, 1996. www.sfgate.com/bayarea/article/S-F-Lawyer-s-Quest -Continues-On-case-since-2986148.php#src=fb.

INDEX